DON'T LIE TO ME

Also by Judge Jeanine Pirro
Published by Center Street

Liars, Leakers, and Liberals:
The Case Against the Anti-Trump Conspiracy

Radicals, Resistance, and Revenge:
The Left's Plot to Remake America

DON'T LIE TO ME

and

STOP TRYING TO STEAL OUR FREEDOM

Judge Jeanine Pirro

CENTER STREET

NEW YORK NASHVILLE

Center Street
Hachette Book Group
1290 Avenue of the Americas, New York, NY 10104
centerstreet.com
twitter.com/centerstreet

First Edition: September 2020

Center Street is a division of Hachette Book Group, Inc. The Center Street name and logo are trademarks of Hachette Book Group, Inc.

The publisher is not responsible for websites (or their content) that are not owned by the publisher.

The Hachette Speakers Bureau provides a wide range of authors for speaking events. To find out more, go to www.HachetteSpeakersBureau.com or call (866) 376-6591.

Print book interior design by Timothy Shaner, NightandDayDesign.biz

Library of Congress Cataloging-in-Publication Data has been applied for.

ISBNs: 978-1-5460-5973-8 (hardcover), 978-1-5460-5972-1 (ebook)

Printed in the United States of America

LSC-W

10 9 8 7 6 5 4 3 2 1

I dedicate this book to one person:

The one person who has stood fast against an incredible onslaught of attacks, insults, and lies; a man with the uncommon stamina, energy and perseverance to fight the dark forces that seek to tear down mankind's greatest experiment in freedom; a man who brings truth, light and transparency to a nation clouded in darkness and chaos; a man who never wavers in his determination to

Make America Proud, Strong, and Yes, Great Again,

President of the United States
Donald J. Trump

CONTENTS

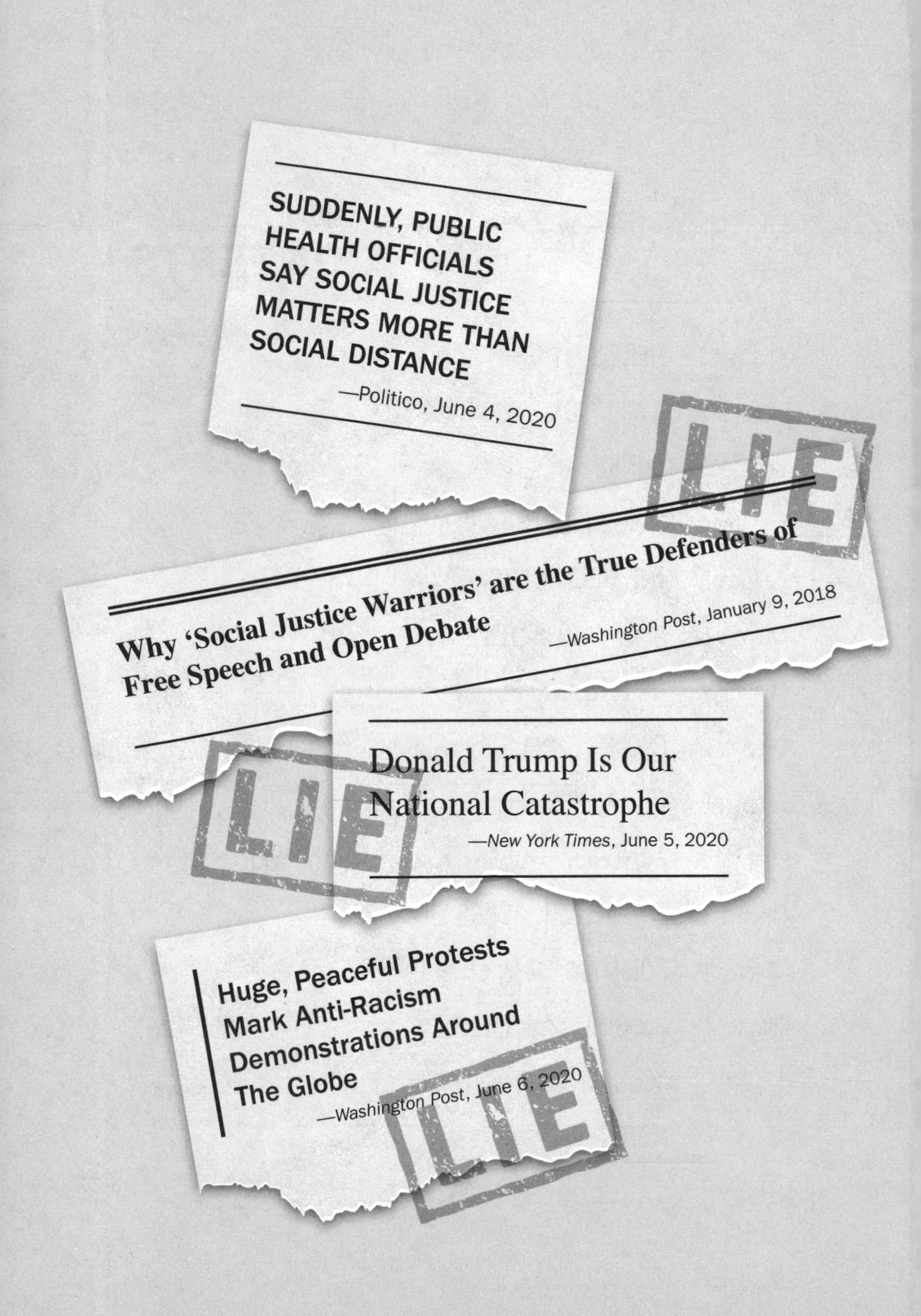
SUDDENLY, PUBLIC HEALTH OFFICIALS SAY SOCIAL JUSTICE MATTERS MORE THAN SOCIAL DISTANCE
—Politico, June 4, 2020
LIE
Why 'Social Justice Warriors' are the True Defenders of Free Speech and Open Debate
—Washington Post, January 9, 2018
LIE
Donald Trump Is Our National Catastrophe
—New York Times, June 5, 2020
Huge, Peaceful Protests Mark Anti-Racism Demonstrations Around The Globe
—Washington Post, June 6, 2020
LIE

Chapter One

HERE'S MY OPEN

We are in the fight of our lives.

It's a fight between good and evil, and a fight between truth and lies. From the beginning, the Left has been waging an all-out war against President Trump. They have attacked him with every weapon in their arsenal, and he's still standing, facing them down like no other man possibly could. Over the years, their attacks have only grown in intensity and frequency. When he was a candidate, they tried to convince us that he was racist and sexist. When that didn't work, they told us that he was Russian agent and a Putin puppet. When *that* didn't work, they told us that he had illegally meddled in the affairs of Ukraine, obstructed justice by trying to defend himself, and committed a thousand offenses against the Constitution along the way.

These were lies, plain and simple.

The liars, leakers, and liberals were lying to us then, and they're lying to us now.

What we have witnessed since the beginning of 2020, from the anxiety over the coronavirus from Wuhan, China to the shameful politicization of the death of George Floyd in Minneapolis, shows that the liars are determined to create havoc and chaos in an effort to stop the reelection of Donald Trump. Somewhere deep in the consciousness of the Left, they know that if President Trump manages to beat them back one more time on election night on November 3, 2020, pulling off an upset victory on the heels of the worst economic crisis that this country has faced since the Great Depression, their efforts will have been for naught.

That's not to say that they won't try, of course. I am always amazed at their capacity to invent false narratives and distort the truth.

But think about it: Considering what they're doing right now, how could they possibly get any more radical? For weeks, Americans saw the virus level as well as the mortality rate drop, and for weeks, Americans begged to be let out to go to work. As I write this, there are violent riots occurring nightly in several major US cities, and the leaders of those cities, nearly all of whom are Democrat mayors, are allowing the violence to occur and continue and insist that the feds be removed from their cities. In states like New York, Michigan, and Illinois, liberal governors flex their pathetic muscles by not allowing law-abiding citizens who peacefully protest to return to work, and they force them to remain indoors. They bully us when we say otherwise by claiming we don't value human life. When we say, "We should open up," they act like we're saying, "I want your grandmother to die." Yet these same governors and mayors allow protestors to gather by the thousands in the streets without any concern for the virus. In fact, they celebrate the protests.

Even the public health community lied to us. Either that or they simply weren't competent enough to recognize the truth when it was right in front of their faces. From the beginning, they told us that two million people would die if we didn't shut down the economy. They told us that the coronavirus could live on surfaces for weeks, that we needed to scrub our groceries with bleach, and that we needed to wear masks everywhere. They told us that the virus couldn't be transmitted from person to person, a lie that we would later learn was spread by China with the help of the World Health Organization.

Now, they've gone beyond lying. They're so brazen in their efforts to control us that when the hypocrisy is blatantly obvious, they simply say that social gatherings for social justice, although risky, are worth the risk.

In fact, on June 5, about 1,200 of the country's top public health experts, who, up to that point, had been telling us that remaining inside and staying away from other people was the only way to stop the coronavirus from spreading, wrote a public letter essentially endorsing the widespread protests. In this letter, they said that they were perfectly fine with the protests.

In fact, they wrote that *racism* is a greater threat to Americans than the coronavrius.

"As public health advocates," they said, "we do not condemn these gatherings as risky for coronavirus transmission. We support them as vital to the national public health and to the threatened health specifically of Black people in the United States."[1] [2]

Over the course of a few weeks in the United States, it became effectively illegal to play catch with your son outside, go to church, or open your business, but perfectly legal to loot, riot, and throw bricks through windows. Suddenly, it was frowned upon to stand in front of your state's capitol building holding a sign reading OPEN UP, but it was perfectly acceptable to put on a ninja outfit, throw milkshakes at people you disagree with, and assault police officers whose only goal was to make sure the protests remain peaceful.

The Left allowed social distance to give way to social justice.

So, my advice? If you're going to head outside during what remains of this pandemic, be sure to pack a picket sign with a hatchet handle, some bricks, and a few Molotov cocktails. If you don't take these precautions, someone might think you're breaking the law.

A LIBERAL'S PARADISE

In some cases, rioting in the streets hasn't been enough for the liberal mob. Neither has looting, burning down buildings, or assaulting members of the National Guard. In some cities, the mob has attempted to *take* the streets, too.

In Seattle, it worked. There, on June 9, a group of militant Leftists overtook a six-block section of the city and claimed it as their own. In a statement, they announced that you were leaving the United States. The Seattle police precinct was turned into the people's precinct.

In this Capitol Hill Autonomous Zone, first known as CHAZ before it was changed to CHOP, for Capitol Hill Organized Protest, we have seen a small example of how far the Left will go to satisfy the progressive extremists and surrender our cities to them. Even as groups like Antifa, a pseudo-military organization of anarchists and Leftists who run around in all-black garb with backpacks full of light weaponry, have moved in and conquered large swaths of our cities, most of our liberal leaders refuse to criticize them. Whether they agree with them or are afraid of being called racists, fascists, or—even worse—beneficiaries of *white privilege*, they've allowed chaos to spread throughout the United States of America.

When Jenny Durkan, the Democrat mayor of Seattle, was asked on June 11 how long she thought the autonomous zones would remain in her city, she reacted like she was at Woodstock.

"I don't know," she said. "We could have a summer of love!"[3]

Well, Jenny, perhaps you might want to get together with Mayor Bill de Blasio's wife Chirlane McCray, who's said that New York City without the NYPD would be "nirvana."[4] But do us a favor, won't you?

Leave your police protection behind.

So, you have a right to ask: If these people don't want to live in the United States anymore, where *do* they want to live?

Well, I can't tell you that. But I can tell you what they want. According to a list of demands published on June 9, the men and women (and nonbinary, gender-nonconforming citizens) of CHAZ/CHOP would like the police completely defunded and abolished. They would like to see all prisons emptied and then shuttered for good. They would like all African American people currently serving prison sentences to be retried for their crimes (which is going to be difficult, considering that they have also demanded that all courts of law be shut down). And even if some people were convicted, there would be no jails to put them in. The residents of this autonomous zone have also demanded that prisons be replaced with restorative, transformative accountability programs. I guess victims should be on notice that they need to have a "transformative accountability session" with their rapist. After all, if these lunatics were ever to get their way, rapists wouldn't be going to prison.

I've often said that if you want to know how a Democrat is going to run this country, you don't have to do much thinking—or, God forbid, elect one of them. All you have to do is take a look at some of the cities they've already been allowed to ruin. In places like San Francisco, Minneapolis, Chicago, and Detroit—all of which have been under Democrat control for decades—you'll find some of the highest crime rates in the nation. You'll also find homelessness on a mass scale, as well as broken needles and human feces in the streets. In fact, according to a list published by *Business Insider* earlier this year, you'll find that the ten most dangerous cities in the country are all run by liberal Democrat mayors.[5] In Baltimore and Detroit, two liberal strongholds, the murder rate is higher than in El Salvador, Guatemala, or even Afghanistan.

If you want *that* for your city, then by all means, cast your vote for feckless Joe Biden. If this appeals to you, then run out and buy yourself a ninja outfit and see if you can get in touch with Antifa.

The Leftist liars and hypocrites will tell you that they hate walls, and yet the first thing they did to secure their un-American utopia was erect large barriers to keep out "fascists." They'll tell you that private citizens shouldn't be allowed to own guns, which should belong only to members of law enforcement. Then, they'll tell you that members of law enforcement are a bunch of violent, racist thugs who shouldn't have guns, either. *Then,* when it's time to give someone the job of protecting their newly made city from outsiders, they stationed armed guards at the gates with AK-47s, rifles, and sidearms.[6]

Of course, it's important to keep in mind that when they say "fascists," what they really mean is anyone who doesn't buy into their deranged, radical agenda. To them, you're a fascist. So am I. Their use of this term, which is a real word with a real meaning, has become so watered down over the years that it includes virtually anyone who disagrees with them. According to the platform of Antifa, words are violence, and anyone who says words you don't like is a fascist.

In fact, as the Left gets more and more radical, you'll find that there are very few people they *don't* think are fascists. In the beginning, it was only Donald Trump and a select few of his advisors. Then it was anyone who worked for him. After some time passed, it was anyone who supported him, and then it was anyone who was *friends* with anyone who supported him.

Clearly, these whack jobs live in their own little world, and you are not a part of it. Nothing can be done to appease them. Just ask Mayor Durkan, who tried and failed to make concessions to the liberal mob. During the early days of the protests, she let these radicals do whatever they wanted to do. While they were destroying the city, she babbled on about a "summer of love." When President Trump criticized her for it in a tweet, saying that the violent takeover of Seattle had to end, she responded "Seattle is fine. Don't be so afraid of democracy."[7]

Less than two weeks after she sent that tweet, the violence began to ramp up. As President Trump predicted, once the looting started, the shooting started. Police, to their credit, previously chased out of their precinct, responded to a 911 call of a shooting as the anarchists refused their entry.

The nineteen-year-old shot that night died. There was no crime scene preservation, no interviewing witnesses; there would simply be no justice in this so-called nirvana. Within 48 hours, there was a second round of shooting in the CHOP zone.

Then a third and a fourth. One of those shot seeking victim status actually claimed the police who had tried to enter repeatedly and were stopped and pelted, claims the police didn't respond quickly enough.

Seattle police then actually released a five-minute video showing police and emergency responders being prevented by a violent crowd from getting to the victim.

Finally, Schizo summer of love Seattle mayor Jenny Durkan asked the occupants to leave—very politely, and without much force. In response, the squatters refused, threatening business owners with retaliation if they even painted over their graffiti.

Only when the protestors showed up in Mayor Durkan's own front yard, holding signs and threatening her property for a change, did she take action. The morning after the protestors held a rally in front of her house, the mayor gave police the full authority to break up the CHOP zone for good.

It was clear within hours.

Today, Capitol Hill businesses and residents are now suing the mayor over the handling of CHOP Zone, claiming that she and the city effectively authorized the actions of these anarchists. And this woman is so tone deaf to the damage she facilitated that she's started her reelect 2021 mayoral campaign early.

THE PETRI DISH

For years, we have been living in a petri dish of lies, deceit, and the makings of a violent revolution.

We began to get a sense of it during the Obama years, when the economy was at an all-time low and many of us felt like things would never improve. Everything seemed out of sync, and every day we were lied to.

We were told that 1 percent GDP growth was "the new normal," and that the economic recovery was moving along at a normal pace, while many Americans were working two or three jobs just to keep food on the table. We were told that ISIS was in full retreat in the Middle East and that our military was more capable than ever of dealing with them. Meanwhile, ISIS was expanding, and the generals on the ground knew it. Obama was calling for a reduction in army staffing to pre–World War II levels. He refused to call radical Islamic terrorism by its proper name, choosing instead to refer to "acts of terror," using a smokescreen of euphemisms and politically correct phrases.

Anyone who dared go against him, such as Lieutenant General Michael T. Flynn, who testified in front of Congress that Al Qaeda was not in any kind of retreat, was marked for retribution and rewarded with an undeniable target on his back.[8]

During the Obama years, things that were blatantly clear to us were steeped in smoke. When a man named Nidal Hassan stepped onto a military base at Ford Hood, shouted "Allahu akbar," and opened fire, killing thirteen people and wounding twenty-eight, we were told it was "workplace violence," not terrorism. Even though Hassan carried business cards that said "soldier of Allah," the liberals refused to see what was right in front of their faces.[9] In Obama's mind, adherents to the religion of Islam were a persecuted minority in this country, and it would have been politically incorrect to suggest that their religion had anything to do with terrorism.

On September 25, 2012, two weeks after the attack on our embassy in Benghazi that left four people dead, including Ambassador Chris Stevens, President Obama addressed the United Nations, saying "the future must not belong to those who slander the prophet of Islam."[10] The comment perplexed me for years, but it was at a national prayer breakfast a few years later that he made it even clearer. There, he told Christians to "get off their high horses" and take a hard look at the shameful acts that had been committed in the name of Jesus Christ.

During those years, we were told to be sensitive to people's feelings—we were told not to say anything that might be offensive to anyone. America watched as its younger generation, recently out of high school and college, was offended by words and ideas. It was the beginning of a new paradigm where the First Amendment gave way to political correctness, when facts gave way to feelings. Young people dictated what others should think, and they threatened social condemnation for anyone who didn't fall in line. On social media, this would become known as "cancel culture," a system in which anyone—even those who agreed with the Left's insane dictates more than 99 percent of the time—could be excommunicated and scrubbed from history for saying the wrong thing, doing the wrong thing, or even *thinking* the wrong thing.

We first watched this play out, ironically, on college campuses, places that were supposed to be the bastions of free speech. At the University of California at Berkeley, offended students broke windows, burned cars, and caused hundreds of thousands of dollars of damage to property. At other universities, students on the Left shut down speakers and incited riots whenever someone said something that hurt their feelings. When a group called Antifa—short for "antifascist"—began showing up at these demonstrations in small numbers, infiltrating peaceful protests, and inciting violence, anyone who was concerned about them was dismissed.

It wasn't just physical violence, either. At Evergreen State University, students held a "day of absence," demanding that all white students and faculty stay home for the day, recording anyone who didn't comply and posting the videos on social media to shame them. In those days, we knew that the "woke" revolution was a problem on college campuses, but we thought it was contained. We thought that once these students headed out into the real world, getting jobs at institutions like the *New York Times,* Google, and Twitter, they would adapt to the ways of the world.

They didn't.

Instead, these oversensitive students went out into the real world and insisted that the world adapt to *them*, not the other way around. Rather than shedding the lessons they had learned in college—about how their feelings were all that mattered and that all conservatives were evil fascists—they doubled down, putting blinders on that blocked out the real world. Some of these former students got jobs at big tech companies in Silicon Valley, where they have been censoring the speech of conservatives using complex algorithms and other shadowy practices. Others went into media, getting jobs at major news outlets like the *New York Times* and CNN. With these people at the helm, the mainstream media grew even more radical than it had been during the early years of the Obama presidency.

Long before we had even heard of the coronavirus, an epidemic known as Trump Derangement Syndrome was spreading—and this generation was patient zero. Under their influence, our media institutions began blaming Donald Trump for anything that went wrong.

In their eyes, President Trump—a man who rebuffed political correctness and identity politics—was dangerous. That's why the liberals expended so much of their energy trying to remove him from office. From the moment he announced he was running for president, it began. They wrote books alleging he was incompetent, dug into his private life, and attacked members of his family and his administration, but none of it stuck. Meanwhile, President Trump never did anything other than give it right back to them, knowing that his astounding record of success would be the best revenge.

For that, they hated him.

All the Democrats could do was sit around, lob more baseless accusations at the president, and hope that something—maybe a meteor or a global pandemic—finally appeared to stop President Trump from succeeding.

Then, out of nowhere, a virus arrived from Wuhan, China—a virus that would halt the country's economy, wreak havoc on our lives, and finally give the Democrats something to hold against the president in the lead-up to Election Day, as if *he* had brought it to the country himself.

For Nancy Pelosi, Joe Biden, and the rest of the liberal establishment, it was perfect.

In fact, this virus couldn't have been any *more* perfect for the Left if it had come wrapped in shiny paper and a bow, with a tag that read: TO: LIBERALS, WITH LOVE, CHINA.

GOING VIRAL

With the coronavirus came the perfect opportunity for the Left to continue its effort to tear down America.

Suddenly, governors and mayors on the Left could force people inside, stop them from working, and make sure they were dependent on the government for everything. It was like a Leftist fever dream. During the pandemic, people were dependent on the government not only for money, which came in the form of unemployment checks and a small one-time stimulus payment, but also for information. Every morning, people were glued to their television screens, looking to their mayors and governors for answers. In the evenings, they would turn to President Trump's briefings with the Coronavirus Task Force—when the liberal media wasn't cutting away from the president in mid-sentence, of course.

During the pandemic, the governors and mayors of this nation had all the power. Although President Trump had made the decision to shut down the economy, he left it up to the governors and mayors to decide whether they would reopen. There was nothing else to do, and there was nowhere else to go—not legally, at least.

In some states, nearly all of which were run by liberals, these attention-seeking politicians seized power and had a very hard time letting it go. All over the country, people who had been exhausted by Sleepy Joe Biden's failing attempts to finish his own sentences looked elsewhere for a liberal hero. In New York City, they found one in Andrew Cuomo, the governor who had never done anything for them. During the pandemic, though, the people of New York seemed to forget all about his past transgressions.

Even when Governor Cuomo signed an executive order that forced thousands of people who'd been infected with the virus into nursing homes all over the state, a decision that caused the deaths of ten or eleven thousand people who we knew were the most vulnerable, the liberal media fawned over him. Even when he wasted time conducting ridiculous interviews with his brother, Chris Cuomo, on CNN, arguing about who makes better meatballs and who has the bigger nose, they kept airing his press conferences. Within weeks, these press conferences had become a shameful vaudeville act that made a mockery of the people who were dying of the virus. But the higher-ups at CNN didn't care. All that mattered to them was ratings.

Meanwhile, reporters on every mainstream media network pushed the lockdown with an almost evangelical zeal. They bombarded us with images of mass graves, packed hospitals, and graphic photographs of people on ventilators. They told us that more than two million people in the United States could die, a number that would later turn out to be based on bad science and faulty modelling.[11] Every day, the media warned us about the dangers of not wearing a mask—of course, that was after they told us we didn't need to wear a mask—social distancing, and not doing your part to stop the virus from spreading. Chris Cuomo, who suddenly became one of the most watched anchors on cable news during the first months of the pandemic—before his ratings took a *big* nosedive in late May—was among the worst of the guilt bullies on the Left. After it became clear that the curve was flattening and people could go outside again, Cuomo took to the airwaves to scold New Yorkers for daring to go for a stroll in the park.

"We are deceiving ourselves," he said on CNN on May 5 as he put up pictures of people sitting in Central Park in Manhattan. "Look at these fools. Fools! I know they wanna be out there. Fools! It's not about you! What about the other people? Look, I'm not gonna castigate you. That's not my job. I'm not your daddy, but we have to think about this. We are rushing to get back out of want, not just out of need...beautiful weather does not make for a beautiful reality."[12]

By the way, at the time Chris Cuomo spoke those words, he was sitting in his house in the Hamptons. He had a job, and he never had to worry about losing it.

In the interim, many people lost everything. Businesses closed, many of which will never reopen. The emotional toll, including depression and suicides, got much worse during the pandemic. Victims forced inside with their abusers and unable to get out caused domestic violence numbers to increase dramatically. Abused and neglected children, who often found respite going to school, suffered physically and emotionally locked at home with an angry parent.

The Left used the virus to stop us from going to church and synagogue. They used it to stop us from seeing our friends and burying our loved ones—those who died from the virus or one of the many afflictions that were ignored during the pandemic.

In liberal states, the rules about what we could and could not do were often as ridiculous as they were harmful. Had the situation not been so deadly serious, these rules might have been comical. In places like Michigan, for example, where Governor Gretchen Whitmer ruled with a tyrannical hammer, people could still go out and buy alcohol and marijuana whenever they wanted. To her, those businesses were considered essential.

As for churches and synagogues? Not so much. The Left's disdain for Christians was evidenced by the fact that many pastors were given tickets for violating social distancing orders when they tried to hold services for those people parked in their cars in parking lots.

During that time, it seemed as though the lockdown might never end. The Left had gotten a taste of power, and they were never going to let it go.

ON A DIME

With every day that leftist politicians continued their hold on our states and cities, extending their lockdowns well past the point of medical necessity, small businesses in America suffered. Many bars and restaurants, which often operate on very thin margins, were forced to close their doors for good. In the small towns of this country, many of the family-owned stores that had been fighting a losing battle with big corporations for decades finally had to give up the fight. The big corporations took in billions of dollars in profit every year; they could afford to weather the pandemic and still pay their employees. Small businesses, many of which barely make enough money to cover rent and labor in the best of times, could not.

One of these small businesses was a restaurant in Minneapolis called Conga Latin Bistro, which sits on Hennepin Avenue on the south side of the city. In 2014, a man named George Floyd had come to Minneapolis from Houston, where he'd worked at a church helping people find housing, to become a security guard at the restaurant and start a new life.[13] However, when the pandemic hit the United States and restaurants all over the country were forced to shut down, Floyd lost his job. In March, he found himself in the same position as millions of other Americans: He was broke and out of work, and most of the places where he would normally have looked for work—the nightclubs, bars, and restaurants around town—were closed down indefinitely.

On May 25, about two months into his unemployment, Floyd walked into a grocery store near his apartment to buy food. According to the man behind the counter, he'd attempted to pay for this food and a few other items with a twenty-dollar bill that appeared to him to be counterfeit. The man behind the counter called the police, and four officers showed up at the scene. They handcuffed Floyd, threw him to the ground, and one of the officers—a sick, sadistic man named Derek Chauvin—put his knee on Floyd's neck for a full eight minutes and forty-six seconds, cutting off his breath and eventually killing him. For almost nine minutes, Floyd tried to get the attention of people standing by.

He yelled, "They're killing me, man!" "Help." "I can't breathe." He cried for his mother.

No one stepped in to help.

Video of the scene quickly went viral, and the sight of Floyd's death soon shocked the nation. It offended virtually everyone, but to the African-American community, seemed all too familiar. George Floyd, a black man, was on the ground. The officer who killed him was white; so were two of the officers who stood by while George was murdered. This combination brought up memories of Eric Garner, Michael Brown, and Freddie Gray, all black men who died while in police custody or immediately thereafter.

I argued that Officer Chauvin should be charged not only with murder in the second degree but murder in the *first* degree. That officer had over eight minutes to change his mind, and he was made aware of the fact that he was killing George Floyd several times. He could have stopped at any time, but he didn't. He kept pushing his knee into the neck of George Floyd.

But on a dime, after George Floyd's death, this country went from a complete state of lockdown to a state of unrest and protest that included destruction, rioting, and looting.

God bless the protestors who remained peaceful. However, we were still in the middle of a pandemic—one that the liberal media had been telling us would kill you if you so much as stepped out your front door.

Now, it didn't matter.

Nobody on the Left accused the people who took to the streets to protest George Floyd's death of putting their fellow Americans in danger or not caring about the health of their grandmothers. The Left didn't tell them that they would have the blood of innocent people on their hands.

Suddenly, in the media, it seemed as though the virus wasn't even a problem anymore—as long as you were a liberal, of course. And if it *did* turn out to be a problem, it certainly wouldn't be the fault of the protestors. No, it would be the fault of all those people who wanted to go out and safely open their businesses up again.

When the protests in Minneapolis took a violent turn, where they were burning down buildings and looting stores, there was no police resistance. Many city leaders supported the protestors-turned-rioters, which essentially allowed them to wreak havoc with impunity. As the Third Precinct was burned down on May 29, police vehicles could be seen leaving the precinct one after another, yet police still needed help to be helicoptered off the roof of the precinct. In downtown Minneapolis, protestors broke into a sports bar that was owned by Korboi "KB" Balla, a black firefighter who'd poured most of his savings and "countless hours" into getting his new business open, and ransacked it.[14]

During the first days of the coronavirus pandemic, with the media pushing a national lockdown of all small businesses, Balla had been forced to delay the grand opening of the bar; then, during the riots—which were conveniently downplayed and ignored by the liberal media—he'd been forced to return to see the damage and the destruction of not just his property but his dream.

"To find out that the countless hours, hard work, late nights away from my kids, and my family had all been for nothing," he said, "was soul-shattering. It's not the material things, more so the time that cannot be reclaimed."[15]

On June 1, during a riot in Richmond, Virginia, protestors blocked a fire truck from reaching a multifamily residence that had been set on fire with a young child inside. When the truck approached, the rioters—who had set fire to the building as well as several others surrounding it—stood in a line and stopped the firefighters from getting through. By the time the truck made it through the line of rioters and got to the burning building, it was almost too late.

Thankfully, the firefighters were able to rescue the child. But they were only seconds away from that not being the case.

At a press conference a few hours later, the chief of police broke down in tears. "When you take a legitimate issue and hijack it for unknown reasons," he said, "that is unacceptable to me, it's unacceptable to the Richmond Police Department, unacceptable to the city of Richmond."[16]

You might think that a story like that would have made the front end of news broadcasts all over the country. But it didn't. As of this writing, only a few online publications, most of them conservative, have written about it.

Instead, two nights later, CNN's Chris Cuomo—the man who'd scolded us all for wanting to go sit in the park when the curve had begun to flatten—decided to *defend* the violent turn that the protests were taking, just a few weeks after he had ridiculed people for having the gall to go outside and get some fresh air in the park.

"Too many see the protests as the problem," he said. "No. The problem is what forced your fellow citizens to take to the streets. Persistent and poisonous inequities and injustice. And please, show me where it says that protests are supposed to be polite and peaceful. Because I can show you that outraged citizens are what made this country what she is and led to any major milestone. To be honest, this is not a tranquil time."[17]

Well, not to rain on your parade, Chris, but it just so happens that I *can* show you where it says protests are supposed to be peaceful. So can anyone who passed the fifth grade. In fact, if you pull out a copy of the Bill of Rights, you'll find the First Amendment on the first page:

> Congress shall make no law respecting an establishment of religion, or prohibiting the free exercise thereof; or abridging the freedom of speech, or of the press; or the right of the people peaceably to assemble, and to petition the Government for a redress of grievances.

Did you catch that, Chris? Right in between *people* and *to* in the last line? That word was *peaceably*, which is close enough to *peaceful* to prove that you don't know what the hell you're talking about.

When the founders of this country wrote the right to protest into the Constitution, they made sure that the assembly was to be peaceful. Not that it matters to anyone on the Left. When the Constitution doesn't work for them, they ignore it, or turn it on its head.

Since these so-called peaceful protests began, the liberal elites in the media and state and local governments have supported them. After all, it's not their windows that are going to be broken by flying bricks when the violence starts; it's not their jobs that will be at risk when the mob sets up a police-free zone on the street in front of their businesses. As this goes to print, progressives on the Left continue to push the lie that these protests are nothing more than a series of grassroots uprisings, coordinated at the local level and carried out by Americans who want racial justice.

Hogwash.

Make no mistake: it is not an accident that in the aftermath of the death of George Floyd, protests and riots broke out in more than 2,000 cities and towns across the United States in a matter of days. Do you believe it's a coincidence that the sites of these protests happened to be loaded up with pallets of bricks and rocks before the gatherings even began? This is not a grassroots uprising. This is not a few concerned citizens marching for the right to have their voices heard. This is a coordinated attack on civil tranquility and the rule of law, orchestrated by foreign actors who are, in the words of Attorney General Bill Barr, "playing all sides to exacerbate the violence." The Democrats know that this violence will lead to pain, suffering, and even death—that's not their concern.

They only want to create chaos going into the November elections.

But the biggest lie of all is the blaming of this unrest on President Trump, who is determined to uphold the Constitution, the rule of law, and his oath to protect America. The truth is that only President Trump is willing to stand up to the radical Left and keep us safe.

Racist Trump Defends Using 'Chinese Virus' to Describe Coronavirus Pandemic

—*Rolling Stone*, March 18, 2020

LIE

INSIDE TRUMP'S FAILURE: THE RUSH TO ABANDON LEADERSHIP ROLE ON THE VIRUS

—*New York Times*, July 24, 2020

LIE

Trump's Iran War Has Begun

—*Vox*, January 3, 2020

LIE

TRUMP LABELS HIMSELF 'A WARTIME PRESIDENT' COMBATING CORONAVIRUS

—*Politico*, March 18, 2020

Chapter Two

A MAN FOR THIS SEASON

On the final evening of 2019, with fireworks about to explode over the skies of Palm Beach, Florida, President Donald Trump walked across the lawn of Mar-a-Lago. First Lady Melania Trump, looking radiant as ever in a sleeveless gold-and-white ballgown, walked alongside him. On the other side of the property, hundreds of guests were waiting for them in the grand ballroom of the resort. At midnight, they would ring in the year 2020 with the President of the United States and his family, clinking champagne glasses, telling stories about the passing year, and looking forward with hope and anticipation to a new decade ahead.

They certainly had a lot to be thankful for. President Trump and his family had a lot to be proud of.

By the end of 2019, the United States was in the best shape of its life. The Dow Jones Industrial Average was sitting at 28,462, the highest number it had ever reached. Our unemployment numbers were lower than they'd ever been. Across the globe, our enemies were in full retreat and our allies were finally paying their fair share for the vital services we provided.

There had never been a better time to be an American.

During his first three years in office, President Trump had worked day and night to make good on every one of the bold promises he'd made during his 2016 campaign—promises that Americans were unaccustomed to having fulfilled. He'd bolstered our economy. He'd begun bringing our soldiers, many of whom had been engaged in seemingly endless foreign wars since they were only eighteen years old, home from the battlefield. Along the way, he had faced down the deep state, the Democrats, and a hateful, hyperpartisan news media, managing to win every time and come out the other side stronger than ever.

By all accounts, his success would only continue. In July 2019, the economy had officially entered its longest period of expansion in history, and it showed no signs of slowing down.[1] On the eve of the new year, it seemed that all President Trump had to do was stay the course and run the country exactly as he'd been running it since 2017, and his reelection in November would be all but assured.

On the other side of the aisle, Democrats had no one who could compete with the president on any level. The Democrat Clown Car, full of long-forgotten bozos like Beto O'Rourke, Cory Booker, and "Mayor Pete" Buttigieg, couldn't even get out of first gear. Together, the Democrat candidates were still cramped together, tripping over their clown shoes while the whole country watched and tried not to laugh (or cry). Barring some horrible natural disaster—say, I don't know, an earthquake, a meteor, maybe a viral pandemic that ripped through our major cities and shut down our economy for months—the election of 2020 would be easier for President Trump to win than a staring contest with Sleepy Joe Biden.

Not only could President Trump run the country like a business, eliminating unnecessary spending and sending our national profits soaring, but he could also protect our nation in times of crisis, making the tough calls when nobody else would. The story of his first term was one of swift and certain decisions, strength, and an unwavering sense of right and wrong. There was no dithering.

In October, President Trump had presided over the targeted killing of the brutal terrorist leader Abu Bakr al-Baghdadi (with some assistance from my pal Conan the hero dog), dealing a crippling blow to ISIS in the Middle East. Years before that, he had fired cruise missiles into Syria after he'd seen video of chemical weapons attacks on civilians, including innocent children, upholding the red line that President Obama wouldn't, couldn't, or just didn't have the courage to enforce himself—or maybe he'd cut his own deal with Russia, whom he'd placed in charge of actually monitoring the chemical weapons stockpiles in Syria.

On the diplomatic front, President Trump had engaged in expert negotiations with Kim Jong-Un on the only level that Kim could understand, embarrassing the dictator on the world stage until he finally agreed to come to the negotiating table. President Trump had also ripped up Obama's disastrous nuclear deal with Iran, keeping yet another one of his key campaign promises and ensuring that Iran would never—not in ten years, twenty years, or thirty years—develop a nuclear weapon. Under the president's watch, the world had come closer to peace than it had been since the end of World War II.

Every day brought a new challenge, and every day he faced it down with grit, fierce determination, and resolve.

* * *

That very evening, for example, he had shut down what might have been a deadly protest at the US embassy in Baghdad. Just a few hours before the party at Mar-a-Lago was set to begin, a group of militants in Iraq had stormed the gates of the embassy, where dozens of Americans had been working. They'd fired guns. They'd broken windows with battering rams, taped up anti-American propaganda, and shouted Arabic slogans.[2] All of this provided an eerie echo of Benghazi, an attack on our embassy in Libya that left a United States ambassador and three people dead. If you're a regular viewer of my show, *Justice with Judge Jeanine,* you know that during that crisis, Barack Obama and Secretary of State Hillary Clinton seemed determined to do nothing, and according to Greg Hicks, the senior person on the ground, everyone was told to stand down. Even though we had stations in North Africa, they said it would take too long to get to Benghazi. Were they going there by camel? There was an effective stand-down. When the press gets there before the United States Army, you have to ask: What was the point? What was Barack Obama trying to say about the massacre in Libya? Why not try to secure the crime scene? Why allow the crime scene to be trampled by the media, of all people? Then they lied about it on every Sunday morning show. Then, Susan Rice, the assistant to the Liar in Chief, the one who told you Bowe Bergdahl was a hero, the one who told you Benghazi was a peaceful protest five times, the one who did nothing about the Rwandans being massacred, has the unmitigated gall to say that anyone who votes for Trump belongs to the trash heap of history.

It was exactly the kind of thing President Trump, when he ran for president, said he would not do.

This time, when the rioters arrived at the US embassy in Baghdad, they found it empty. President Trump had ordered a complete evacuation earlier that afternoon, and he'd sent in a unit of US Marines to stop the violence before it could even begin.[3] Thanks to his focus on protecting Americans around the world and asserting our military prowess when necessary, the whole thing was over in less time than it took Hillary Clinton to pull on one of her pantsuits during the Benghazi crisis in 2012.

Today, the attack on our embassy in Baghdad is a small footnote in our history. I'm sure you'd already forgotten about it. But make no mistake: With a less competent president in charge, it would have been catastrophic. If President Trump had made one wrong move, hesitated for even a second too long, hundreds of people might have died. President Trump was working every day to keep us safe.

At the door of the ballroom, President Trump stopped for a moment to answer questions from the reporters of the White House Correspondents' Association who'd traveled to Mar-a-Lago with him. One reporter asked about the status of trade negotiations with China, which had finally begun to bear fruit after months of back-and-forth fighting on tariffs. At the time, President Trump was preparing to sign phase one of a historic trade agreement with China, fulfilling yet another of the promises he'd made during the campaign.

When asked about the situation with our embassy in Iraq, he assured them it was under control. Unlike in 2012, when the

Obama administration had told them the same thing, this time they could take the president's word for it. The Obama administration lied to us; President Trump didn't.

He turned to leave.

Then, just before he entered the room, a reporter asked President Trump to share his New Year's resolution. President Trump politely refused, indicating that once you say a resolution out loud, you risk it not coming true.

"I can't say it," he said. "I think when you do that, you jinx it. I don't want to jinx it."[4]

Well, I don't know what else happened that evening. Maybe President Trump slipped up and shouted his resolution from the rooftops or spilled some salt on the table. Maybe when he walked away, one of those reporters stuck a few extra pins in their President Trump voodoo doll.

What I do know is that within three weeks of hosting that gala at Mar-a-Lago, President Trump would be faced with a test unlike anything an American president had ever endured. He would be placed, suddenly and with very little warning, into a wartime posture, forced to defend the United States from an invisible, invading enemy.

Eventually, he will bring us out of this crisis stronger than ever, proving once and for all that he is a man who can lead not only in times of peace and prosperity but in times of suffering, distress, and upheaval, too. I'm sure you've heard the phrase "a man for all seasons," first used to describe the English statesman Thomas More during the reign of King Henry VIII. Today, that phrase is used to refer to someone who can adapt at will to any circumstances, changing their demeanor and mood to fit whatever is happening.

Well, by the end of the coronavirus pandemic, President Trump would prove that he is much more than that—not just a man for all seasons, but a man specifically for *this* season, seemingly put on earth to be president at this very moment in our history.

* * *

That night, as the fireworks were going off and the partygoers of Mar-a-Lago were celebrating, officials from the city of Wuhan, China, informed the World Health Organization of a deadly virus that had been spreading around their city for a few weeks. "The evidence is highly suggestive," they wrote, "that the outbreak is associated with exposures in one seafood market of Wuhan."[5]

By the time anyone outside China learned about this virus, it would be too late. In a matter of days, this deadly virus would be spreading the world like wildfire. Even President Trump, who has always been able to look ahead and see with remarkable accuracy what was coming around the corner, could not have predicted the horrible toll that China's actions, or lack thereof, would take, both on the United States and the world.

At the beginning of January, the greatest test a president had ever faced began.

THE VIRUS ARRIVES

By now, you've probably read mainstream media stories about how President Trump did not do enough to handle this crisis, especially during these crucial early days. As the election marches toward its conclusion, this is sure to become a major talking point for the loony Left. In fact, Nancy Pelosi and Adam Schiff have demanded we set up a commission like the one that was used after the terror attacks of September 11, 2001, to determine how President Trump failed this country in the early stages of the crisis.

That's a lie!

If you look at the facts, you will see that from the very beginning, President Trump handled this crisis exactly the way he'd handled so many others. He saw the problem, weighed his options, and acted quickly and certainly without fear or favor. In spite of the fact that he had a trade deal in the mix, he made the decision to cut all flights from mainland China.

It's impossible to tell how much worse it could have been if he hadn't taken drastic steps so early in the process.

You want an after-action report, Nancy? Read this.

JUDGE JEANINE'S HANDY AFTER-ACTION REPORT

As far as we know, the first case of the virus that would come to be known as the coronavirus and then Covid-19 reached our shores on January 21, 2020. That day, a thirty-five-year-old man from Washington state got off a plane from Wuhan, China, and carried the virus back to his home in Snohomish County, a suburban location near Seattle.

Recent studies have shown that the virus also landed in major cities like New York, Los Angeles, and Boston, coming in from Europe and Italy before those countries barred travel to the United States. But according to a report in the *New York Times*, despite President Trump's early attempts to implement vital screening procedures at airports in those cities, some of the federal agencies in charge of implementing his orders were much too slow in setting them up.[6] The virus was able to penetrate our borders because we were not testing people soon enough.

Less than eight days after the first case of the virus appeared, while the liberal media and the Democrats in Congress were still laser-focused on his impeachment, President Trump formed the Coronavirus Task Force. This was a team of the most renowned experts on infectious disease in the country, all of whom reported directly to Vice President Mike Pence.

On January 29, President Trump read a report by Peter Navarro, the White House's world-renowned expert on the Chinese supply chain, trade deals, and all things Asia, and grew concerned. According to Navarro's report, "the lack of immune protection or an existing cure or vaccine would leave Americans defenseless in the case of a full-blown coronavirus outbreak on U.S. soil. This lack of protection elevates the risk of the coronavirus evolving into a full-blown pandemic, imperiling the lives of millions of Americans."[7]

Two days later, on January 31, President Trump took the decisive step of shutting down all flights from mainland China to the United States, an unprecedented move not done since 9/11. There is really no way of knowing how many lives were saved by this action. I would venture a guess that there were many people in the White House who were against this. There were political, social, and economic implications. But President Trump, as always, was true to his fundamental belief that Americans come first. Damn the torpedoes.

I also know that Democrats, particularly the ones who have been against President Trump since day one, didn't seem to like it. As soon as Sleepy Joe Biden found out, he nearly blew a gasket, telling supporters at a rally in Iowa that President Trump's actions were "racist."

"This is no time," he said, "for Donald Trump's record of hysteria xenophobia [*sic*], hysterical xenophobia, and fear-mongering to lead the way instead of science."[8]

When Representative Ami Bera, a Democrat from California, heard about the president's travel ban, he called it racist, too.

"This is a virus that happened to pop up in China," he said. "But the virus doesn't discriminate between Asian versus non-Asian. In our response, we can't create prejudices and harbor anxieties toward one population."[9]

Well, Mr. Bera and Mr. Biden, maybe you two are right. Is it possible that if we'd been a little more sensitive in our response, the virus would have skipped right over us and gone on to the next country? Did I miss the study that concluded that the virus was "woke" and down with identity politics?

Of course not!

For the entire month of January, this virus was assaulting our shores like an invading army; closing down our borders was a necessary step in making that assault stop. We should be glad President Trump closed them when he did.

For the next few weeks, despite being attacked constantly by Democrats in Congress, President Trump kept a close eye on the situation. During his second State of the Union address on February 4, 2020, he warned the country about what was to come.

"Protecting Americans' health also means fighting infectious diseases," he said. "My administration will take all necessary steps to safeguard our citizens from this threat."[10]

When the president finished his speech, Nancy Pelosi showed her interest in what the president said by repeatedly ripping her copy of the speech in half. Apparently, Nancy didn't think this virus was going to be that big of a deal. She couldn't have been more blasé about it if she'd been out shopping for wombats in Wuhan. On February 24, Nancy and a few of her legislative aides walked through Chinatown with a group of reporters—you probably know that Nancy doesn't go *anywhere* without a camera crew—and took one last shot at President Trump for shutting down travel with China.

"We should come to Chinatown. Precautions have been taken by our city. We know that there is a concern about tourism, traveling all throughout the world, but we think it's very safe to be in Chinatown and hope that others will come."

Earlier in the month, even New York City's public health commissioner had let everyone know that it would be perfectly safe to celebrate the Lunar New year there, too.

> @NYCHealthCommr: As we gear up to celebrate the #LunarNewYear in NYC, I want to assure New Yorkers that there is no reason for anyone to change their holiday plans, avoid the subway, or certain parts of the city because of #coronavirus.

Then, she followed it up with this:

> I want to be clear, this is about a virus, not a group of people. There is NO excuse for anyone to discriminate or stigmatize people of Asian heritage. We are here today to urge all New Yorkers to continue to live their lives as usual.[11]

A few days later, on March 3, Mayor Bill de Blasio of New York City tweeted this:

> @BilldeBlasio: Since I'm encouraging New Yorkers to go on with your lives + get out on the town despite Coronavirus, I thought I would offer some suggestions. Here's the first: thru Thurs 3/5 go see "The Traitor" @ FilmLinc. If "The Wire" was a true story + set in Italy, it would be this film.

I'm sorry—*who* failed to respond adequately to this crisis, again? And by the way, isn't sending a message to #Resist not just contraindicated, isn't it putting public health in danger to send a contrary message?

Throughout the beginning of this crisis, both of these people would berate President Trump for not acting quickly enough in the beginning. In one of the many interviews she'd give on CNN, Nancy Pelosi would say that the president's failure to act early was "deadly."

Well, here comes the boomerang: Point one accusatory finger at someone else, and there are three pointing right back at you.

While they were telling people to go on with their lives as normal, President Trump was closely monitoring the situation with the virus and taking crucial steps to try to prevent its spread. But even his best efforts couldn't stop the virus. In an investigation conducted early in the month of April, the *New York Times* found that more than 430,000 people managed to slip into the United States from China and Europe in the early months of 2020. Even with President Trump's travel ban on China, the most drastic step ever taken by the United States to combat the spread of a virus, we could not stop it from coming.

I don't know if anyone could have.

LOCKDOWN

Beginning on March 22, the United States entered a state of lockdown that was truly surreal. For everyone, life was different. All of us in television experienced a new reality: working from home.

In the beginning, I mostly stayed in my house, cleaned constantly, I couldn't stop mopping my floors and filmed my show in the city. When the city shut down, too, I started filming from home. During one memorable taping, I was placed into a dark van in my driveway with no monitor, a teleprompter that was running backward, and a crew that didn't appear to notice. Like many, I was required to do my own makeup for the show, which clearly is not my forte. Let's just say that the following week, I started doing my hair and makeup on Wednesday for my Saturday show!

And by the way, to anyone who made fun of me on Twitter: *You* try walking into a dark van, turning your phone upside down, and attempting to read it while you're talking through an earpiece to somebody you can't even see.

But it wasn't all bad. During the first months of the shutdown, for instance, I finally got to try some of my mother's old recipes, including her pineapple upside down cake, which filled the house with a sweet smell for a few hours and reminded me of her. I also baked an angel food birthday cake for my son Alex, who was quarantined in New York City, then sent him a picture of it and then proceeded to eat the whole thing myself. There was also a cream cheese cherry pie. As the weeks went on, I went through all the jam in my pantry—and then went out and bought more, posting each one on social media as I consumed it. All of us were buying stuff that we would never have even *considered* pre-lockdown.

The real doozy was when I had to put on my bathing suit and jump into the shower to wash my standard poodles, Stella and Sir Lancelot because the groomer was closed. Sir Lancelot is a gentleman and he will do anything I say. Stella, my rescue dog, on the other hand, has the strength to resist. She listens to her own inner voice, certainly not mine! I was convinced that it would be no big deal. Trust me. It was a *disaster.* Each one flew out of the shower soaking wet, and when I finally got a chance to blow-dry their hair, I thought they would look perfect. The truth? They smelled great, but they looked like hell.

In a sense, this period at home was a blessing for me. I had time to think about my life and the blessings that I have as an American, and the opportunity to reflect on all that God has given me.

Unfortunately, too many Americans did not have the same experience. For many people, the lockdown was catastrophic. They were afraid they wouldn't have the ability to provide for their families. For the first time, people who wanted to work not only couldn't work but were prevented from working. The economy that Donald Trump had provided for us, and to which we had become so accustomed, had become elusive. Restaurant owners all over the country, no longer able to fill their establishments with patrons, laid off workers in droves. Thousands of hotel workers were furloughed indefinitely, deprived of their weekly wages and uncertain of their future employment status. A study conducted months later showed that in March alone, 701,000 people lost their jobs lost their jobs—which was nothing compared to what lay ahead.[12] The quarantine let depression, anxiety, and desperation set in.

Over the course of a single day, the Dow Jones Industrial Average fell 2,352 points, the most precipitous declines since 1987.[13]

This was an economic crisis unlike anything the United States had seen since the Great Depression, and, to harden the blow, it was caused by an earth-shattering public health catastrophe. Because of this deadly combination, none of our government's previous efforts were going to work against it. We couldn't send people back to work with government-funded jobs, as we did during the Great Depression. We couldn't send people out to shopping malls and Disney World, as we did after the terror attacks of 9/11, because crowds weren't allowed to gather and the shops were all closed. Clearly, this would require a different kind of solution—one that Americans had never seen before.

It was going to take grit, creativity, and patience. Most important, it was going to take time.

During the German bombing raids of 1940, citizens of London were placed under similar circumstances. They awakened every morning knowing that today might be the day their families were killed in their homes. Because of this, they held each other close and enjoyed the company of their fellow citizens. Picture a scene from *Cabaret*. But during the deadly coronavirus pandemic, we couldn't do this. Many families were forced to take shelter miles apart from each other. Grown children couldn't see their elderly parents, and young grandchildren couldn't see their grandparents. It was like we were living in a bubble.

During this tumultuous time, President Trump was sitting behind the Resolute Desk. He was a man inspired by Winston Churchill, of whom he keeps a bust in the Oval Office at all times.

And thank God he was.

A LEADER FOR OUR TIME

In more ways than one, President Trump was the leader we desperately needed during these dark days. Not only because he has the capacity to work twenty-four hours a day, seven days a week, staying in the fight long after many much younger members of his staff had fallen down from exhaustion. Not only because he'd been working tirelessly during his first years in office to provide the nation more than ten thousand points of economic cushion, so that when the most precipitous decline in the history of the stock market *did* finally occur on his watch—through no fault of his own—the lowest figure the Dow ever hit was 18,591. That's still about two thousand points higher than it was on the very *best* day under President Barack Obama, the man who told us you'd need a magic wand to get the kind of growth President Trump has given us.[14] It wasn't simply his amazing commitment to American business, or his playful sense of humor, or the way he had of talking straight to the press, even in the midst of a crisis.

No. President Trump was the leader we needed because more than anyone else—certainly more than anyone who's held the office during my lifetime—he understands America and her place in history. He understands what Americans want, what they need, and he is dedicated to improving their lives at all costs. He knows what regular Americans care about. Ever since he was inaugurated in January 2017, his main goal has been ensuring that all Americans, no matter their race, creed, or nationality, are allowed to share in the success of their nation, and so far, he has met that goal with amazing results.

In 2015, Donald Trump ran for president to help the very same people who would be hit the hardest by the catastrophic coronavirus outbreak almost five years later. He ran to help the plumbers, electricians, and dock workers of the world; the carpenters and car dealers and restaurant owners who awakened every morning of this crisis in a state of dread and uncertainty, not knowing when their businesses would reopen and jobs would return or their paychecks would start coming again. President Trump heard their cries for help loud and clear, and vowed to act swiftly in their defense.

So, when it finally became clear that coronavirus would hit the United States much harder than it had hit any other country in the world, including China, South Korea, and Italy, the president called on his decades of experience in business for a quick, comprehensive solution. He did not wait for the dithering bozos in Congress to bring him a bill that would solve America's problems. He didn't use focus groups or poll tests to find out what kind of executive response would be most palatable to the public. He sure as hell didn't count on mayors like New York City's Bill de Blasio, Los Angeles's Eric Garcetti, or Chicago's Lori Lightfoot to figure it out for him.

Instead, on March 13, President Trump held a press conference in the Rose Garden of the White House, speaking directly to the American people as he always had. By his side were Dr. Anthony Fauci, the man who is heralded for bringing the country through the AIDS epidemic of the 1980s (although we still don't have a vaccine for it), and Dr. Deborah Birx, one of the world's most renowned experts on infectious disease.

He also included several leaders of private-sector laboratories, all of whom assured us that they were working around the clock to get tests into the hands of people who needed them. Their inclusion in the response to this crisis sent a clear message to the country and to the world that America would remain open for business no matter what came our way. These people also made it clear that the solutions to this crisis, whether vaccines, ventilators, or testing equipment, were going to come as a result of capitalism and American ingenuity, not the bureaucracy of the federal government.

It is often said that in moments of great uncertainty, people show us who they really are. Crisis, as the old adage goes, reveals character. Time and time again, over a long career that has involved a great deal of pain and trauma, I have found this to be the case. It was certainly true during the first days of the coronavirus pandemic, as the country entered panic mode and our leaders were forced to act.

During those crucial first months, President Trump certainly revealed who he really is. So did Vice President Mike Pence, the man to whom President Trump entrusted so much responsibility when he named him the head of the Coronavirus Task Force. Both men showed the kind of calm, resolve, and unflagging determination that few world leaders could have mustered in that trying moment.

But it wasn't only them.

All over the world, people showed parts of themselves that inspired me. When the National Basketball Association, for instance, announced that all further games would be canceled for the season, a nineteen-year-old rookie on the New Orleans Pelicans named Zion Williamson promised to pay the salaries of every worker at the Smoothie King Center, the stadium where his team would have played if it hadn't been for the pandemic.[15] In rural Oregon, when the school district shut down, school bus drivers went around delivering paper-bag lunches to children who couldn't afford to eat at home.[16]

But not everyone showed such courage. In fact, some people, mostly those who dwell in the dirty swamp of Washington, DC, and its shadowy environs, saw the tragedy as nothing more than a chance to advance their own personal agendas. They used it, as they've used every major event since November 8, 2016, to hurt the president. They used it to sow division and discord or, in the worst cases, to benefit themselves.

NAME GAMES

About a month into the worst of the crisis, President Trump made the decision to hold daily briefings from the press briefing room, a space that hadn't been used to brief the press in eleven months when the coronavirus crisis began. You might remember that in the beginning of the president's first term, that room had been the site of several nasty back-and-forth fights with White House reporters. It's where CNN's Jim Acosta had made his rambling, almost Bidenesque speeches about the Statue of Liberty and immigrants and American values; where Sarah Huckabee Sanders, a quick-witted woman who could handle anything thrown at her (and did), had been forced to deal with lies and false stories every day.

In a crisis, though, public safety takes precedence over politics, at least when there's a real leader in charge. So, President Trump, knowing that it was important to talk to the American people directly, would bring the experts to answer questions and lay out what they felt was the best course of action for the American people. This had nothing to do with politics, although the press constantly tried to turn it into a political game. He said that the American people are entitled to transparency. He opened up the briefing room to reporters, giving them direct access to him and the newly formed Coronavirus Task Force. It's no different from what Winston Churchill did during World War II or what Franklin Delano Roosevelt did with his "fireside chats" in the years following the Great Depression. Donald Trump wanted the American public to get the news, and he wanted them to get it directly from him, the President of the United States, and from the team of experts he had assembled.

Walking into the press room on March 15 at the beginning of the pandemic, I'm sure the president expected the same hate and vitriol he'd had to endure from reporters since his first day in office. After all, the moment they had been waiting for during the three years, two months, and twenty-six days of the president's first term had finally arrived: The stock market was in trouble, and they could *finally* write a negative story about President Trump that had some shred of truth to it. I'm sure Paul Krugman, the columnist for the *New York Times* who predicted on Election Day 2016 that "markets would tumble" celebrated the fulfillment of his prophecy—albeit a few years too late. I wouldn't be surprised if CNN threw a big party in their boardroom.

Surprisingly, though, things got off to a pretty civil beginning. For a while, the reporters in the room managed to contain their excitement with an air of poise, at least when the cameras were pointed at them. Maybe it's because they all had to sit six feet apart. (Stupidity, much like the coronavirus, is believed to be highly contagious.) As the first days of the crisis unfolded, reporters asked about steps that ordinary Americans could take to prevent the crisis. They inquired about infection rates and testing kits. They asked for a rough timeline of the country's response—all the things you'd expect these servants of the people to ask about during a public health emergency.

Then, on day six of the briefings, as the body counts were piling up and Americans were being laid off in historic numbers, a reporter from ABC News named Cecilia Vega decided that now, in the middle of a crisis, was her moment to risk it all and go for the gold in the Fake News Olympics, vaulting over all the lying liberal luminaries of briefings past. That's right Paul Krugman, Chris Matthews, and Jim Acosta: Move over, because Cecilia was about to come in hot!

Toward the end of the briefing, really hamming up her fake panic and concern for the cameras, she decided to ask the president this: "Why do you keep calling this the Chinese virus?" she asked. "There are reports of dozens of incidents of bias against Chinese Americans in this country."[17]

That's right. Not a word from this woman about the soaring death rate or the preventive steps we could have taken to stop it from climbing higher. Nothing about the fact that at the very moment she was asking the question, the Chinese government had just finished printing thousands of pamphlets falsely blaming the United States Army for spreading the virus. No. Instead, she was worried, as the Left in this country always seems to be, about *racism*, whether it's real or not, and whether some ethnic, religious, or other minority group is feeling offended by something.

President Trump, somehow managing to keep his cool, responded, "Because it comes from China. It's not racist at all. It comes from China."

Apparently, Cecilia wasn't alone. The next day during the briefing, a reporter named Yamiche Alcindor indicated that a member of the White House staff had referred to the coronavirus as the "Kung-flu" and asked whether that was "acceptable at this time."

Again, President Trump refused to take the bait.

"It comes from China," he said. "That's why they call it the Chinese virus."

Well, Yamiche and Cecilia, I have a few follow-up questions, if you'll permit me.

First of all, *are you stupid*? You're going to use up vital time during a presidential briefing—in an unprecedented national emergency, no less—to ask questions about feelings and identity politics, and then have the nerve to act like the president is the one who's being irresponsible? Please. Even if your questions *had* been pertinent, which they weren't, a five-year-old could have told you that there is nothing racist about calling a virus that comes from China a Chinese virus, just as there's nothing wrong with calling a correspondent from CNN a CNN correspondent.

If you need proof, take a look at some of your colleagues from the liberal media. When the virus first hit, *they* certainly had no problem calling it the Chinese virus. On January 20, CNN published a story called "Vaccine for New Chinese Coronavirus in the Works."[18] The next day, *BuzzFeed* reported that "The First Case of the Chinese Coronavirus" had hit the United States.[19] Over the next two weeks, outlets from the *Washington Post* and the BBC to *Business Insider, USA Today,* and National Public Radio would all reference either the "Chinese Coronavirus" or the "Wuhan Coronavirus"—or both.[20]

Also, since it would appear you two didn't do your typical fifteen seconds of Google research before beginning to report on this epidemic, here's a primer on viruses and how they have historically been named: Other than a few guidelines from the World Health Organization that discourage naming diseases for places, people, or other geographic locations, which were created in 2015, there are no rules for naming a virus.[21] Usually, when the time comes to decide what to call these things, the people who would do so are busy, you know, *saving lives*. Unlike you two, they have real jobs, and when they don't do those jobs, people die.

Since you both seem so concerned, though, you might be interested to know that when it does come time to name a virus, it is not uncommon—in fact, it is *extremely* common—to name it after the place where that virus first appeared, or the group of people who first contracted it. Consider the Spanish Flu of 1918, or the Hong Kong Flu of 1968. Do you think anyone who came down with those were expressing racism against the Spanish or the people of Hong Kong? Of course not! Back then, names were only names, not complex signifiers of power, gender, and patriarchy, or whatever you lunatics are calling it these days.

Here, if you're interested, is a far-from-complete list of viruses that were named after people or places:

- West Nile virus
- Rocky Mountain spotted fever
- Lyme disease
- Ross River fever
- Ebola
- Zika fever
- Japanese encephalitis
- German measles
- Spanish flu
- Hong Kong flu
- Lassa fever[22]

Convinced yet? Do you think we named Lyme disease so we could spread racism against people who lived in the small town of Lyme, Connecticut? Or do you think that a band of evil Republicans came together in the 1970s to be racist against the people who, let's see, "contracted lung infections after attending the annual American Legion convention in Philadelphia?" Give me a break.

Still, this little snafu between reporters and the president in the briefing room was enough to attract national media attention. Within days, instead of reporting on how to combat the spread of the coronavirus, news outlets were settling into their old habit of calling everything the president does racist, fanning the flames of the culture war when they should have been focused on the war against this deadly epidemic. The *New York Times* said that the president was using the podium to "spew hate" and "rewrite history."[23] *HuffPost* ran a story about why we don't give viruses racist names.[24] The focus shifted from China's role in this crisis to potential racism against Asian Americans, just as the media wanted.[25]

From there, it only spiraled. Reporters started asking the kinds of hateful, unhelpful questions at a clip that surprised even me. For days, he endured these questions with an uncharacteristic restraint. Then he started giving it right back to them, as he had since the beginning of his administration. Asked what advice he had for Americans by a smug reporter from NBC who'd been hammering him with unfair questions for days, the president replied, hilariously, "I'd say you're a terrible reporter, that's what I'd say."

Before long, our strong showing of national unity had devolved back into the media's war against Trump. It was like jumping back in time two years, back to when the press briefing room was open every day and the press was free to write whatever lies it wanted to about the administration. No wonder they closed it down in the first place.

But President Trump accepted this new state of affairs with a good sense of humor. He never got off course or allowed the press to bait him into petty fights. Instead, he shut down their absurd, irrelevant, and politically charged questions quickly and then got back to business. Even when the press tried to write stories that fomented mass hysteria and panic, the president still answered questions and gave them information—something he was not required to do and which took valuable time away from actually working. What was important to him was that the American people hear the news directly from him.

Of course, the press conferences were only the beginning.

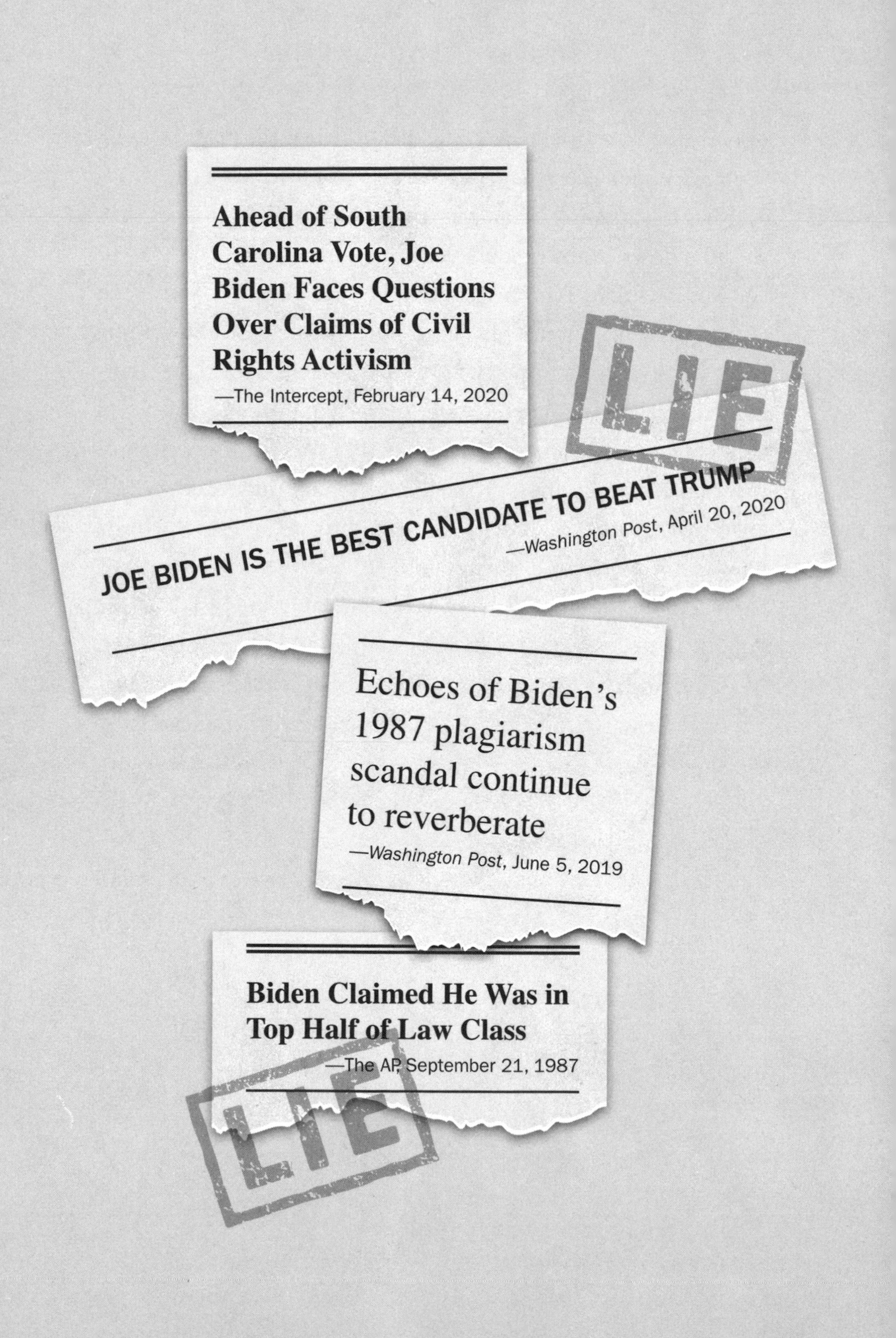
Ahead of South Carolina Vote, Joe Biden Faces Questions Over Claims of Civil Rights Activism
—The Intercept, February 14, 2020
LIE
JOE BIDEN IS THE BEST CANDIDATE TO BEAT TRUMP
—Washington Post, April 20, 2020
Echoes of Biden's 1987 plagiarism scandal continue to reverberate
—Washington Post, June 5, 2019
Biden Claimed He Was in Top Half of Law Class
—The AP, September 21, 1987
LIE

Chapter Three

BUNKER BIDEN

Around the beginning of March, it seemed like the coronavirus had taken over the world. Even if we didn't have it, this little pathogen had somehow burrowed its way into our brains, making it almost impossible to think about anything else. When you turned on the television, there it was. When you opened a newspaper, there it was. By St. Patrick's Day, we were practically begging for relief.

Then, suddenly, like an answer to our prayers, a small careening object came slowly into view on the road ahead, weaving crazily as it swerved in and out of the lanes.

Was it a bird?

A plane?

Nope! That, ladies and gentlemen, was the world-famous Democrat Clown Car, ripping through the country one last time before it finally slowed to a crawl to dispense one last lonely liberal bozo.

And boy, was it *roomy* in there!

Alone in the front seat at last was Sleepy Joe Biden, the seventy-five-year-old senator from Delaware. Over the past year, seemingly against all odds, Sleepy Joe had overcome his age, obvious mental issues, and the fact that nobody really liked him anymore to become the presumptive Democrat nominee for president. All he had to do was not screw up for a few more months, and the nomination would be his.

Of course, there was one final hoop for him to jump through.

Behind him in the back seat sat Senator Bernie Sanders, the crazy-haired comrade from Burlington, Vermont, who'd promised us free college, free healthcare, and . . . well, free everything, really. He was going to redistribute the wealth of America, tax us into oblivion, and scold us the whole time he was doing it. Together, these two represented the absolute best that the Democrat Party had to offer this country in the year 2020.

Yep, seriously.

Long gone were the crazy clowns of yesteryear who'd kept us so entertained during the early stages of the primary. Almost as soon as the race had begun, they'd started to drop like flies.

Political lightweights like Robert "Beto" O'Rourke and Mayor Bill de Blasio had been among the first to go. The car had barely begun to speed up when these two Democlowns opened up the doors on either side and jumped out together, rolling down the road in a cloud of dust and white makeup. After them, everyone's fun aunt, Kamala Harris, also had to leave the party early, taking with her that hysterical parody of her that Maya Rudolph used to perform on *Saturday Night Live*. Which, as I'm sure you know, left more space in the program for them to dust off other timeless characters such as . . . oh, I don't know, *me*! (Thanks a lot, Kamala.)

But it wasn't only the big names. Along the way, we also lost such forgettable liberals as Deval Patrick, John Delaney, Jim Connelly, Michael Bennet, and Tom Steyer. And if you're wondering just *how* forgettable these guys were, consider this: I made one of those names up as I was typing this, and you're probably not even sure which one it is!

By the time the real contenders for the nomination had been forced out—your Mayor Petes, your Elizabeth Warrens, your Amy Klobuchars—the world was wondering if it could really be true that in the year 2020, the Democrats had come up with nobody better than Bernie and Biden. The same group of people who preached identity politics, diversity, and inclusion was now going to pin all their hopes on two old white guys from the United States Senate.

By their own self-imposed diversity standards, almost *any* other candidate would have been better. Mayor Pete would have been the first gay president. Kamala Harris would have been the first black woman. Andrew Yang, the tech billionaire who promised everyone $1,000 a month, would have been the first Asian American. Even Bernie Sanders, if he'd hung in a little longer, could have become the first Jewish nominee for president—although, considering how liberals in Congress like Rashida Tlaib and Ilhan Omar feel about Israel, a Jewish nominee is probably not something the radical Left would have bragged about.

Sadly, though, it seemed that none of those other clowns had quite what the Democrat voters of this country were looking for in the year 2020—a certain *pop*, if you will, that crazy look in the eye that says, *Hurry up! Elect me now! I don't know how much longer my brain is still going to be working!*

ONE LAST DEBATE

On March 15, 2020, with these two clowns still fighting over the wheel, the clown car finally pulled into a parking space in the lot behind a small CNN studio in Washington, DC, the site of the final Democrat primary debate. Because of the growing pandemic, the debate had been moved from its original venue in Phoenix to this cramped little studio in the swamp, where it would take place without an audience. This meant that Bernie Sanders could no longer rely on energetic, free-stuff-loving Bernie bros to applaud when he made his insane points about socialism, and Joe Biden . . . well, actually, for Sleepy Joe, it'd probably be about the same. Between his never-ending stories, his dopey demeanor, and his tendency to SPEAK AT AN ALARMINGLY HIGH VOLUME during the first couple of debates, he wasn't getting a whole lot of applause anyway.

That night, at eight o'clock on the big red nose, the candidates came out, bumped elbows, and stood at podiums that had been placed six feet away from each other. Anyone who'd been hoping for fireworks—or at least some sign of life—would be severely disappointed. In the end, the debate only served to prove that even in the midst of a global pandemic, the Democrats can still manage to bore you to tears.

Over the course of two hours—which felt more like twenty years—they yelled at each other about voting records, policy details, and their respective ideas about how to combat the coronavirus, which, by that evening, had infected 3,487 Americans.[1] Bernie said Medicare for all was the answer. Biden was noncommittal on that point, as always, but he didn't offer a plan of his own. Instead, he tried to remind the viewers at home that yes, in case you somehow forgot, he *did* used to work in the White House. According to a count kept by *New York* magazine, Biden mentioned the White House Situation Room, where he got to sit during some of the O-Biden administration's biggest crises, six times during the debate; he said he would be ready to act "right now" because of that experience sixteen times, repeating the phrase over and over.[2]

When it came to policy, they talked about healthcare, and trade, and . . .

You know what? I can't do this anymore. To be honest, I have *no* idea what else these two bozos talked about that night. By the ten-minute mark of this two-hour clown show, I felt like I'd need ten gallons of coffee just to stay awake. I'd be surprised if even *they* remember a single detail of what they said.

Looking back, one of the only things that sticks out about the whole debate is Joe Biden's "surprise" announcement that he would name a female vice president when he became the nominee. Other than that, the whole thing was a snooze. In fact, if social distancing really starts to stress you out during these next few months, pull up a few clips from this debate on YouTube and try to watch for five minutes; I guarantee it'll put you right to sleep.

In the end, it didn't matter anyway. The *New York Times* reported that the audience for the debate was only 10.7 million, nearly half of what the first two had gotten, and I'd be surprised if half that number made it to the final elbow bump at the end.[3] As you can see, even with people literally trapped in their homes, these two couldn't make the country care about what they had to say.

For all intents and purposes, the coronavirus had effectively ended the Democrat primaries. The debate only served to prove it. By the next morning, more than 4,226 people in the United States had been infected by the coronavirus virus and forty-five had died. That number was rising exponentially. We were in a state of emergency, and nobody had the time to care about who the Democrats were going to run against President Trump, especially when they were so clearly going to end up losing anyway. The country wanted to make their decision and get it over with, looking for something old, boring, and comfortable. Clearly, Joe Biden was their guy.

Much like an old sweater from the attic, he brought comfort to those who needed it. Was he the best thing in the world? No. Was he itchy? Sure. But he was the best they could do during a hard time.

So, under the stress of this deadly pandemic, the country seemed to decide with near-unanimous consent that it would be Sleepy Joe Biden, not Crazy Bernie, who would take the final custard pie to the face on election night. Even though Crazy Bernie wouldn't "officially" drop out for another month or so—and even then, he would keep his delegates for the convention—the hours after that final debate were when it all ended for him.

And thus, the Democrat primaries of 2020 ended not with a bang, but with a whimper. Or, to be more accurate, it ended with the faint sound of Joe Biden, and most of the country, saying, *Wait, really?*

SLEEPY JOE IN THE SHADOWS

If you were surprised to see Joe Biden finally become the Democrat nominee for president, imagine how *he* felt.

When he looked over at the passenger seat of the beat-up Democrat clown car—Joe doesn't drive so well—and finally found it empty, I'm sure Biden gripped that wheel hard and wondered how, of all the qualified Democrats in the country, it was he, a seventy-seven-year-old white guy who could barely remember his own name, who'd be forced to stand opposite President Trump on a debate stage in the fall. I'll bet he needed to change his Depends after that one! Do you think money expended on Depends can be deducted as a campaign expense? After all, he had given us plenty of reasons not to vote for him. He had screwed up names, fumbled through speeches, and thrown in more nonsensical references to old schoolyard fights than I'd ever heard in my life.

Whatever he was thinking, I know *I* was confused.

After watching Joe Biden on the stump during the months leading up to the coronavirus pandemic, the idea that he was going to step into the ring with President Trump on debate night was baffling to me. As I'm sure you know, the president is a man who can take even the most seasoned political debaters in the world—Ted Cruz, Marco Rubio, and Crooked Hillary Clinton—and make mincemeat out of them. And clearly, Sleepy Joe was nowhere near their level. I couldn't believe the kind of carnage that would almost surely occur at a Biden-Trump debate was even *legal*, let alone something you could televise in primetime.

Every time he got the chance, Sleepy Joe let us know that he was not up to the job. In the month of February 2020 alone, he had already trailed off in the middle of countless stories. He had obviously forgotten where he was during a speech in Columbus, Ohio, pausing for a full six seconds and staring off into the distance like he'd just seen an alien in the back of the audience.[4] He had announced several times that he was running for the United States Senate, not the presidency.[5] He had also mixed up the names of his wife and sister more than once—which must create problems in their household that I don't even want to *think* about—and he'd forgotten the name of Barack Obama, who, apparently, had forgotten to endorse him.[6] I wonder why!

Want to run through a few more? Don't worry, I can do this all day.

A few days after his first rally in Columbus, Biden had tried to quote the Declaration of Independence during a campaign speech, saying, and I'm quoting exactly here, "We hold these truths to be self-evident." Long pause. "All men and women created by the . . . you know, you know, the thing." (Is that how it goes? Maybe I learned it wrong in elementary school.) Speaking in Iowa, he had referred to Margaret Thatcher when he meant Theresa May.[7]

Here, if you're interested, is a running list of some of Joe Biden's other greatest hits, transcribed here in the man's own words:

May 22, 2020: *"If you have a problem figuring our whether you're for me or Trump, then you ain't black."*

August 9, 2019: *"Poor kids are just as bright and just as talented as white kids."*

July 9, 2020: *"I got a lot of—I got hairy legs that turn . . . blonde in the sun. And the kids used to come up and reach in the pool and rub my leg down so it was straight and then watch the hair come back up again. They'd look at it. So, I learned about roaches. I learned about kids jumping on my lap. And I've loved kids jumping on my lap. And I tell you what, the men are now all men. The guys I worked with down here, and they're all guys all the time, they're all good men."*

May 18, 2020: *"We choose truth over facts."*

September 9, 2008: *"Uh, uh, Chuck Graham, state senator, is here. Stand up, Chuck! Let 'em see ya! Oh, God love ya, what am I talking about."*

[For context, I should probably say that Chuck Graham, the state senator to whom Biden was speaking at the time, had been in a wheelchair since he was in high school.]

I'm sorry folks, but there are gaffes, and then there are . . . well, whatever the hell *those* are.

By the beginning of March, it got so bad that even the liberal media—who'd always been Biden's biggest defenders—were calling him out on it. The *Washington Post*, which had previously defended Biden's grave errors in judgment as nothing more than cute little gaffes, published a column titled "It's Fair to Speculate Whether Biden Is Mentally Fit to Be President."[8] The *New Yorker* published an article called "Why Joe Biden's Gaffes Matter," citing a writer named Michael Kinsley who defined a gaffe this way: "A [gaffe] occurs when a politician tells the truth—some obvious truth he isn't supposed to say."[9]

His problem, if I may be blunt about it, is that his mind is not quite what it used to be.

Compared to President Trump, who during his first campaign never missed a beat, even when he was doing three campaign stops a day, giving hour-long speeches at every one without looking at a single note, Biden looked like an amateur. If he'd been forced to tag along with the Trump campaign for even two days in 2015, he'd have jumped out of the plane somewhere over Michigan.

And just think: If that's what the stress of a campaign did to that man's brain, what on earth is the United States presidency going to do to him? Even the strongest men come out of that job looking like they've aged twenty years, and Sleepy Joe barely looks like he's got twenty more *minutes* of fight left in him. If, by some miracle, he gets elected and he ends up having to deal with even *half* of what President Trump has already dealt with, he'll be out on the White House lawn in no time singing show tunes. The job would break his brain, simple as that.

So, you might say that the emergence of the coronavirus came as something of a blessing to the Biden campaign. With the whole country shut down, Sleepy Joe could no longer make those famous "gaffes" of his. He couldn't say stupid things to people because he wouldn't be allowed to *talk* to people. With campaign events suspended and crowds unable to gather, he wouldn't be able to creepily rub the shoulders of female voters or whisper in people's ears because he wouldn't be allowed within six feet of anyone!

As a campaign strategy, it was perfect.

In fact, if I didn't know better, I'd say Joe Biden cooked this virus up himself.

As soon as the virus hit, the Biden campaign had a similar thought. With Joe Biden confined to his house in Wilmington, Delaware, according to a report in *Politico*, his top campaign aides advised him not to attack the president for a few days, assuming (correctly) that taking shots at the commander in chief while you're sitting alone in your basement tends to make a guy look . . . well, stupid.[10]

So, almost immediately after he gave a tightly scripted, surprisingly presidential press conference on March 13, Bunker Joe went into full-on hibernation mode. During that time, the presumptive Democrat nominee became harder to find than one of Hillary Clinton's emails, and the country was much better off for it.

Politically speaking, it was probably the best move he could have made. Anyone who's seen Joe Biden give a speech in public—listening to his odd references, his long digressions, and all those old stories about Corn Pop and Skeeter and dog-faced horse ponies (or horse-faced pony dogs, or whatever he actually said that day)—knows that the less this man is allowed to speak, the better.

I'm sure that somewhere, buried deep in the recesses of the former vice president's brain, Bunker Biden knows that this is true. Somewhere deep down, he must be painfully aware that he does not have what it takes to run this country or even to see his long, calamitous campaign through to the end. Maybe that's the part that keeps making him trip over basic words or trail off in the middle of sentences. Maybe that's why all his strange tough-guy stories end up making no sense, or why he can't ever seem to tell where he is at any given moment.

Maybe, while he was deep in hibernation down in his basement in Delaware, that part of his brain kicked into overdrive, showing Bunker Joe a little slideshow of all the gaffes, wrong moves, and grave mistakes that led him to this point in the first place. Maybe as he slept, he saw the plagiarism scandals, the Anita Hill hearings, the accusations of inappropriate touching, and his family's corrupt deals with foreign governments.

Let's take a look, shall we?

A CAMPAIGN OF LIES

Did the pages get all blurry? Good.

That, ladies and gentlemen, was us traveling back in time to the year 1987, when Sleepy Joe Biden first threw his floppy clown wig in the ring and decided to run for president.

As you probably know, the world was a much different place back then. The stock market had just taken a big dip, bringing the Dow Jones Industrial Average from 2,630 to just under 1,800 in just one day. There was a Republican—George H. W. Bush—running to bring our economy back. Against him, there were seven candidates for president, none of whom were very impressive. A newspaper columnist had dubbed them "the seven dwarves," and the name stuck. In New York, a governor named Cuomo—as in Mario, Andrew's father—was wringing his hands about whether he should join the fray and run for president himself. He had given a speech in 1984 at the Democrat National Convention that had blown the roof off the place, and people were practically begging him to run. In the end, he'd decide not to.

You know what? Now that I've written it all out, maybe things aren't so different from today after all.

Anyway, in Washington, Joe Biden was on fire.

Since the beginning of his career, Biden had billed himself as a young, hip, blue-collar hotshot from Delaware. When he won his first senate race, he was only twenty-nine years old, and he ran on a platform of hope and radical change, unseating a stodgy old establishment politician named J. Caleb Boggs. Every morning, Biden rode the Amtrak train into Washington, often sitting in the engine car with the conductors, and he liked to be called Six Pack Joe.

During that first campaign for president, Biden would often say that American politics moved in two cycles, each one driven by two very different groups. First, you had the young, angsty reformers who came in and made radical change; then, you had the stodgy old political class who would come in, calm everyone down, and allow America to "catch its breath."[11]

Obviously, Biden thought he was in the first group. He fancied himself a liberal reformer in the tradition of Franklin Delano Roosevelt, John F. Kennedy, and Lyndon Johnson—men who could smash through legislation whether the old establishment politicians liked it or not. He was going to go to Washington, shake things up—today, you might even say "drain the swamp"—and support the interests of the working-class people he grew up with. Obviously, Biden was not always the shady, backroom-dealing Washington insider we know today.

In the beginning, he actually believed in things.

Or so he claimed.

Whenever he gave a speech during the race for the 1988 presidential primary, Biden leaned hard on his blue-collar roots, and he spoke often about the small role he'd played in the famous civil rights marches of the 1960s.

Here he is speaking to a crowd in New Hampshire in February 1987: "When I marched in the civil rights movement, I did not march with a twelve-point program. I marched with tens of thousands of others to change attitudes. And we changed attitudes."

Well, I have to admit, he was partially right about that. Joe Biden certainly did not march in the civil rights movement with a twelve-point program. In fact, he didn't march in the civil rights movement *at all.* At no point during Biden's time at the

University of Delaware or Syracuse University College of Law did he participate in a single civil rights march, let alone one with "tens of thousands of others." He'd only admit this years later, telling reporters in a press gaggle in the 1990s that he "was never part of that. I wore sport coats."

According to interviews they'd give in later years to the *New York Times*, Biden's campaign aides at the time used to point out this pesky little lie about the marches whenever their candidate would start riffing on his fake experience in the civil rights movement. He would, according to these aides, "[assure] them he understood—then [keep] telling the story anyway."[12] In other words, he lied.

If Twitter had existed back then, that might have been the end of the road for Lyin' Joe. But back in the 1980s, smaller gaffes like this were easy to hide. We didn't have people watching over us all the time, so old-school politicians like Biden could get away with a lot more. And if the recent revelations about inappropriate touching and sniffing are any indication, there is probably much more to come.

Back then, with his young brain still firing on all cylinders, I'm sure that one-man-force-of-nature approach to campaigning was charming. No wonder that when he finally announced his candidacy in 1987, his poll numbers were respectable.

As the campaign wore on, Biden performed relatively well. He connected with crowds, often using that signature touch-the-shoulders, whisper-in-the-ear method of getting his message out (especially when he was imparting that message to pretty and young women). With no #MeToo movement to shut down that kind of behavior, things moved right along for Lyin' Joe.

But the gaffes started piling up. During one speech, he plagiarized Robert F. Kennedy without proper attribution. He got in a fight with a man who'd questioned his academic record, yelling, "I probably have a much higher IQ than you do!"

That was all bad, sure, but it wasn't until a debate in Iowa in February 1987 that Biden finally sealed his fate for good.

During his closing statement, the young senator made a wonderful, eloquent speech about his upbringing, his education, and his roots in the coal mines of Pennsylvania. Joe may have an excuse for mental mix-ups today, but in 1987, when he was running for president, another failed effort, he chose to steal words instead of being creative enough to write his own. You tell me if this isn't plagiarism.

It really brought down the house, and for good reason.

Here's an excerpt:

> I started thinking as I was coming over here, why is it that Joe Biden is the first in his family ever to go to a university? Why is it that my wife who is sitting out there in the audience is the first in her family ever to go to college? Is it because our fathers and mothers were not bright? Is it because I'm the first Biden in a thousand generations to get a college and a graduate degree that I was smarter than the rest?
>
> Those same people who read poetry and wrote poetry and taught me how to sing verse? Is it because they didn't work hard? My ancestors, who worked in the coal mines of Northeast Pennsylvania and would come up after twelve hours and play football for hours?

No, it's not because they weren't as smart. It's not because they didn't work as hard. It's because they didn't have a platform on which to stand.

Nice, right?

Well, if you liked that, you're going to *love* this speech by Neil Kinnock, a British politician who was then the head of the Labour Party in the United Kingdom.

In a campaign ad filmed a few months before Biden began running for president, Kinnock delivered this message, which became popular in both the United States and the UK (and, apparently, in Joe Biden's living room).

You'll want to pay special attention to the parts in bold.

> **Why am I the first Kinnock in a thousand generations to be able to get to university? Why is Glenys the first woman in her family in a thousand generations to be able to get to a university?** Was it because all our predecessors were thick?
>
> **Did they lack talent? Those people who could sing and play and recite poetry?** Those people who could make wonderful beautiful things with their hands? Those people who could dream dreams, see visions? Why didn't they get it? Was it because they were weak? **Those people who could work eight hours underground and then come up and play football?** Weak?
>
> Does anybody really think that they didn't get what we had because they didn't have the talent or the strength or the endurance or commitment? **Of course not. It was because there was no platform upon which they could stand.**

Apparently, Lyin' Joe had been given a VHS tape of this address during the campaign, and he'd liked it so much that he began lifting from it liberally during his stump speeches. He did it so often and got such a positive response that when it was time to write a closing speech for the debate in Iowa, he just went ahead and used it again!

As many people have pointed out since then, it would have been one thing for Biden simply to have lifted the phrasing from Kinnock's speech—the questions at the beginning, the piece about the "platform upon which they could stand" at the end. But it was quite another thing for him to copy the guy's entire life story and claim it as his own. You might not know, for instance, that Neil Kinnock's father really was a coal miner in Wales. Joe Biden's was a car salesman. In fact, as far back as people have been able to trace the Biden genealogy, we've yet to find a single person who "worked for twelve hours in the mines" or "came up after to play football."

Much like his experiences in the civil rights movement, this story came right out of the vice president's rear end.

Now, if it were just a few silly mistakes, that'd be fine. I know from experience that political campaigns are long, and even the best of us can make egregious errors without even realizing we've made them. Personally, I've found that the best approach is to apologize and move on.

In Lyin' Biden's past, however, there is a record of lies, distortions, and insane behavior that should have disqualified him from holding political office a long time ago. These minor scandals from the 1988 race for the presidency—a race he'd been forced to drop out of shortly after the Iowa debate debacle became public—were only the beginning.

JOE SIX PACK JOINS THE SWAMP

Over the fifty years he spent in Washington, Lyin' Joe Biden underwent a remarkable transformation. During his long career in the senate, it seemed that with each passing year, another layer of the brash, confident reformer who'd come to Washington to shake the place up would fall slowly away, revealing the slimy green swamp creature skin that lay underneath.

Over the years, though, Joe Biden seems to have lost track of what brought him to Washington in the first place. (Hell, if he remembered some of the reasons he ran for office back in the 1970s—to break up the established order, to drain the swamp, to fight for the working class people of the United States—he might just go ahead and jump on the Trump Train with us!) He is no longer the revolutionary who wanted to change the status quo. These days, he *is* the status quo.

If you look at his voting record, you'll find a man who's voted solidly with the liberals in every major policy decision since the 1970s. His career has been about as interesting and revolutionary as a read through the Wilmington, Delaware, phonebook.

And when it comes to corruption, it's hard to know where to start. In fact, there's virtually a playbook for it. Here's how it works: A big corporation gives Joe Biden some money; then, in return, Joe Biden does whatever they want. He is beholden to special interests, and he makes no attempt to hide it.

All throughout his career, for instance, Biden has taken massive donations from the credit card industry. In return, he wrote a bill that made it harder for Americans to reduce their debts—something credit card companies had been trying to get passed for years—and voted down any amendments that would have hurt the companies themselves.[13] At a fundraiser in 2019, he told a group of Wall Street executives that if he became president, "nothing would fundamentally change for them." Many of the bankers who were in the audience that day are now funding his campaign.[14]

So much for Six Pack Joe.

JUST WHEN I THINK I'M OUT . . .

When historians look back on this election, I'm sure the narrative will seem simple. Joe Biden, the mild-mannered senator from Delaware, was pulled back into the last race of his life because the Democrat establishment couldn't stand to see Bernie Sanders become their nominee. Sometime around the third or fourth primary, knowing that Crazy Bernie was really going to step in and tax them into oblivion if something didn't get done fast, the big-money donors and Wall Street billionaires who really call the shots for the Democrat Party recruited Biden.

And if you think for a second that the establishment—meaning the donors, the super PACS, and the Democrat National Committee—don't have that kind of power, consider that this isn't the first time they've screwed over poor old Comrade Bernie. In the lead-up to the 2016 election, the Democrat National Committee was blatantly in the tank for Hillary Clinton and openly hostile toward Bernie Sanders. They allowed Clinton to make staffing decisions at the organization before she became the nominee.[15] It's no surprise that when 2020 rolled around and they found themselves without a strong establishment candidate to support, they went out and found one themselves.

It couldn't have come at a worse time for Joe Biden. From his memoirs, his public statements, and his general demeanor, we could already tell that he probably would have been fine not ever running for president again.

Even Barack Obama, a man he's called his "brother," had discouraged him.

In Biden's memoir *Promise Me, Dad,* written in the aftermath of the death of his son Beau, he writes that he and Obama had engaged in a frank conversation about whether the vice president should ever try his hand at the big job again. He had, after all, given it one more shot in 2008, losing to the very man who'd eventually become his boss for eight years, and he had never quite given up on his lifelong dream of occupying the Oval Office himself. For a while, during his second term in the White house, Obama had encouraged his aides to "give Joe space" and let him think about whether he was going to run or not.

When they finally sat down to talk about it, Biden writes, "the president was not encouraging."[16]

Afterward, to really drive the point home, Obama had arranged a meeting between Biden and David Plouffe, the man who'd helped manage Obama's first campaign in 2008. In liberal circles, this man is revered. It's said that he can get anyone elected. According to people familiar with their conversation who spoke to *The Atlantic* a few years earlier, Plouffe told Biden this: "Mr. Vice President, you've had a great career, you've been such an asset to this administration—and we love you. Do you really want it to end in a hotel room in Des Moines, coming in third to Bernie Sanders?"[17]

I never thought I'd see the day when David Plouffe and I saw eye to eye on something, but he's absolutely right.

I mean, think about it. Lyin' Biden—who is not exactly the most talented guy in the world—had managed to become one of the longest-serving senators in the history of the United States. During his career, he had witnessed everything from the civil rights movement to Watergate and three impeachment hearings; he'd greeted ambassadors and kings and foreign ministers as Barack Obama's vice president. Toward the end of that administration, he'd even become a funny meme on the internet, the "guy next to Obama" who was beloved by liberals everywhere. He'd also been awarded (for reasons that make no sense to me) the Presidential Medal of Freedom, in a ceremony that *was* genuinely touching, by Obama.

By any measure, that's a good career. He should have been proud to hang it up there.

In fact, I'm sure Six-Pack Joe would have loved nothing more than to spend his golden years kicked back on his porch in Delaware with a few cold beers, doing exactly what he'd done when he was Barack Obama's vice president.

Nothing.

He could have sat on the sidelines, maybe taken a commentator job on CNN, and lived out the rest of his days in peace.

Instead, he became exactly the opposite of everything he used to represent. Today, he is the one being called on by the establishment to let the country "catch its breath" after the revolutionary first term of President Trump. As he slept through the first few days of the coronavirus crisis in his basement, I'm sure Bunker Biden thought hard, realized what he had become, and started getting angry.

It certainly would explain what happened next.

WAKE-UP CALL

I don't know at what point during this whole ordeal that Bunker Joe Biden finally came out of hibernation, but I do know that he did—and *boy*, was he cranky. But rather than stepping outside, seeing his shadow, and then going back to sleep for six more weeks as he should have, Biden decided that now was his time to take command and start trying to look presidential.

Better late than never, I guess.

On March 20, Biden got on a conference call with reporters (presumably after somebody dialed the phone for him) and told them he was planning his own briefings, which would be done right from his living room in Wilmington, Delaware.

One reporter called them "shadow briefings," and the name stuck.[18]

Here's a little taste of what he said on the call, if you can decipher it: "President Trump, stop saying false things, will ya? People are worried they are really frightened, when these things don't come through."[19]

Now, that wasn't English, but that's not why it was stupid. It was stupid because at no point during President Trump's briefings had he allowed a single piece of false information to be uttered from the podium. He did what he was supposed to do, laying out the facts, giving guidance, and, when necessary, answering questions from a press corps that was waiting for him to slip up at any second. But slip up he did not. This is just what we've come to expect from the president.

Still, a few days after his prefatory remarks on the crisis, there were television cameras and wires all over the Biden living room in Wilmington, and Bunker Biden was staring straight into one of those cameras, desperately trying to deliver a press conference via webcast. Like a confused old grandfather trying to sign up for his first Facebook account, he fumbled with his notes and tripped over his words, but eventually he got going.

And the results, according to even the most liberal of the liberal media outlets, were "disastrous."

One newspaper said he got off to a "rocky start," which I think was an understatement, given the circumstances. Apparently, the only thing worse than letting Joe Biden talk to people is letting him talk to himself in his living room. Who knew? Over the course of the webcast, there were problems with the lights, problems with the script, and more interrupted sentences than you'd find on an old, scratchy vinyl record. And that's *before* you consider what he was actually saying—or, more interestingly, what he was *not* saying.

For instance, you might find it interesting, as I do, that at no point in Joe Biden's shadow briefing did he mention that this disease came from Wuhan, China. He didn't mention that our economy is in substantially better shape than it would have been if President Trump had not enacted an unprecedented trade war against that country and their corrupt communist government, reducing our dependence on Chinese supply chains and putting us on the road to independence. Maybe that's because this was a trade war, as I'm sure Joe Biden knows, that the president undertook against the advice of elitists and liberals everywhere. In other words, had this disease hit our shores under the administration of Biden and Barack Obama, who sucked up to China and other authoritarian regimes at every turn, our economy would have been annihilated.

Or maybe Biden's silence on this point might have something to do with the fact that in 2013, Joe Biden and his son Hunter took a trip to China on Air Force Two that ended with Hunter somehow getting just over $400 million for a small investment fund he'd started.[20] On that trip, Hunter met with officials of the Chinese Communist Party, and there are pictures of them all shaking hands. I wonder what that was about! Were there deals being made? To this day, Hunter Biden remains on the board of BHR Equity Investment Fund Management Co., a shadowy investment company with ties to the Communist Party of China. I'm sure they wouldn't be too happy if Hunter's dad started taking a tough stance on China, now, would they?

At one memorable point in the speech, Biden read a scripted line from his jumbled notes and, for once, didn't mess it up. This line, as is always the case with the focus-grouped, tightly scripted sayings, was the moment that made headlines. "Trump keeps saying that he's a wartime president," said Biden. "Well, start to act like one. To paraphrase a frustrated President Lincoln writing to an inactive General McClellan during the Civil War, 'If you don't want to use the army, may I borrow it?'"[21]

Good joke, Joe. But there is one problem. At the very moment you were delivering that hack line in your living room, speaking in front of black-and-white framed photographs of yourself back when you could actually get things done, President Trump was making plans to have the Army Corps of Engineers outfit several hospitals, arenas, and convention centers around the country with makeshift medical equipment to combat the spread of coronavirus. He was supervising those plans personally with Lieutenant General Todd Semonite, making it so that when those hospitals were up and running, patients could be transported in immediately.

By March 26, less than a week after Joe Biden's first shadow briefing, the entire Javits Center in New York was a makeshift hospital, all thanks to the brave men and women of our National

Guard. I don't know about you, but I'd say the president is making fine use of our army.

You know what, Joe? I think I understand. If I had to sit in my house dreaming all day about finally becoming president, but all I could actually do was sit and watch a *real* leader on television, I probably wouldn't be happy either. You're like a washed-up boxer who sits around watching old heavyweight title fights all day, telling yourself that someday you might step in the ring again. But you won't, and you know it.

Next time, Joe, why don't you stay in the shadows. As long as you don't try to jump out and sniff anyone again, maybe—just *maybe*—you'll still be your party's nominee this November.

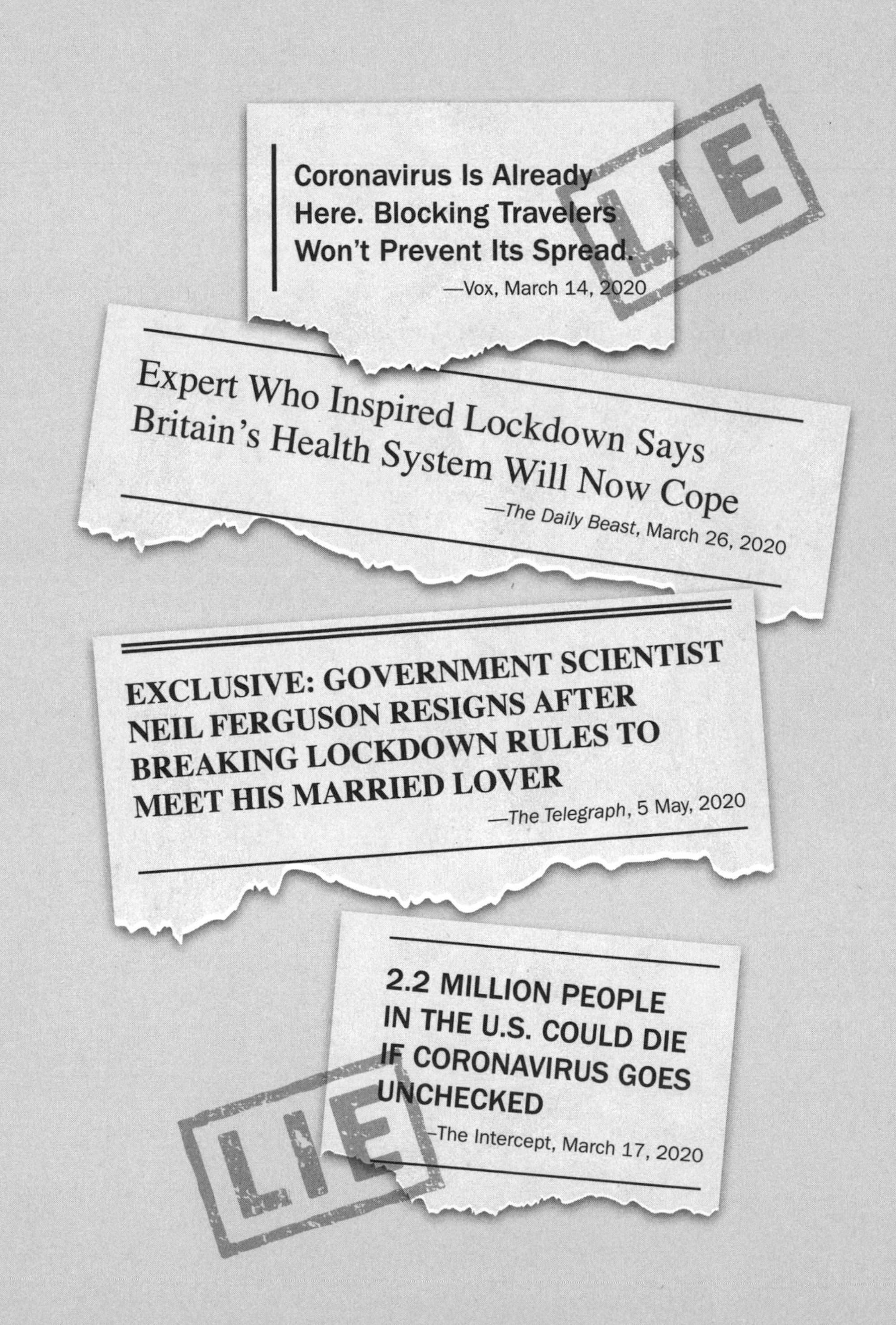
Coronavirus Is Already Here. Blocking Travelers Won't Prevent Its Spread.
—Vox, March 14, 2020
LIE
Expert Who Inspired Lockdown Says Britain's Health System Will Now Cope
—The Daily Beast, March 26, 2020
EXCLUSIVE: GOVERNMENT SCIENTIST NEIL FERGUSON RESIGNS AFTER BREAKING LOCKDOWN RULES TO MEET HIS MARRIED LOVER
—The Telegraph, 5 May, 2020
2.2 MILLION PEOPLE IN THE U.S. COULD DIE IF CORONAVIRUS GOES UNCHECKED
—The Intercept, March 17, 2020
LIE

Chapter Four

FAKE NEWS GOES VIRAL

The pandemic was hard on everyone. Millions of people lost their jobs, and many more suffered from drug addiction, alcoholism, and depression. We are only beginning to get a sense of the damage.

However, that's not the worst part.

The worst part, if you ask liberal media commentators like CNN's Brian Stelter, is that the coronavirus pandemic made some of his fellow journalists very, *very* sad.

On April 18, at the beginning of his weekly newsletter, written primarily for other high-powered journalists and elite media insiders, Stelter had a small breakdown in print, lamenting the fact that he had—and please skip this next part if you're squeamish or sensitive to horrible misfortune—*missed a deadline* for the first time in years.

Gasp! The horror!

"Truth is," Stelter wrote, "I crawled in bed and cried for our pre-pandemic lives. I think those tears had been waiting a month to escape."

Well, Brian, I don't think I have to tell you that at the time you were typing those words, you *did* have a job. So did the rest of your crew at CNN. In fact, given that your entire career has been built around nothing other than gossiping about what other reporters are doing, I don't think your job was ever really in danger. You didn't have to leave your home, you were getting paid, and you had a reason to get up in the morning. Meanwhile, just over 22 million Americans had lost their jobs and had no idea what they would be facing if the pandemic finally let up.

So, you want to cry like a baby? I get it. I don't have a problem with men expressing their emotions. But you should cry for the people who have no hope, no reason to get up, no job to go to, and no one to talk to. Rather than crying for yourself and your friends in the media, you should thank God and your lucky stars that you had a reason to get out of bed and get paid. You should think of all those locked at home, such as the battered women who are trapped with their abusers with no place to go, or the children who are being abused and neglected and can't fight for themselves.

Your pathetic claim at victimization rings hollow.

Then again, I don't expect much from people who work at CNN.

THE PERFECT STORM

By the time the coronavirus pandemic hit the United States, the liberal media was fresh out of catastrophes. For five years, they had been predicting that President Trump would bring about either a recession or the apocalypse—or both—neither of which happened.

In the weeks leading up to the 2016 election, when they told us Trump supporters were going to take to the streets and incite violent race riots if our candidate lost? On April 9, 2015, the *Boston Globe* published a whole fake front page predicting what the newspaper might look like if Donald Trump won the presidency. In a story on the left-hand side of the page, they predicted "mass riots" and curfews in multiple cities. On the right, they ran a headline reading MARKETS SINK AS TRADE WAR LOOMS. Other stories on this imaginary front page predicted shadowy deportation forces roaming the streets and a complete breakdown of the American economy. A few months later, over at the *New York Times,* the editorial board predicted that when—not *if*, but *when*—Donald Trump lost the election, his supporters, whom they described as "on edge and quick to lash out," would bring about a "violent conflict" in the streets."[1]

Of course, we all know that the only people who participated in anything close to a "violent conflict" that night were the supposedly calm, "peaceful" supporters of Hillary Clinton. Throughout the evening, they were the ones who screamed and broke windows and damaged property. They were the ones who flipped over garbage cans and cursed at police officers in front of Trump Tower. In New York City, when I left the Hilton hotel in the early morning hours after the election, I was cursed at by a group of protestors. One in particular was yelling at me, "Fuck you!" My eyes started at the Converse sneakers up to the black tights and the tutu that he was wearing, and I responded in kind. There was a whole line of police officers opposite that person on Sixth Avenue. Thank God for the police, who were out there almost shoulder to shoulder. It was not easy getting to my car. And apparently, those protestors really enjoyed themselves, because they've been doing it ever since.

Throughout President Trump's first term, this pattern played itself out again and again. Whenever the man made a move on the world stage, whether it was the start of a trade war or the decertification of the horrible nuclear deal with Iran, the media predicted that the end of the world was imminent. When he pulled us out of the Paris Accords, they told us that we'd all die of global warming. When he went back and forth with Kim Jong-Un of North Korea on nuclear weapons, they told us to put on our helmets and stock up on canned foods, because the nuclear holocaust was on its way.

In a sense, this isn't their fault. It's their business model. When a news network runs stories about death and destruction, more people watch. A recent study in *Adweek* showed that people are about 30 percent more likely to click on a story that has a negative superlative—*worst*, *most dangerous*, *most deadly*—in the headline than they are to click on one with positive words—things like *growth*, *prosperity*, *all-time high*.[2] In newspapers, the mentality is *if it bleeds, it leads:* The worst stories all go on the front page, and the positive ones get shuffled to the back of the paper. In short, nobody really cares about good news.

Unfortunately for the news business, most of the stories of President Trump's first term—the ones that weren't lies—were positive stories. The stock market was breaking records, unemployment was lower than it had ever been, and we were deescalating conflicts overseas that had been raging for decades. For us, that was all great. But for the mainstream media, which depends on riots, recessions, and robberies to keep the lights on in their newsrooms, it wasn't. After all, they couldn't send war correspondents to cover all the bloody conflicts that *weren't* breaking out in the Middle East. They couldn't send a reporter to get the inside scoop on all the people who were getting up, going to work, and providing for their families now that they were employed.

It was great news, but it was terrible television. So they lied, and they created the Russia Collusion Delusion, the Impeachment Hoax, and dozens of other fake conspiracies.

And when the coronavirus hit the shores of the United States, the media saw their chance to report on a genuine crisis—one they believed would involve overflowing hospitals, mass deaths, and bodies in the streets—and pin the whole thing on President Trump. No matter what he did to respond to the threat of this pandemic, they were going to say it was wrong. When he enacted a travel ban from China, they said it wasn't going to work. Reporters at *BuzzFeed* wrote that "barring foreign travelers from China . . . likely violated civil rights laws, without leading to any real lowered risk of a U.S. outbreak."[3] *Vox* published a story titled "Coronavirus is already here. Blocking travelers won't prevent its spread."[4]

When it became clear that the virus was here to stay, however, the media got to work making things seem as grim as possible, knowing that every bad headline and news clip stood to make President Trump look bad. Life under Trump was impossible. Sometimes, they were *so* eager to make things look bad that they lied. On March 22, for example, CBS News ran a story about how horrible the conditions were in New York City's hospitals, playing scary-looking clips over one of Governor Andrew Cuomo's press conferences. One piece of the footage showed a small hospital corridor with nearly a dozen beds packed into it. Patients were on ventilators, and there didn't seem to be nearly enough doctors to tend to them all. Looking at it, you'd think it was footage of a city in Italy, where the outbreak really did reach near-apocalyptic levels.

As it turns out, the clip *was* from Italy—from one of the worst-hit hospitals in that country, in fact.[5] When CBS was caught red-handed using the doctored footage, they called it "an editing error" and said they wouldn't use it again. Then, just over a week later, they *did* use it again, this time during a report about hospital conditions in Philadelphia. If they had done it once, I might be willing to believe it really was just an editing mistake. But they did it again, knowing full well that the clip wasn't from anywhere near the United States. The people at CBS News who ran those stories knew that there *were* no hospitals in the United States where conditions were as bad as in Italy. Even in New York City, which became the epicenter of the virus, hospitalizations peaked on April 7, and our healthcare system was never overwhelmed in any serious way.

Even if the first time they ran that clip *was* a mistake, the second time it wasn't. It was a lie.

But it didn't stop at the headlines. During the pandemic, even the deaths of American citizens could be used as weapons against President Trump. On March 24, a man in Arizona died after drinking fish tank cleaner that contained the chemical chloroquine phosphate. His wife, who'd also drank the liquid, said that they'd done it because President Trump said it was okay. A few days earlier, President Trump had discussed the possibility that a drug called hydroxychloroquine, which is often used to treat malaria patients, might be effective against the coronavirus. He had spoken specifically about the *medically supervised* use of this drug, of course, and never mentioned the chemical that was in this man's fish tank cleaner.

But that didn't stop the liberal media from pinning the man's death on the president. The day after the man's death, *Axios* reported that "a man has died after ingesting chloroquine phosphate—one of the anti-malarial drugs that Trump has mentioned in recent days."[6] Several other news outlets posted similar messages. When it was revealed to them that chloroquine phosphate and hydroxychloroquine are completely different substances which have virtually nothing in common besides the sound of their names, some of these outlets posted corrections to their false stories. Axios took down their original tweet and posted a correction, which read "We have deleted this tweet and corrected our story because it did not reflect the full nature of the self-medication done with an additive commonly used to clean fish tanks."[7]

Gee, that's an awfully roundabout way of saying "We lied."

In the end, the correction didn't make much of a difference. You see, when Axios posted its original tweet—which blamed the president for a man's death, making all the wildest fantasies of liberals on Twitter come true—that tweet went viral. It was shared and retweeted more than fifty thousand times. Tweets about the same event from other news outlets got similar treatment. So, this unchecked lie was allowed to spread around the internet for a full sixteen hours before anyone bothered to correct it. When *Axios* did post a correction, that correction was only shared about five thousand times, which is nothing compared to the hundreds of thousands of impressions that the original tweet got.

In the modern media landscape, stories aren't judged by how correct they are. They're not judged on how good they are, or how many sources spoke on the record to corroborate the facts within. Today, they're judged by their ability to go viral and attract eyeballs on social media platforms like Twitter and Facebook. In fact, reporters at *BuzzFeed*—the online outlet that famously published the Steele dossier in full—are given weekly breakdowns of every story they publish. These reports tell the writers how many "natural views" a story got and how many "viral views" it got. When the second number is high, they're told that the story was a success. Usually, the stories that go viral are the ones that contain negative information. They're especially likely to go viral if they confirm something that their leftist readers and viewers already believe—hatred of President Trump, for example.

During the pandemic, plenty of stories "went viral" because of the Left's hatred for President Trump. Many of them contained lies. I'm sure you heard, for instance, that the drug hydroxychloroquine was potentially lethal, according to scientists who published in some of this country's best medical journals. In the eyes of the media, if President Trump was saying that something might be helpful, it must be poison. However, I think it's much less likely that you read the story letting people know that two of those prestigious medical journals, *The Lancet* and the *New England Journal of Medicine,* were forced to retract their research about the dangers of hydroxychloroquine when it was revealed that their research didn't stand up to scientific scrutiny. According to the editors of these journals, the data that had been collected from hospitals around the world "wasn't properly analyzed."[8]

Again, it's a strange way of saying "We lied." Hydroxychloroquine is *not* potentially lethal, and I'll take it. There were repeated testaments of doctors and nurses on the front lines who were using it as a prophylactic.

If you watched television during the first days of the pandemic, you probably heard the number 2.2 million tossed around. That, according to the liberal media, was the number of people who could die if we didn't get control of this pandemic by locking down our economy indefinitely. On March 16, the *New York Times* wrote a front-page story that read: "Sweeping new federal recommendations announced on Monday for Americans to sharply limit their activities appeared to draw on a dire scientific report warning that, without action by the government and individuals to slow the spread of coronavirus and suppress new cases, 2.2 million people in the United States could die."[9]

On CNN's *State of the Union,* Dr. Anthony Fauci told Brianna Keilar that "millions of people could die in the U.S. from the coronavirus."[10]

In *The Intercept*, a headline read: 2.2 MILLION PEOPLE IN THE U.S. COULD DIE IF CORONAVIRUS GOES UNCHECKED.

So, you might be wondering, now that it appears we're *not* looking for places to bury 2.2 million Americans, where on earth did that number come from in the first place? Was there some kind of a fake news summit we didn't know about? Did they get it in another fake dossier from Russia?

Well, strap in. This is the biggest lie of them all.

THE MASTER OF DISASTER

In the middle of March, with the notion of a national lockdown just beginning to take hold in the United States, a fifty-one-year-old professor named Neil Ferguson walked under the awning of 10 Downing Street in London, straight into the office of Prime Minister Boris Johnson.[11] That morning, there were only 152 known cases of coronavirus in the United Kingdom, and 872 known cases in the United States.

Professor Ferguson had terrible news.

For the past thirty days or so, he and a team of researchers at Imperial College London had been studying the coronavirus, trying to determine how many people might be at risk if the disease ever became a full-blown pandemic. Using a computer model that Ferguson had designed back in 2003, these researchers had been trying to arrive at a series of predictions about the pathogen, which had just been renamed coronavirus. They wanted to know where it might spread, how lethal it could be, and what, if anything, could be done to stop it.[12] Working in a laboratory all by themselves, this team of researchers would plug various statistics about different countries into the computer program, add what little they knew about the virus, and then draw conclusions based on whatever numbers the computer spit out. Nobody but Neil Ferguson had ever reviewed this computer program, and according to several experts in epidemiology and computer programming, his code—the language spoken by the computer to make its models—was full of holes.[13]

Big holes.

According to an expert named David Richards, who would review the programming a few months later, after Ferguson was finally forced to make it public for the first time, the predictive model was "a buggy mess that looks more like a bowl of angel hair pasta than a finely tuned piece of programming."[14] Richards would also add that his company, one of the most respected data analysis firms in Britain, "would fire anyone for developing code like this and any business that relied on it to produce software for sale would likely go bust."[15] Another expert would call Ferguson's model "totally unreliable," saying it was "something you wouldn't stake your life on."[16]

Now, I'm not a computer scientist. But I do know that if you claim to be conducting state-of-the-art research, and you pass that research on to the most powerful heads of state in the world in an attempt to influence global policy, it's probably not a good idea to be relying on something that's *seventeen years old.* In the world of computers, it's generally accepted that any given technology—including the lines of code that make up predictive models—is usually about twice as sophisticated at any given moment as it was two years earlier.[17] So, in technological terms, the seventeen years between 2003, when Ferguson wrote this code, and the year 2020, when he finally got around to using it, might as well have been three centuries. In the end, he might have been better consulting the works of Shakespeare or a medical textbook from the 1800s.

However, you didn't need to dig through thousands of lines of code to realize that something was very, *very* wrong with Neil Ferguson. All you had to do was take a quick look at his résumé. Over the years, this professor had been making predictions about all kinds of diseases, usually forecasting doom, gloom, and death. Then, once the diseases actually came and went, it would become clear that he had botched his predictions in spectacular fashion.

Unfortunately for all of us, the coronavirus pandemic was not this man's first rodeo.

In 2001, for instance, during a small outbreak of foot-and-mouth disease—not to be confused with foot-*in*-mouth disease, an ailment that Sleepy Joe Biden seems to have come down with in a big way—Ferguson advised the British government on how it should respond. After studying a few samples of cattle, swine, and deer, After studying a few samples of cattle, swine, and deer, the team at Imperial College said it was hopeless, and they predicted that an epidemic was imminent. According to their calculations, the only thing the government could do if they wanted to survive was round up the usual suspects—meaning the cattle who might have been infected—and shoot them.

Over a period of four months in 2001, acting on the advice of Ferguson and his colleagues, farmers in the UK slaughtered or starved nearly 11 million sheep and cattle on their farms.

Speaking to reporters about the incident a few years later, a farmer named Charlotte Reid, who lived a few doors down from one of these farms, described what it was like.

"I remember that appalling time," she said. "Sheep were left starving in fields near us. Then came the open-air slaughter. The poor animals were panic stricken. It was one of the worst things I've witnessed. And all based on a model—ifs, buts, and maybes."[18]

In the years following that incident, researchers questioned the validity of Ferguson's arguments. They noticed inconsistencies in his modeling, problems with his methods, and big mistakes in the computer code he'd been using.[19] In short, they said he'd been extremely cavalier with his predictions, always managing to predict the worst-case scenario.

But by then, the professor—who would later earn the nickname "the master of disaster" for his, shall we say, *gloomy* approach to the job—had moved on to other things.

In 2005, he claimed that up to 200 million people would be killed worldwide as a result of the bird flu, often comparing it in interviews to the infamous Spanish flu pandemic of 1918. (This is a talking point he would refer to quite often during the coronavirus pandemic as well.) "There are six times more people on the planet now," he said, referring to the death figures from Spanish influenza during an interview with *The Guardian*. "So, you could scale it up to around 200 million people probably."[20]

In the end, exactly 282 people died.[21]

In 2009, during an outbreak of swine flu, Ferguson predicted that sixty-five thousand people might die from the disease in Britain.[22] The real number? Four hundred fifty-seven.[23]

Look. If this guy had been off by a couple hundred lives, or even a few *thousand* lives, I'd be willing to write him off as an otherwise qualified expert who sometimes makes mistakes. I don't imagine the calculations he's trying to make are easy, or that it's possible to arrive at an exact right answer in these situations. But clearly, this is different. Even when you consider how difficult the situation was, or the fact that Ferguson and his team were dealing with viruses that we knew very little about at the time, the sheer magnitude of this man's ineptitude is stunning. After all, there are plenty of professions that involve making detailed predictions, and they all seem to have higher standards than Ferguson's chosen field of biostatistics.

Imagine, for example, that instead of becoming the United Kingdom's leading authority on viruses, Neil Ferguson became a local weatherman in Boulder, Colorado. How many times do you think he'd be allowed to get on television, throw his laser pointer in the air, and yell, "Hurricane! Tomorrow! This is it! We're all gonna die!" before they finally stopped him from going on the air ever again? If he were a stockbroker, do you think he'd be allowed to invest anyone's money again after betting the house on not one, not two, not three, but *four* different companies that all ended up going bust?

Probably not.

Beyond the numbers, the man's audacity is stunning. Any person who's willing to allow millions of animals to be slaughtered on what his colleagues agree was essentially a glorified hunch, then *keep* making ridiculous predictions long after your first one has been disproven is . . . Well, let's just say he's not somebody who should be trusted to make life-and-death decisions about the world economy (or to tie his own shoes correctly).

But in the chaos and confusion that came during the first days of the coronavirus, nobody wanted to ask questions. The elites told us that it was time to trust the experts, believe the science, and bow down at the altar of statistics and government-approved models. They told us we had to sign away our freedom, our rational minds, and eventually all our rights in order to stop the spread of a disease that was, they assured us, deadly, and coming for us at any moment.

So, what did the "expert" have to say?

Not surprisingly, according to the results of Ferguson's coronavirus research—and I'm using the term "research" *very* loosely—we were in *big* trouble. So much trouble, in fact, that Ferguson begged Boris Johnson for a meeting, hoping he could convince the prime minister to reverse course on his stated plan for fighting the virus.

A few days earlier, Johnson had announced that the UK, unlike some of its neighbors in Europe, would attempt to contain the coronavirus through a strategy known as herd immunity, hoping that if enough young, able-bodied people got the disease and recovered, the whole population would become virtually immune. Rather than shutting down the economy and forcing everyone inside, the United Kingdom would protect vulnerable populations, take basic precautions, and try to delay the spread of the virus so they could "flatten the curve," keeping the hospital system from getting overwhelmed. It was an interesting thought, and it would have been enlightening to see it play out in practice.

Unfortunately, we never got the chance.

On the afternoon of March 16, Neil Ferguson did his usual doomsday song and dance in the front offices of 10 Downing Street, assuring the prime minister that the four horsemen of the apocalypse were saddling up at that very moment. He couldn't have been any less subtle if he'd knocked on the front door in a black robe with a scythe in his hand.

Even without the dreadful details, the numbers alone were enough to make you wince.

According to the results of the Imperial College's research, which Ferguson carried with him in the form of a twenty-page report called *Report 9: Impact of Non-Pharmaceutical Interventions (NPIs) to Reduce coronavirus Mortality and Healthcare Demand*, there would be just over 550,000 deaths in the United Kingdom from the coronavirus, even *with* social distancing measures in place.[24]

In the United States, the numbers were much worse. Apparently, no matter what kind of preventive measures were taken in the US—whether it be sheltering in place, compulsive handwashing, or a complete and total lockdown of all nonessential businesses—the death count could still surpass *2 million* by the beginning of summer.[25] That, as the experts never tired of reminding us during those early days, is more Americans than have died in every war since 1776.[26]

Scary, right?

Boris Johnson certainly thought so. Within a few hours of hearing Neil Ferguson's chilling report, the prime minister announced a strict set of social distancing measures for the United Kingdom, completely reversing his position on herd immunity. He said that the economy needed to stop, the streets needed to empty, and the businesses all needed to close their doors until it was safe to get going again. And how could he not? This man had just heard from someone he believed to be the world's leading expert in his field that half a million citizens were going to die on his watch. He couldn't just sit back and let it happen!

In a matter of days, the news of Ferguson's report had traveled the globe faster than any virus ever could. Many countries, including the United States, decided to act based on his predictions, shutting down their economies and forcing hundreds of thousands of small businesses to shutter and eventually go bankrupt?

As of this writing, we may never know how far off the mark Neil Ferguson truly was. What we know is that his twenty-page paper on the subject, which has come to be known simply as the "Imperial College Report," is probably the single most influential piece of scientific research this century. It is also, according to Johan Giesecke, the former chief scientist for the European equivalent of the CDC, "one of the most wrong."[27]

As of this writing, just over 140,000 people have died from coronavirus in the United States.[28] In the United Kingdom, that number is about 45,000.[29] That is a tragedy, and I would never dream of saying otherwise. But it is *not* what the models predicted. According to Neil Ferguson and his doomsday crew at

Imperial College, both the United States and the United Kingdom were supposed to run out of hospital beds within weeks of the first reported cases. We were supposed to experience an unprecedented wave of devastation.

These were predictions that the mainstream media were all too happy to go along with. By the middle of March, news anchors in the United States were predicting the end of the world—which, of course, is what they'd been doing since the day President Trump was inaugurated. On April 2, CNN's Jake Tapper quoted the model to predict that "two million people could die." Over at MSNBC, Rachel Maddow, who repeatedly called it the "Wuhan Virus from China," said this:

> "The projections are terrible in terms of the numbers of American deaths out there...ultimately, the pace at which U.S. hospital capacity is going to be overrun is daunting and terrible. Ultimately, what that will mean is that severely ill patients who need to be in a hospital to try to keep themselves alive, they will not have hospital beds. The projections are just terrible."[30]

In a matter of weeks, complete and total lockdown became the only effective strategy to combat the coronavirus. Anyone who suggested something else—or dared question the blue-state mayors and governors who were leaning into the idea of a lockdown with such obvious glee—was labeled a science denier, a conspiracy theorist, or a cold, unfeeling monster who didn't value human life and was intent on killing your grandmother.

It was emotional bullying of the worst kind, and it would be months before we finally got the urge to stand up and fight back.

THE WALK BACK

In the midst of all that chaos, during which time the United Kingdom was taking the advice of the Imperial College's Neil Ferguson, around ten million people in the United States had filed for unemployment. Thousands of businesses had been forced to close down, many of them ultimately for good. In the United Kingdom, which hadn't been in lockdown quite as long as the United States, the unemployment rate was rising rapidly, hitting 10 percent in the second quarter of 2020.

Sadly, Neil Ferguson was still employed.

On March 26, when he was asked in front of Parliament whether he felt Britain was ready to combat the virus, he did not launch into the same doomsday song and dance that he'd performed for Boris Johnson. He didn't talk about dead bodies in the streets, ventilator shortages, or hospitals that couldn't cope with all the infected people. In fact, he looked positively unfazed by all of it.

"I am reasonably confident," he said, "that the health service [in the United Kingdom] will be able to cope when the peak of the epidemic arrives in two to three weeks."[31] Ferguson also said that thanks to "the restrictions that had recently been put in place," the death rate in the United Kingdom probably wouldn't go above, say, twenty thousand.

Really, Neil?

After running with guns blazing into the offices of your prime minister and *begging* him to shut the country down, you realize that maybe things aren't quite as bad as you thought? Also, these "restrictions" you mentioned were only put in place *two days* before you were speaking. Even according to your own models, which several experts have said vastly overestimated the effectiveness of shelter-in-place measures, such rules would take at least six to eight weeks to begin having any discernible effect on the transmission of the disease.

Clearly, Neil Ferguson knew that what he was saying that morning wasn't true. He was trying to cover himself, and in doing so, he found out what all liars eventually do: If you just tell the truth, you don't have to remember what you said.

It's also worth noting that the walk-back of Ferguson's claims didn't get nearly as far as his original numbers. The truth rarely does.

Incidentally, Ferguson would eventually be relieved of his position in the British government—but not for getting his models wrong or for misrepresenting the results of his research in front of Parliament. No, he would step down because on May 5, while the rest of his country was huddling indoors under a strict lockdown that he helped create, this man snuck his married lover—whom he'd met on the online dating site OkCupid—into his apartment. Because he wasn't in the United States, where Dr. Fauci seemed perfectly fine with Tinder hookups during quarantine, he was promptly fired.

Oh, and one other thing. A few days after Neil Ferguson visited 10 Downing Street, he woke up with a cough, fever, and shortness of breath. Within hours, Ferguson tested positive for coronavirus. A few days after *that,* Prime Minister Boris Johnson tested positive for the disease. At the hospital, Ferguson admitted that he'd had "recent contact" with the prime minister, admitting there was "a slight risk I may have infected somebody, but it is probably quite slight."

Well, Neil, considering your record, I wouldn't count on it.

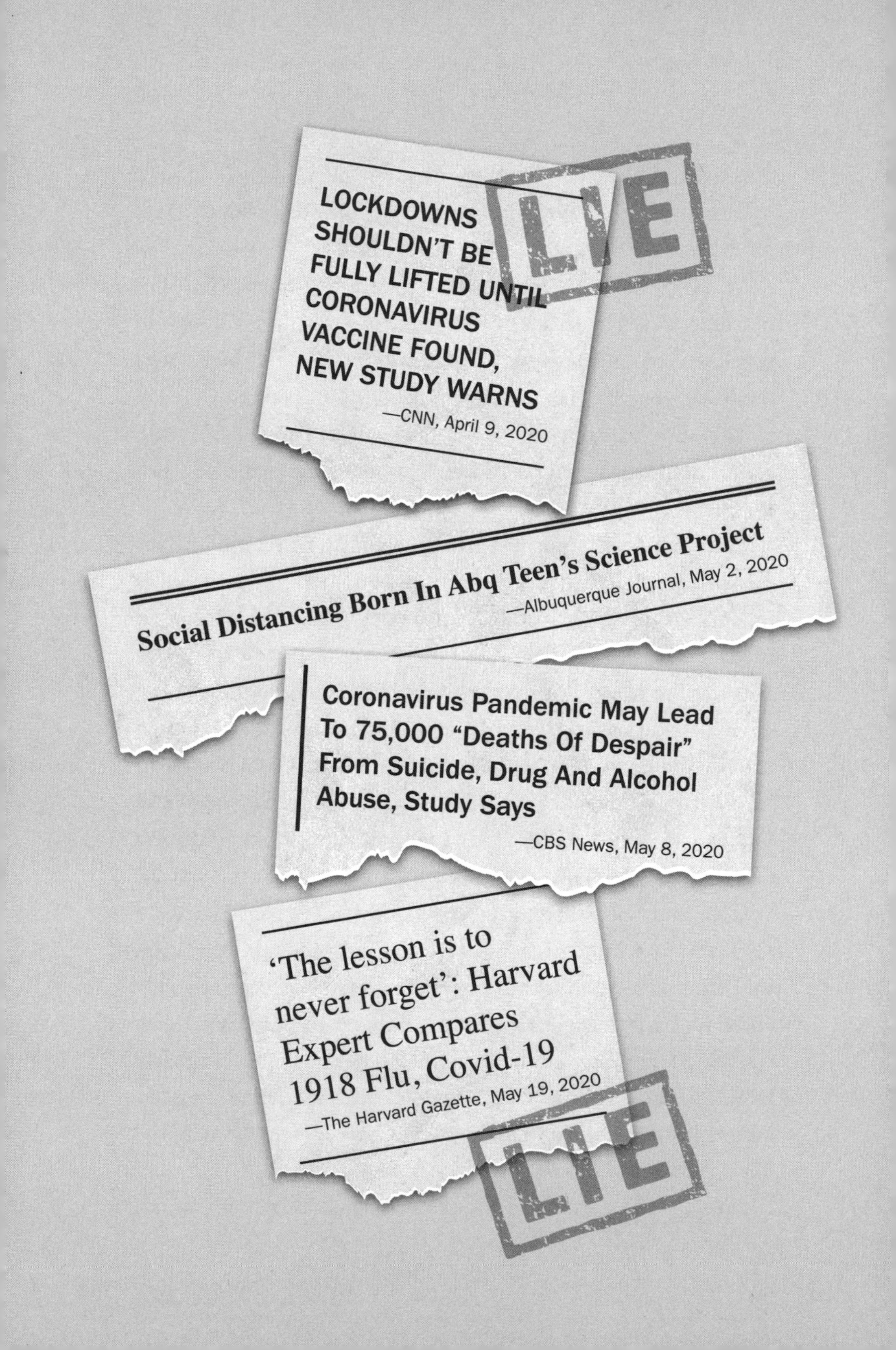
LOCKDOWNS SHOULDN'T BE FULLY LIFTED UNTIL CORONAVIRUS VACCINE FOUND, NEW STUDY WARNS
—CNN, April 9, 2020
LIE
Social Distancing Born In Abq Teen's Science Project
—Albuquerque Journal, May 2, 2020
Coronavirus Pandemic May Lead To 75,000 "Deaths Of Despair" From Suicide, Drug And Alcohol Abuse, Study Says
—CBS News, May 8, 2020
'The lesson is to never forget': Harvard Expert Compares 1918 Flu, Covid-19
—The Harvard Gazette, May 19, 2020
LIE

Chapter Five

THE LIBERAL LOCKDOWN

You can't keep Americans down. Born of rebellion and revolution, we are ready to fight. It's in our DNA. We are ready to fight this virus. We are ready to fight to get back to work. We are ready to fight to get our kids back to school. We are ready to fight to reopen our country in a safe and strategic way.

We get it. We aren't stupid. We know to wash our hands, wear a mask, and keep our distance. We know to look for signs of the virus. We look to protect the vulnerable. We appreciate that the numbers need to be contained as we go through the phases of reopening. We know that the virus can come back—in fact, we have seen it come back in some states—but we continue to be ever vigilant to make sure a complete reopening is dependent upon the data.

But the truth is, we have been locked down, waiting, and sheltering in place for months. We are *not* children. We are capable of using our God-given common sense to protect ourselves and others. But there has to be a balance between physical safety and economic survival. Every day these statewide lockdowns are allowed to continue—every time a state slides back into complete and total panic mode because of an uptick in cases, as happened in Florida, Georgia, and Texas at the beginning of July—the misery continues. Sure, the unemployment rate has fallen from nearly 15 percent to 11 percent, and things are beginning to show signs of improvement. Thanks to President Trump's decision to open the country again, millions of people have been able to get back to work safely. Still, too many are suffering. As I write this, close to 18 million people are still without work, many of them living in blue states with governors who have consistently insisted on keeping states locked down.[1] For too many, their livelihoods and their dreams have disappeared for good. For some who have been forced to keep their businesses closed, there will simply be no business to rebuild, especially after the supposedly "peaceful" protests that destroyed countless stores around the country after the death of George Floyd. For others, there will be no coming back from the depths of depression, alcohol, drug abuse, or domestic violence.

Medical experts agree. On May 20, a group of six hundred doctors wrote a letter to President Trump warning of the horrible toll that the lockdown would have on citizens of the United States.

"In medical terms, the shutdown was a mass casualty incident," they wrote. "Suicide hotline phone calls have increased 600 percent. We are alarmed at what appears to be the lack of consideration for the future health of our patients . . . The millions of casualties of a continued shutdown will be hiding in plain sight, but they will be called alcoholism, homelessness, suicide, heart attack, stroke, or kidney failure. In youths it will be called financial instability, unemployment, despair, drug addiction, unplanned pregnancies, poverty, and abuse."[2]

During the first week of shelter in place orders, consumption of hard liquor increased by 55 percent compared to the same week last year.[3] All over the country, instances of domestic violence increased dramatically. In Chicago, for example, a city that endured one of the strictest lockdowns after New York City, calls to a local domestic violence hotline skyrocketed. During the first week of March, there were around 380 calls to report domestic violence a week. By the end of April, according to the *New York Times,* the weekly number was about 550.[4]

We've always known that domestic violence, in general, increases in intensity and severity as time goes on. There is no doubt that putting the batterer with his victim day in and day out exacerbates that scenario, because there is no way she is ever out of his sight if they are in one house or one apartment. And as for abused and neglected children, for most of them, the best place they could be is out of the home, where they are abused by the very person who gave birth to them or fathered them or is living with them in a parental situation. At least in school, a teacher can identify unusual behavior or bruises and is then mandated to call in Child Protective Services or the Bureau of Child Welfare. But if that child is home, no one knows about the extent of the abuse, and the child is incapable of being identified as a victim.

Enough!

For months now, we have had to listen to inflated numbers, bad predictions, and the opinions of so-called experts who obviously didn't know what they were talking about. We've had enough of this lockdown. The Declaration of Independence gives us the right to life, liberty, and the pursuit of happiness. Included in that is the right to survive, live freely, and care for our families. It doesn't give governors—and certainly not mayors—the right to impose nanny states, reduce liberties, and enlarge governmental power. Of course, government has the authority to protect public health during a pandemic. But that power cannot be used to nullify Constitutional rights, including the right of peaceful protest when civil liberties are at stake.

Enough of these small-time politicians using this pandemic to flex their pathetic muscles in order to gain attention. Like ticketing citizens for attending drive-in church services on church property in their own cars. Like arresting and handcuffing a father in front of his son, with whom he was playing catch outdoors. Like prohibiting citizens from purchasing firearms despite talk of abolishing the police.

Over in New Jersey, Governor Phil Murphy couldn't explain why he allowed stores selling beer, liquor, and weed to remain open as "essential businesses" but sought to punish churches and synagogues for providing religious services. When Fox News's Tucker Carlson asked him whether he had considered the Bill of Rights before handing down his orders about what businesses would be shown mercy during the lockdown, the governor said he "wasn't thinking of the Bill of Rights." He said it was "above my pay grade."

Above your pay grade? Are you stupid? You forgot the Constitution? Did you forget you took an oath to uphold it?

During the pandemic, places of worship were singled out as parishioners met in parking lots on Easter Sunday to listen to church services over their car radios and were targeted for lockdown violations. A federal court had to halt Democrat Kentucky governor Andy Beshear's ban on gatherings at churches. Democrat governor John Bel Edwards ordered congregants not to gather in more than minimal numbers in a church in Louisiana. That pastor said his church is cleaner than a gas station, Walmart, and Sam's Club—all of which were open for business during the pandemic.

So, let me get this straight: Gas is essential, but God isn't?

In Florida, a megachurch pastor who was arrested for holding services in a packed church was granted a reprieve by Republican governor Ron DeSantis, who said church services were essential and religious institutions could be open to the public.

Now *there's* a smart governor, who understands the Bill of Rights.

The Left criticizes the Right, who clearly wants to open up sooner rather than later, by saying that they're science deniers and that they're not listening to science. This is not about science. It was never about science. This is about the Left and the Right digging in. The Left is dug in to make sure that we are sheltered in place for as long as possible. The Leftist progressive Democrats see a silver lining in this: Instill fear, stop this country at all costs, and shut it down until election day in November. If the country stays locked down and people keep losing their jobs, they know that Bunker Biden might not even have to come out of his basement until long after they've already elected him president. To make sure that happens, they have extended the lockdown in order to destroy Donald Trump's signature piece of his first four years: the economy. Those who say that it's too dangerous to vote at a polling place argue that mail-in ballots are essential. Nancy Pelosi even put a requirement for mail-in ballots, versus absentee ballots, in her $3 trillion stimulus bill.

The Left, acting under the guise of a science that has been more wrong than right and with a guilt-laden accusation that we don't care about the health of others, are doing so as part of their effort to turn us into a socialist country. They want us locked down, waiting around, receiving government money, and literally dependent on the government to tell us when we can act, how we can act, and where we can act. They want to use this pandemic and the pain that it has caused to convince us that it's time to embrace their socialist agenda, most importantly Medicare for All, which would give the federal government complete control of our healthcare system. What they *don't* want us to do is ask questions about whether this lockdown was even necessary in the first place.

They don't want us to ask, for example, why we shut down the entire country—quarantining *healthy* people with the sick for the first time since the Middle Ages—instead of trying to institute mild social distancing and protecting at-risk populations. They don't want us to ask how a short-term emergency measure to "flatten the curve" and protect our hospital capacity turned into months and months of virtual house arrest, or why they are still refusing to open schools despite the fact that for children—and anyone under the age of thirty—the virus poses virtually no serious risk.

Once we start asking those questions, the whole picture begins to unravel. It starts to become clear that our scientists and doctors—most notably "Dr. Deep State" himself, Dr. Anthony Fauci—actually knew very little about what this virus does or how we should respond to it. Dr. Fauci said that hydroxychloroquine could be very dangerous but there are many doctors on the front lines who disagree with him. [2a] Dr. Fauci said we would never be able to shake hands again, and then he told us that it was fine to go on Tinder for hookups. [2b] Dr. Fauci says we shouldn't open up again, that we should stay inside until there is a vaccine.

Considering Dr. Fauci's track record of abject failure in the production of vaccines, especially since he's director of the National Institute of Allergies and Infectious Diseases for viruses like Ebola, norovirus, MERS, Zika, West Nile, and considering that coronavirus might be a dress rehearsal, as he's said, for the next bad virus, wouldn't the effort be better spent working to harness a therapeutic to treat the disease in a generalized way? What is the obsession with a vaccine? Why now? This man has never been able to create a vaccine for any of the diseases written above.

He's the one who said hydroxychloroquine was unproven, that its safety was not proven, but he's willing to put a vaccine into tens of millions, or even hundreds of millions, of people without years of safety data. At least hydroxychloroquine has been around for years. And the amazing part of this is that in countries that are affected by malaria, which is a disease for which Hydroxychloroquine is prescribed, the Covid rate is extremely low compared to countries where there is no Hydroxychloroquine use. [2c]

So, since they were lying about that, what else have they been lying about?

Well, let's take a look at where this idea came from. You tell me whether it's based on science.

THE SCIENCE PROJECT

Remember the bird flu?

Unless you're one of the 282 people in the world who actually *had* it, I'm sure you don't. But back in 2005, this virus was on everyone's mind. It had spread from a small village in Vietnam, traveling on the backs of migratory birds to places like Kazakhstan, Mongolia, and Russia, killing millions of animals along the way. For the most part, the virus only affected birds and livestock. But experts warned that if it ever made the jump from birds to humans, the results could be deadly.

On September 29, a model commissioned by the United Nations warned that if the virus ever became a full-blown pandemic, it might kill somewhere between 5 and 150 million people.[5] In the United Kingdom, our old pal Neil Ferguson did a few calculations in his head and determined that the virus would kill *at least* 150 million people, maybe more.[6]

At the White House, President George W. Bush grew especially concerned. During a vacation in late July, he had read a book about the 1918 Spanish Flu pandemic called *The Great Influenza*, which painted a, shall we say, *grim* picture of the United States during the two or three years that it had to deal with that disease. Flipping through the pages out on his ranch in Texas, President Bush read about a disease that had infiltrated the United States and killed millions, spreading despite the country's best efforts to contain it.

On page 139 of the hardcover edition, he'd have come across this paragraph, a description of a hospital ward in St. Louis:

> Corpses were wrapped in sheets, pushed into corners, left there sometimes for days, the horror of it sinking

> in deeper each hour, people too sick to cook for themselves, too sick to clean themselves, too sick to move the corpse off the bed, lying alive on the same bed with the corpse. The dead lay there for days, while the living lived with them, were horrified by them, and, perhaps most horribly, became accustomed to them.[7]

Yikes. You know, Mr. President, when the rest of us go on vacation, we usually stick with a great Nelson DeMille thriller or a romantic beach read.

Still, with the images of the 1918 pandemic in his head and word of the bird flu spreading outward from Asia, President Bush became obsessed with preparing the United States for the next big pandemic. In September 2005, he asked Congress to approve $7.1 billion in funding for vaccines, therapeutics, and medical supplies. He also increased funding for the nation's Strategic National Stockpile, a collection of masks, vaccines, and other tools for dealing with disasters. (Oddly enough, this stockpile was created by President Bill Clinton in 1998 after *he* read a novel called *The Cobra Event*, which told the story of a fictional virus that ripped through New York City and killed millions.)

In late September, President Bush called on two doctors in the federal government to come up with another plan—one that would give us the ability to handle a virus for which there was no known therapeutic or vaccine—telling them to "think outside the box." In response, these two doctors, a VA doctor named Richard Hatchett and a former oncologist named Carter Mecher, both of whom had been working in the federal government for about twenty years, started looking around the country for "outside-the-box" ideas. Neither of them had degrees in epidemiology, and neither of them had ever worked with infectious diseases before. Hatchett was a general physician, and Mecher was a former oncologist. Sometime that fall, these two doctors got a message from a complex systems analyst in New Mexico named Robert J. Glass, who had an idea.

That November, Glass's fifteen-year-old daughter had entered a science fair with a project about the H5N1 bird flu. According to a computer model that she'd built with help from her father for the science fair, the best way to stop a disease like the bird flu from spreading was to shut down all schools in the area, lock the students in their homes, and wait until there was a vaccine.[8] In a story published during the science fair, the local newspaper described her work this way:

> Laura, with some guidance from her dad, devised a computer simulation that showed how people—family members, co-workers, students in schools, people in social situations—interact. What she discovered was that school kids come in contact with about 140 people a day, more than any other group. Based on that finding, her program showed that in a hypothetical town of 10,000 people, 5,000 would be infected during a pandemic if no measures were taken, but only 500 would be infected if the schools were closed.

She came in third.

Her father, however, took the computer model she had written and ran with it. Just a few weeks later, he had used the model as the basis for a scientific paper called "Targeted Social

Distancing Designs for Pandemic Influenza." In the paper, Robert Glass and his colleagues call for the same school closures that his daughter had suggested in her science project, writing that such measures "must be imposed for the duration of the local epidemic and possibly until a strain-specific vaccine is developed and distributed. If compliance with the strategy is high over this period, an epidemic within a community can be averted."[9] Unlike the science project, however, this paper didn't only call for school closures. The most terrifying part comes at the very end, where the authors point out that "if neighboring communities do not also use these interventions, infected neighbors will continue to introduce influenza and prolong the local epidemic."

In other words, either you lock down everything, everywhere, for a very long time, or it's not going to work.

Somehow, in the fall of 2005, this paper made its way to the desks of Hatchett and Mecher, who fell in love at first sight. According to a story in the *New York Times* about the project, when Mecher received the results at his office in Washington, he was "amazed."[10] Within weeks, they were pushing the paper around the federal bureaucracy—to the CDC, Dr. Fauci's NIH, and other agencies—trying to get it onto the president's desk and make it official government policy.

At the time, though, the idea of a national lockdown seemed absurd. It didn't matter how severe the disease in question was. After all, this was something that hadn't been done since the days of King Henry VIII, and even *then* it hadn't worked. The initial workup of the idea, which is still available online, is long, but you can sum up its recommendations like this:

Step 1: Go inside.
Step 2: Stay there.
Step 3 (optional): Don't starve.

According to the two doctors, it was met with "skepticism and a degree of ridicule by senior officials."[11] Remembering the initial stages of the process, one doctor who'd worked on the project as part of a team at the Pentagon said that whenever he described what he was working on to someone, "there were two words between 'shut' and 'up.'"[12]

For a while, it went nowhere. The report, and the recommendations that these two doctors had made based on its findings, sat on various desks at federal agencies gathering dust.

In the meantime, on November 1, 2005, the president traveled to the National Institutes of Health in Bethesda, Maryland, and gave a speech. After thanking Dr. Anthony Fauci, who was in the audience that day, President Bush described the efforts he and his administration had been making:

> Our strategy is designed to meet three critical goals: First, we must detect outbreaks that occur anywhere in the world; second, we must protect the American people by stockpiling vaccines and antiviral drugs, and improve our ability to rapidly produce new vaccines against a pandemic strain; and, third, we must be ready to respond at the federal, state and local levels in the event that a pandemic reaches our shores.
>
> To meet these three goals, our strategy will require the combined efforts of government officials in public health, medical, veterinary and law enforcement com-

> munities and the private sector. It will require the active participation of the American people. And it will require the immediate attention of the United States Congress so we can have the resources in place to begin implementing this strategy right away.

You'll notice that at no point during this speech does President Bush mention a national lockdown, social distancing, or quarantines. He doesn't talk about governors instituting "pause" measures or telling their citizens that they can't go to work or keep their businesses open. Like everyone else at the time, he assumed that when a pandemic arrived, we would quarantine the sick, protect vulnerable populations, and focus all our energies on developing therapeutics for treatment and getting those out to communities in need. For decades, that had been official government strategy.

It's what we did in 1957 during an outbreak of the H2N2 virus. It's what we did in 1968, when the Hong Kong flu pandemic reached the United States.

As he was speaking, though, his two advisors were still trying to turn their plan into government policy. The problem, as it turned out, was that the actual doctors—meaning the ones with degrees in infectious disease and experience dealing with it—didn't think it was a good idea. One of the fiercest critics was a man named D. A. Henderson—the only person in this story so far who actually has a degree in epidemiology—who said that the plan would "result in significant disruption of the social functioning of communities and result in possibly serious economic problems."[13] Instead, he proposed that we "let the pandemic spread, treat people who get sick, and work quickly to develop a vaccine to prevent it from coming back." But what does he know? After all, Dr. Henderson only spearheaded the international effort that led to the eradication of smallpox in 1980, one of the greatest achievements in the history of public health.

In another academic paper warning about the dangers of the lockdown idea, he and a group of professors from Johns Hopkins University wrote this:

> There are no historical observations or scientific studies that support the confinement by quarantine of groups of possibly infected people for extended periods in order to slow the spread of influenza . . . It is difficult to identify circumstances in the past half-century when large-scale quarantine has been effectively used in the control of any disease. The negative consequences of large-scale quarantine are so extreme (forced confinement of sick people with the well; complete restriction of movement of large populations; difficulty in getting critical supplies, medicines, and food to people inside the quarantine zone) that this mitigation measure should be eliminated from serious consideration.

For a while, warnings like this were enough to keep the lockdown idea from becoming law. At no point do any economists, businesspeople, or legal experts appear to have been consulted about this plan. It was all government bureaucrats and computer modelers—the same people who would get us into trouble in 2020 with their alarmist predictions about coronavirus.

Then, slowly, as the hysteria surrounding the bird flu faded and fewer people were paying attention, the plan started moving again. Late in the year 2006, Carter Mecher and Richard Hatchett met with government public health officials, including Lisa Koonin, who was working at the CDC, and presented the plan "over burgers and beer."

Then, in February 2007, the Centers for Disease Control and Prevention took this plan—which still read like the bare bones of a high school science project—and made it official government policy. When it came time to think of a name for it, they didn't call it "total shutdown of the country," which would have been true. Instead, they called it a group of "non-pharmaceutical interventions," or "NPIs," which, admittedly, sounds a little less threatening.

For fourteen years, this plan sat around, virtually untouched. In 2009, President Barack Obama put a very minor version of the plan into practice when he closed some schools in response to the H1N1 outbreak. It was also during that crisis that President Obama severely depleted the Strategic National Stockpile that President Bush had built up, making no effort to replenish it. Thanks to his incompetence, the country was left with a dangerous lack of N95 masks and other supplies when the coronavirus pandemic began.[14]

In 2013, the Obama administration began a five-year review of the old science-project plan, then published an updated document called "Community Guidelines to Prevent Pandemic Influenza" in 2017, which contained some updated guidelines about what to do in the event of a pandemic.[15] For another three years, the plan sat in someone's desk drawer gathering dust.

Then, out of nowhere, came the Wuhan Coronavirus, a virus that had the bad luck to occur in the midst of a perfect storm. Finally, there was a virus deadly enough—and a medical bureaucracy tangled enough—that the government finally had a chance to give this wacky plan a shot and shut down the country indefinitely.

One of the loudest cheerleaders for this plan was Dr. Anthony Fauci.

PAGING DR. DEEP STATE (TO THE BRIEFING ROOM)!

In the beginning, we all thought we could trust Dr. Anthony Fauci. He had a friendly face, a calm demeanor, and one of the most impressive resumes we had ever seen. (We knew because he said so every twenty minutes.) During his first briefings about coronavirus, it seemed as if Dr. Fauci might be perfectly willing to sit back and let President Trump take the lead, only jumping up to the microphone when called upon to do so.

As the months went on, however, it became clear that Dr. Fauci *loved* the microphone—loved it so much, in fact, that the one in the White House briefing room wasn't enough to satisfy him. Even in the early days of the crisis, before the shutdowns began and the virus became politicized by the Left, Dr. Fauci was always on camera somewhere, sometimes doing more than a dozen interviews a day. During the first interviews, the doctor didn't seem all that concerned about coronavirus, which, in those days, was still perfectly fine to refer to as the "Wuhan coronavirus." On January 21, he went on Newsmax TV and said, "This is not a major threat to the people of the United States, and this is not something that the citizens of the United States right now should be worried about."[16] On January 26, he told a radio host that "The American people should not be worried or frightened by [the virus]. It's a very, very low risk to the United States, but it's something we, as public health officials, need to take very seriously."[17]

On March 8, during an appearance on *60 Minutes*, he was asked about whether people in the United States should be wearing masks.

"Right now in the United States," he said, "people should not be wearing masks."

"You're sure of it?" asked the host. "Because people are listening really closely to this."

"Yes. Right now, there is no reason to be walking around with a mask. When you're in the middle of an outbreak, wearing a mask might make you feel better, and it *might* even block . . . a droplet. But it is *not* providing the perfect protection that people think it is. And often, there are unintended consequences—people keep fiddling with the mask, and they keep touching their face."[18]

This was a lie.

While he was speaking, Dr. Fauci knew that masks were an effective deterrent against the coronavirus. He knew that widespread availability of masks is a key factor in preventing the spread of a disease. But he also knew that if regular people—you and me—went out and bought masks, they might not be available to frontline healthcare workers. So, he lied, and he lied right to our faces.

Now he stands up and has the audacity to get upset with the American public for not taking every word he says as gospel. Here he is on June 19, speaking with a radio host from the Department of Health and Human Services: "One of the problems we face in the United States is that unfortunately, there is a combination of anti-science bias that people are—for reasons that sometimes are . . . inconceivable and not understandable, they just don't believe science, and they don't believe authority."[19]

Well, doc, if it really is "inconceivable" to you, allow me to explain a few things. First of all, it isn't "science" that people don't trust.

It's *you.*

We are more than willing to listen to hard data about what this virus does, how it works, and what we can to do prevent its spread. If you gave us real information about the virus or how to avoid it, we would be happy to listen. But that is *not* what you've been giving us. Instead, you have served up predictions that have been wrong at every turn.

Throughout January and February, you told us that the coronavirus posed "no serious risk" to people in the United States.[20] Then, in March you trotted out models telling us that more than two milion people could die, predicting piles of bodies and overflowing hospital corridors if we didn't do *exactly* what you told us to do. On March 16, the day President Trump made his first recommendations on social distancing from the White House podium, you and Dr. Deborah Birx referenced Neil Ferguson's infamous Imperial College model, this time warning us that more than two million people could die in the United States. In January, you said that China was handling the pandemic with "great transparency." Then, in April, you said that China's "delay in transparency" prevented the rest of the world from adequately preparing to deal with the virus. Could it be that between January and April, Dr. Fauci, it became clear that the World Health Organization had been lying to us and you were relying on them for your information?

If you're a fan of Dr. Fauci, you might brush these lies aside—he says you can go on Tinder, but then he says you can never shake hands again—and say that he didn't know any better than the rest of us, that he was learning as we were and trying to make the best of a bad situation.

Hogwash.

The whole reason we put Dr. Fauci on television in the first place is because he's supposed to know *more* than us. He is supposed to be an expert in infectious disease, having had the title of the head of that department for more than forty years—which he never tires of pointing out—and he is supposed to give expert guidance that the rest of us don't have. If he only knows what we know, then he shouldn't be on television. He *definitely* shouldn't be making sweeping proclamations about how "this is going to get much worse" or how "schools can't open up," projecting an air of ultimate authority the whole time, if he's just going to turn around and say *oops* when he turns out to be wrong.

Of course, Dr. Fauci was only one swamp creature among many.

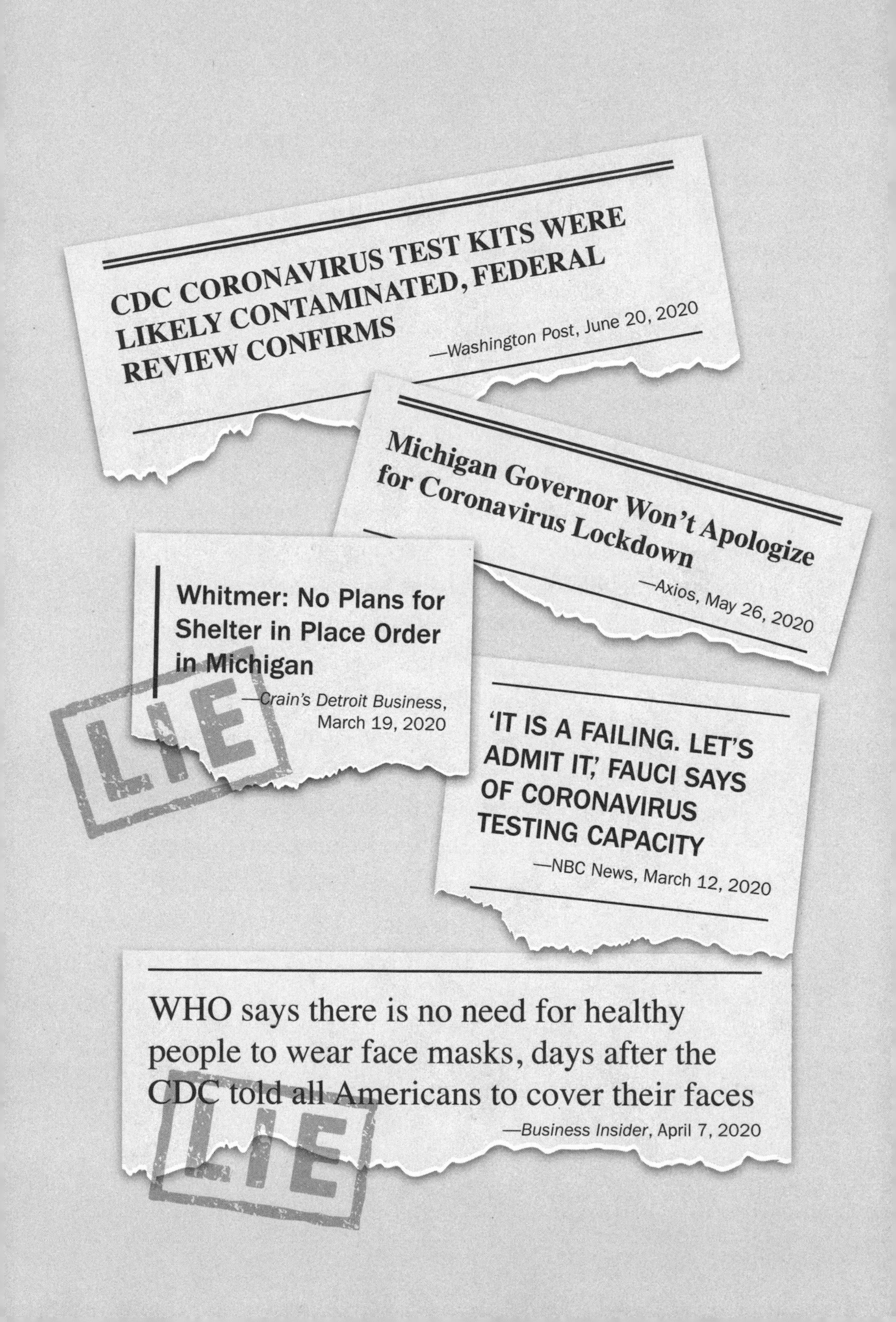
CDC CORONAVIRUS TEST KITS WERE LIKELY CONTAMINATED, FEDERAL REVIEW CONFIRMS
—Washington Post, June 20, 2020
Michigan Governor Won't Apologize for Coronavirus Lockdown
—Axios, May 26, 2020
Whitmer: No Plans for Shelter in Place Order in Michigan
—Crain's Detroit Business, March 19, 2020
LIE
'IT IS A FAILING. LET'S ADMIT IT,' FAUCI SAYS OF CORONAVIRUS TESTING CAPACITY
—NBC News, March 12, 2020
WHO says there is no need for healthy people to wear face masks, days after the CDC told all Americans to cover their faces
—Business Insider, April 7, 2020
LIE

Chapter Six

A SWAMP OF LIES

When President Trump took office, he also took control of a vast government bureaucracy that had been growing for decades. During the administration of President Bush, it increased by 6 percent; under Obama, it increased by 8 percent.[1] During the campaign, President Trump promised to raise the standards for people working in our government and to clear out the dead weight, and he was right in the middle of making good on this promise at the end of his first term. The budget he'd proposed for 2021 included about $1.9 trillion in cuts to nondiscretionary spending programs, which would have eliminated several levels of unnecessary bureaucracy.

Then the pandemic arrived.

For the first time in his presidency, President Trump was forced to wade out into the deepest part of the swamp, working *with* the very people he'd been working against for nearly four years. The country was facing an unprecedented crisis, and there was no time to go around the federal bureaucracy and find a new way to react. President Trump had to work with the federal agencies, and he had to do it while dealing with a hostile press, an incompetent Congress, and petulant governors on the Left who made the wrong decisions at every turn. Eventually, he was able to wrangle this unruly bureaucracy and coordinate a sensible response to the crisis. But in the beginning, before anyone was paying attention, the lack of action on the part of agencies like the CDC, the Food and Drug Administration, and the NIH were deadly.

Here's what happened.

"IT WAS A FAILING, LET'S ADMIT IT."

In early January, three days after the Chinese government locked down the city of Wuhan, a thirty-five-year-old man walked into an urgent care clinic in Seattle, Washington, complaining of a slight fever and a cough. When doctors asked for his medical history, he said that he'd been out of the country for about two weeks, traveling around Asia on business. Three days earlier, he said, he'd come back to the US on one of the last direct flights from Wuhan, China.

As soon as he said those words, the alarm bells went off. People in the local public health community who'd been keeping a close eye on the virus knew that it was only a matter of time before more cases began showing up. They also knew, according to interviews they would give in the months to come, that they needed to act quickly in order to stop the virus from spreading. The more tests they could perform, the better they could trace the virus; the better they could trace the virus, the easier it would be to contain it. They knew that if we got a hold on the number of cases early, quarantining the sick and protecting at-risk populations, we might be able to prevent a full-on lockdown of the sort that occurred in China, Italy, and South Korea. Given the fact that the United States had some of the best private-sector laboratories in the world, our chances seemed pretty good.

Then the bureaucrats of the federal government—people who operated in the dark at various government agencies, well out of sight of President Trump—got in the way.

In late January, a doctor in Seattle named Helen Chu called the Centers for Disease Control with an idea. She told them she'd been working on a local study of the flu for a few months, and during that study, she'd been able to collect thousands of samples from people in the Seattle area. According to a report in the *New York Times,* Dr. Chu said that if she and her team could modify some of the tests they'd already been using for the flu and use them to test for the Wuhan virus, as it was then called, then they might be able to produce the country's first working map of how far the virus had spread. Using the results of those tests, Dr. Chu could contact affected people, stop them from going out and spreading the virus, and dramatically decrease the chances that the United States would have to suffer from a full-blown pandemic.

The CDC refused.

They did not refuse on the grounds that Dr. Chu's tests were unsafe or unreliable or that they might do some unnecessary harm to her samples, all of which might have been good reasons for denying her. They didn't refuse because they had a better or more efficient test in their own laboratories. In fact, it would be weeks before they would be able to develop a test that was reliable enough to ship out to labs across the country. No, they refused, according to a report published in the *New York Times,* because the lab in which Dr. Chu and her team had proposed conducting the tests "was not certified as a clinical laboratory under regulations established by the Centers for Medicare & Medicaid Services."[2]

In short, she didn't have the proper ministerial paperwork.

Even though the tests that Dr. Chu was planning on performing could have sounded the alarm about the severity of the virus months before someone actually did, allowing some of the earliest patients to hunker down and get treatment rather than walking around and infecting thousands of other people, the CDC decided to follow the letter of the law instead, probably costing hundreds of lives in the process. During those first two months, there was a fire in our living room, and this woman was standing in front of it with a fully functional fire extinguisher. Yet the government was telling her she couldn't use it because she hadn't filed the proper paperwork to use it.

This was only the tip of the bureaucratic iceberg.

In the days that followed, that fire in the living room would spread to the kitchen, dining room, and eventually the whole second floor of the house. Public health experts in various state governments would watch while the map of the United States slowly filled with glowing red and yellow splotches, all of which represented new clusters of the coronavirus. What began as a few cases in Washington and New York soon grew to a national pandemic, and nobody knew the extent of the spread.

But there was nothing local officials could do.

For the first month of this crisis, while President Trump was trying to stop the flow of the disease through travel bans and a close study of the virus's RNA sequence, the bureaucrats at the CDC dragged their feet. This agency, which was created in the 1940s for the sole purpose of preparing for a global pandemic like the one we are living through right now, managed to screw up at every turn. They refused help from local officials, sent out tests that weren't ready, and maintained a complete stranglehold on our country's response to the virus. Half of those tests provided inaccurate results. Elsewhere in the federal government, the FDA kept up a byzantine set of regulations that very few companies knew how to navigate.

When the CDC finally *did* get their own test approved and ready to send out to the states, it was a complete mess. Local officials who received the first round of tests from the CDC in early February noticed that the results from the tests were all over the place. On one occasion, scientists in New York got the same results when they tested a person they already knew to be Covid-positive as they did when they tested a puddle of distilled water.[3] In other states, the tests would come back positive no matter what the scientists fed them. It would be weeks before the CDC was able to fix these problems, and months before we had an accurate system of determining who did and did not have Covid.

Time and time again, as they assured President Trump that they were doing all they could to deal with this crisis, the low-level bureaucrats at the CDC refused help from private companies and universities that could have helped.

"We have the skills and resources as a community," wrote the medical director of an academic laboratory in Utah in an email on February 27, "but we are collectively paralyzed by a bloated bureaucratic/administrative process."[4]

In some cases, people who worked in private laboratories were forced to go behind the backs of the government in order to conduct tests. On February 25, Dr. Chu and her colleagues started performing tests on people in Seattle without government approval, and the results were shocking. Within a few hours, they had gotten a positive result from a local teenager who hadn't been out of the country. They also learned that seven patients at a local nursing home who hadn't set foot out of the facility in months had come down with the virus. A few weeks later, one of those patients became the first person to die in the United States from COVID, but not before having daily visits with friends and family in his room at the nursing home.

A few days later, government bureaucrats from the CDC and the FDA got on the phone with Dr. Chu and her team—but not to congratulate them. Instead, they called to ask them to cease all testing and run it through the central office of the CDC instead. On February 29, they finally agreed to allow American biotech companies and other private labs to begin testing for the virus, but it was too late.

The disease had already spread to thousands of people. It was present in all fifty states, and thanks to the unwillingness of government agencies to coordinate with the private sector, we had absolutely no way of knowing how many people might be at risk or where in the United States they might be.

On March 12, just a few days before the first US cities would be given their first shelter-in-place orders, Dr. Fauci testified in front of Congress about the first steps the government had taken in response to the virus. He said, according to a transcript of the testimony, that the testing debacle had exposed "deep structural problems in the nation's public health system."[5]

"Yeah," he said. "It's a failing, let's admit it. The idea of anybody getting it easily the way people in other countries are doing it, we're not set up for that. Do I think we should be? Yes, but we're not."[6]

Really, Dr. Fauci? Over the course of your entire life, you've had exactly *one* job, and that's been to make sure the United States is prepared to deal with a severe infectious disease outbreak. Now that it's finally here, you're just going to throw up your hands and say, *Oh, well, we gave it our best shot*?

But maybe Dr. Fauci has *another* reason for keeping us all inside until there is a vaccine. After all, unlike many other people in positions like his, Fauci can make money off of the drugs he is promoting—particularly vaccines.

He's done it before.

In 2005, Fauci's NIH was conducting clinical trials for a drug called Proleukin. Dr. Fauci's name was listed on the patent for the drug. If it ever became widely used, he stood to earn a profit.

Perhaps that is why his organization reacted so poorly when, in late 2005, an employee at the NIH named Jonathan Fishbein came forward to say that the drug was causing "adverse" affects in test subjects, including "capillary leak and suicidal ideation."[6a] This man, who was in charge of ensuring compliance at the NIH, noted that test subjects were not being informed of these risks.

Fishbein was fired.

Eventually, he was reinstated, and it became public that Dr. Fauci stood to make money off a drug he was promoting. In the end, Fauci agreed to donate the proceeds to charity.

CREEPING SOCIALISM

After we were required to follow these statewide quarantines, we realized that there was not an end in sight. We knew the goal, and we were happy to work together to meet it. At the time, we thought that if we did nothing, more than two million people could lose their lives. We believed that our hospitals and nursing homes might be overwhelmed in a matter of days if we didn't act immediately. It would later turn out that we made these decisions based on models that were severely overblown, models that assumed that the virus had a much higher death rate than it actually did. Based on the information that Dr. Fauci was presenting, nobody was asking questions. The president was relying on a man who had advised five other presidents. Under the guidance of Dr. Fauci, Dr. Robert Redfield, and Dr. Birx—who later turned out not to be the geniuses they were made out to be—President Trump issued a set of guidelines called "15 Days to Slow the Spread."

These guidelines, which were not nearly as strict as some of the restrictions that would come later, told Americans to stay home if they were sick, to avoid large crowds, and to "do their part" to fight the virus by not going out as much as they used to.[7] They were based in part on the CDC's general recommendations to help prevent the spread of the virus, and they were sensible.

Then, the governors took over.

In their speeches announcing their shelter-in-place orders, governors all over the country told us we needed to lock down for as long as it would take to keep our hospitals from getting overwhelmed. In a tweet announcing a "stay at home" order for California on March 19, Governor Gavin Newsom said we needed to "meet this moment and flatten the curve together."[8]

Three days earlier, Governor Phil Murphy of New Jersey had announced his own statewide shelter-in-place order, using similar language. "In many respects," he said, "this is day one of life in New Jersey under the measures we put in place yesterday to ensure social distancing and help flatten the curve and slow the spread of coronavirus. And again, as we said yesterday and was said many times, the extent to which we can, through social distancing, flatten the curve over here, we take the pressure off the healthcare system over here and save lives and health in the process."[9]

You'll notice that neither of these governors said anything about waiting for a vaccine or a cure for coronavirus. They didn't say anything about waiting for a day when we saw zero new cases, or a week where no one in the world died from the disease. They only spoke about this all-important curve. They failed, however, to explain what that term really meant.

I'm sure you know what the curve looks like. Picture it now. On the left, you'll see what the experts told us would happen if we did nothing. There's a giant peak like a mountain, which gets very tall on the left-hand side and then slopes rapidly downward to almost zero. In this scenario, according to the experts, the virus would spread very quickly throughout our cities, and as a result, people would all develop symptoms at the same time, which could result in our hospitals getting overwhelmed. That, they told us, could lead to unnecessary deaths. On the right, you'll see what they told us would happen—what *did* happen—if we took proper precautions. The curve stayed low, but it lasted longer, reaching zero at a much later date. Because we came into contact with fewer people, the virus spread more slowly, which allowed our hospitals to treat everyone who needed treatment.

You'll also notice that no matter what that curve does, the number of people infected doesn't change. The same number of people get the virus in the doomsday scenario as they do in the shelter-in-place scenario. The only difference is that in the shelter-in-place scenario, those people get it over the course of weeks and months rather than days, which prevents total catastrophe.

Flattening the curve was never about making the virus go away forever. It wasn't even about bringing the number of cases down to zero. From the beginning, it was about making sure it spread in a way that let us keep our businesses open, our hospital beds empty, and our most vulnerable populations protected. It was about making sure that the death rate stayed close to zero even as the number of cases went up—which is exactly what's happening now.

At least that's what they *said.*

As it turns out, once governors—particularly the ones on the Left—get a hold of power, they have a very hard time letting it go.

GOVERNOR GRETCHEN

By now, you're probably aware that the coronavirus virus doesn't affect everyone equally. When young people come down with the disease, they are generally able to recover quickly. Most of them don't even need to go to a hospital for treatment. They just sit in bed by themselves for a few days eating chicken soup, and within a week they're fine. The real trouble, we have come to find, occurs when someone who is already sick with underlying conditions—like cancer, diabetes, or heart disease—is infected. These additional conditions are called comorbidities, and *they* are what make coronavirus such a serious problem. In fact, a recent study estimates that of all the people in the United States who have been hospitalized with the disease so far, roughly 90 percent of them were seriously ill with something else when they got it.[10]

The same was true of our states and cities. Sometimes, the virus would come to town and nothing of note would happen; other times, it would find a series of underlying conditions and exploit them ruthlessly.

When coronavirus arrived in Michigan, for example, it found a state riddled with underlying conditions. That state was run by a woman named Gretchen Whitmer, who'd been governor of the state for just under a year. In that time, she had done very little other than raise taxes, push her Medicare for All policies, and make long, impassioned speeches about how the men and women of ICE were "immoral" and "acting against the wishes of people in the state."[12] Before the pandemic, this woman was just one more liberal nutjob ranting to nobody.

But when Joe Biden announced that he was on the lookout for a female running mate, Governor Gretchen must have gotten her hopes up. Suddenly, she began to believe that maybe *she* might be the one who got to stand beside Joe Biden on the campaign trail, finish his sentences for him, and explain, from a woman's perspective, why all that touching and groping and sniffing wasn't really all that bad. In the beginning, this was probably little more than a fever dream. After all, nobody had ever heard of Gretchen Whitmer before the pandemic began, and when they *did* get to know her, they wished they'd never heard of her. As of

February 2020, she had a 42 percent approval rating, and that was before she'd begun to trample on the constitutional rights of Michiganders.[13]

But when the first cases of Covid began appearing in Michigan, Whitmer saw her opening. All she had to do was get tougher on the virus than anyone, making lots of noise while she did it, and maybe Bunker Biden would notice her. Of course, knowing that the competition was stiff in the liberal grandstanding department—with the *Andrew Cuomo Variety Hour* still playing day in and day out on every television screen in the nation—this woman had to go big to get ahead.

And go big she did.

All throughout the pandemic, Governor Gretchen issued nonsensical, illogical, and absurd guidelines that were certainly capable of attracting national attention—in fact, national outrage. They would have been laughable if the situation hadn't been so deadly serious.

In April, she ordered all citizens of Michigan to remain in their homes unless they were doing activities that she deemed "necessary to sustain or protect life."[14]

"If you're not buying food or medicine or other essential items," she said, "you should not be going to the store."[15]

So, you might be wondering: What could possibly engender the outrage to such a benign-sounding statement? What does Governor Gretchen consider an item that is "necessary to sustain or protect life"?

Well, for starters, booze. In Governor Gretchen's fiefdom during the lockdown, it was always permissible to buy beer and whiskey, but it was never permissible to buy household items like grass seed or vegetable seed. If you wanted to buy weed, as in marijuana, you had her blessing. If you wanted to buy weed *killer* for your garden, though, you were, sadly, out of luck. Starting in late March, Governor Gretchen ordered people to stay in their homes indefinitely, and she prevented them from buying carpeting for their floors or paint for their walls while they were stuck inside staring at them. In mid-April, she decreed that home improvement stores could open, but they would have to cordon off their paint, flooring, and outdoor gardening sections with yellow caution tape before anyone would be allowed into the store. These restrictions were outrageous, and they didn't make any sense whatsoever.

But compared to what came next, Gretchen's little list of "forbidden items" was kid stuff.

On April 16, in an unsettling turn toward authoritarianism, the governor's team began looking into software that could help them perform contact tracing on the citizens of Michigan. This technology would allow the governor to find infected people in the state, set up an infrastructure for tracking them, and then find anyone they'd come into contact with. It would require collecting massive amounts of data about American citizens.[16]

At the time, dozens of companies could have helped them do this. But Governor Gretchen, ever loyal to the state Democrat Party that got her elected in the first place, decided to use a company called Great Lakes Community Engagement instead. This group, according to their website, specialized in "outreach campaigns to engage citizens."[17] What they really were, though, was a liberal advocacy organization run by a well-known Democrat consultant named Michael Kolehouse. In the past, Kolehouse had been an Occupy Wall Street protestor. Since then, he'd become a complete unhinged lunatic who posted all day about how much he hated President Trump. When the coronavirus was first spreading through the United States, he wrote on Facebook that he hoped President Trump would "get Coronavirus ASAP" and said that someone should "do the country a favor and cough on that man."[18]

Out of all the public health experts in the world—all the qualified citizens of Michigan who would have been happy to help the government track the spread of Covid—*this* is the person to whom Gretchen Whitmer wanted to give unbelievable amounts of data about the citizens of Michigan. She wanted to give it to him so much, in fact, that she skipped the normal protocols for awarding government contracts and created a special back door for him, awarding Kolehouse's company over $190,000 for their future services.

When the local press caught her, pointing out correctly that the governor probably shouldn't be giving out prized government contracts to political hacks like Kolehouse—especially when those jobs involve handling sensitive information about Americans—Governor Gretchen lied. First, she said that she had never approved the hiring of Kolehouse. Then, when they produced emails proving that she had, in fact, approved the whole plan, she moved to cancel the contract. After that, she lied *again,* claiming that she canceled the contract as soon as she found out what was going on.[19]

Maybe Governor Gretchen was confused. After all, she was very busy during those first few months. On April 15, for instance, she signed an executive order mandating that all nursing homes in the state that were at less than 80 percent capacity create dedicated units for "coronavirus affected residents," and then ordered them to take new patients so long as they had a minimum amount of PPE for employees. To this day, we are not sure how many people died in nursing homes as a result of that order. We do know that more than 1,372 deaths came from nursing homes in Detroit alone, which is a number, according to calculations done by PJ Media, that represents 33 percent of all deaths in Michigan.

In the middle of those two executive orders, citizens of Michigan took to the streets in order to protest the governor's stay-at-home orders. They held signs, chanted, and remained largely peaceful throughout the entire demonstration.

In response, Governor Gretchen called them "irresponsible."[20] Then, she said that if they kept it up, she would have to "think about extending the stay-at-home orders, which is supposedly what they were protesting."[21] In some of the other interviews she did during those days—none of which involved the people she was killing with her executive order on nursing homes—the governor called the rallies "political" and implied that they were "racist and misogynistic."

Well, governor, either you were looking at the wrong protests or you were flat-out lying. There was nothing racist going on. There were people begging you to let them have their lives back. Many of them were people of color.

I'll tell you what *is* racist: sitting in your mansion and decreeing that people who live paycheck to paycheck, of all races, are no longer allowed to go to work.

HYPOCRISY, HATE, AND HYSTERIA

When these liberals passed their laws, they weren't thinking about you and me. I'm sure none of them gave a moment's thought to what their draconian rules would do to average people around the United States. They knew that they wouldn't have to follow their own rules, which is why they had no problem making those rules as cruel and restrictive as possible.

Just before Memorial Day weekend, for example, Governor Gretchen posted this message about some of the waterfront areas of Michigan, which are popular destinations for vacations: "If you don't live in these regions, think long and hard before you take a trip into them . . . A small spike could put the hospital system in dire straits pretty quickly. That's precisely why we're asking everyone to continue doing their part. Don't descend on [waterfront] Traverse City from all regions of the state."[22]

For some reason, she believed that people would be safer in their homes than they would be floating out on the open water thousands of feet from one another.

Did this apply to Gretchen Whitmer's family? Her husband certainly didn't think so. A few days after that order went up, he went down to the docks to try to get the family's boat in the water. When the docking company refused him, he said, "I am the husband to the governor, will this make a difference?"[23]

It wasn't just Gretchen.

In April, Mayor Lori Lightfoot of Chicago issued an order titled *Stay at Home, Save Lives,* and said "getting your roots done is not essential." Then, just a few days later, she got her hair cut. Asked about it, she said, "I'm a person who, I take my personal hygiene very seriously. As I said, I felt like I needed to have a haircut . . . I'm not able to do that myself, so I got a haircut. You want to talk more about that?"

Why, yes, Mrs. Mayor, in fact I do. When you impose ridiculous rules for citizens of your city—rules that you said have to be "iron clad" when it came to enforcement—and then you don't follow them yourself, you send a message that not only are you a hypocrite, but you are so dug in on your imperiousness that you don't care if anyone knows it. Just like Mayor Bill de Blasio, who went to the gym during the first day of lockdown in New York, or Neil Ferguson, who had an affair with a married woman in London, these elites believe they can impose their will on the rest of us and never have to adhere to the same rules themselves.

All of us on television were forced to do our own hair and makeup before millions watched us. This woman, who was issuing the orders, is concerned about how she looks and is willing to be the first to violate her own order for vanity.

And if *that* kind of hypocrisy blows your hair back, wait until you see what the Democrat governors and mayors of this country did when the *real* dangerous protests began.

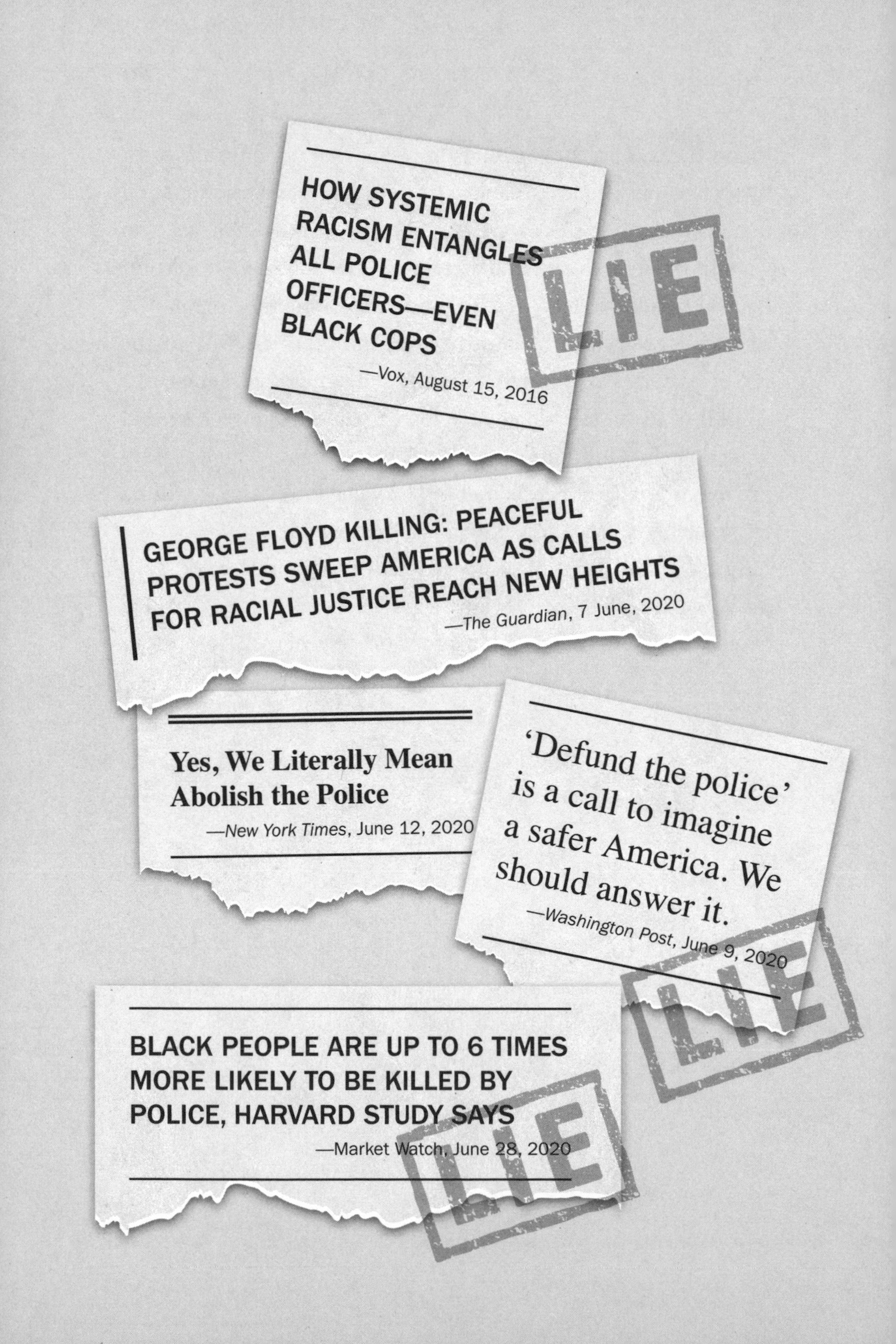
HOW SYSTEMIC RACISM ENTANGLES ALL POLICE OFFICERS—EVEN BLACK COPS
—Vox, August 15, 2016
LIE
GEORGE FLOYD KILLING: PEACEFUL PROTESTS SWEEP AMERICA AS CALLS FOR RACIAL JUSTICE REACH NEW HEIGHTS
—The Guardian, 7 June, 2020
Yes, We Literally Mean Abolish the Police
—New York Times, June 12, 2020
'Defund the police' is a call to imagine a safer America. We should answer it.
—Washington Post, June 9, 2020
LIE
BLACK PEOPLE ARE UP TO 6 TIMES MORE LIKELY TO BE KILLED BY POLICE, HARVARD STUDY SAYS
—Market Watch, June 28, 2020
LIE

Chapter Seven

DE-*FEND* THE POLICE

Law and order is essential.

It's real simple. Without law and order, there is no freedom. Without law and order, freedom ends. Without law and order, there is anarchy.

Don't get me wrong. What happened to George Floyd was a torturous and sadistic murder that has been etched into our national consciousness. It can only be handled in one way: with zero tolerance.

Zero tolerance.

Within days of the incident, Hennepin County attorney Mike Freeman, an accomplished veteran prosecutor, charged police officer Derek Chauvin with murder. The three other officers on the scene have been charged with aiding and abetting manslaughter and murder.

But might Chauvin have been charged with murder one? The one element that distinguishes murder one from murder two for which he is presently charged, is the causing of death with premeditation. The sentence changes from under forty years to life imprisonment.

Some say murder one is too high a charge, that a jury will compromise, that racism is reflected in jury verdicts. But when I was the district attorney, my office prosecuted an off-duty white New York City police officer for shooting and killing a black man. They said murder one was too high a charge. They said it couldn't be done. The jury in my case didn't think murder was too high a charge. Neither did the highest court in New York.

Unbeknownst to me, after the verdict, I learned it was the first conviction of its kind in New York State history—the first time a white police officers had been convicted of killing a black man.

Officer Chauvin's actions were beyond reckless and beyond depraved—beyond a simple intentional murder. George Floyd was not resisting arrest. He was compliant. Even more egregious, he wasn't being arrested for a violent crime, but for allegedly using a counterfeit twenty-dollar bill to buy food during a pandemic.

As to premeditation: Like intent, it can be formed in seconds, simultaneous with the act itself. Consider what was going on during the eight minutes and forty-six seconds while Officer Chauvin had his knee on George Floyd's neck. That knee stayed on Floyd's neck until after he expired. He never let up. Floyd begged him not once, not twice—not five times or ten times—but *sixteen* times to allow him to breathe. He repeatedly and continuously pleaded, "I can't breathe. I can't breathe. Please."

All that was in the first five minutes. The other new police officers, actually kneeling on his back and legs, asked Chauvin if they should roll George on his side, which would have given him some breathing room. Chauvin , the senior police officer on the scene, said no and continued to press his knee into George's neck. In the video recording of the incident, you can see Chauvin shift periodically to get maximum leverage from his left knee onto George's neck while the other officers are on George's back and legs suppressing his diaphragm, making it even more difficult for him to breathe. George continues to plead for his life.

Again, an officer asks if they could roll George onto his side. Chauvin says no, readjusting his knee into George's neck as Chauvin's own right foot moves freely, proving that the full weight of his body was leveraged through his left knee onto George's neck.

At least a dozen witnesses separately yell at police, "He can't breathe!"

They implore Tou Thao, the officer standing, to do something and for Chauvin to get off Floyd's neck. They beg the officer to check George's pulse.

As this is taking place, George says, "I'm through." He repeats, "I'm through, I'm through." Then, he cries in pain.

"They're going to kill me, please, please."

He continues to wail, crying out please, please, begging, "Please, man," and then wails again in pain. The passersby continue to say, "You got him down, let him breathe."

As they plead with Chauvin, George says, "Please, your knee is on my neck."

Chauvin's response reveals his state of mind. Chauvin says, "Get up and get in the car." He mocks George repeatedly. George responds, "You can't win man. My stomach, my neck."

George's nose is bleeding now. The witnesses watching in horror say, "Look at his nose, he's bleeding. He's not resisting.

He ain't doing anything. How long are you going to hold him down? Put him in the car."

George wails, "Mama!" He cries again, "Mama!"

The witness yells, "You're trapping his breathing, bro. I trained in the academy. You're stopping him from breathing."

They repeatedly tell Chauvin that George can't breathe. They then start yelling, "Get him off the ground." Chauvin just keeps his head focused on his knee in the neck of George and then stares at the passersby. One witness who's been watching calls out to Chauvin and says, "He's enjoying that. You're enjoying that, you bum. You are stopping his breathing. You are a bum."

The witnesses then approach to look at George and say, "Look at his head."

Chauvin takes out his mace and points it toward at least two of them. One of them says he's not responsive, but Chauvin continues to keep his knee on him. The witness says, "Check his pulse," and starts yelling. "He's dead! Check his pulse. They fucking killed him! Get off his neck! He's not moving."

They look at Thao. "Are you going to let him keep doing that?"

Folks, this is not just recklessness. This is not just depraved indifference to human life. This is not just intentional murder. This is premeditated murder one. Chauvin was reminded over and over again that he was snuffing the life out of George Floyd. He was reminded by George Floyd begging and wailing for his life. He was reminded by the witnesses and passersby. He was reminded as he felt the life of George Floyd being expelled under his knee. This is not a man who didn't comprehend or understand the depravity. Again and again, he was called upon to stop, to check, to roll him off his back, to check his pulse, to see that his nose was bleeding, to put him in the car. At every one of these points, his attention was drawn to what he was doing and he had a chance to stop. Every one of these alerts was a trigger that alerted him to the consequences of his actions, a point of premeditation after which he made the conscious decision to continue.

So, at what point did the premeditation begin? Did it begin when Chauvin first decided to put his knee on George's neck? There is no policy, procedure, or practice that allows police to do this. Did it begin when he refused to take his knee from his neck? This is a question of fact for the jury to decide. In the courtroom, you tell them to close their eyes in silence for eight minutes and forty-six seconds. That is a long time to form premeditation—a long time to consider it, a long time to reconsider it, a long time to continue it.

Long enough to steal George Floyd's life from him.

Yes, zero tolerance. Bad cops like Chauvin deserve zero tolerance. Every prosecutor, police officer, and judge I know said that what happened to George Floyd was a crime, and it was murder. We all agreed it was a tragedy, and that protests were appropriate.

But I'll bet you never heard the name David Dorn.

He, too, was a black man murdered, shot to death by looters during the so-called "peaceful" protests over George Floyd's death. Captain Dorn was murdered by rioters as he protected his friend's pawn shop in St. Louis. He was a retired seventy-seven-year-old black police captain. As with George, there is a video of him dying, bleeding out at 2:30 in the morning. We need to honor David's life, too. We should be crying for him, too. But why not? He deserves justice.

Murder must not be defined depending upon who kills you.

No one is above the law, and no one is below it. That doesn't just apply to the accused. It applies to both victims here. Both black, both unjustifiably killed. The outrage, however, is only for one. David Dorn's life mattered, too. There must be zero tolerance for his killer as well.

THE WAR ON POLICE

In the days after George Floyd's killing, Americans rose up, incensed at what they saw. The issue was police brutality.

But it morphed into racism.

In the beginning, these protestors took to the streets in anger, and they did so protected by the Constitution. They peaceably assembled, asserting that no American should ever be violently murdered by a police officer, as happened to George Floyd.

The question was how we would handle it. The way the protestors, the Left, and the Democrats handled it was to turn it into a war on police.

In Minneapolis, where the murder of George Floyd had occurred, the protests began peacefully. People marched in the streets and voiced their outrage in a way that was calm, respectful, and nonviolent. However, it soon became clear that Mayor Jacob Frey, a civil rights attorney who was on the side of the protestors, would make no effort to maintain law and order in his city. His silence spoke volumes. Throughout the evening of May 27, the protests devolved into riots, and the crowds became violent. Around ten o'clock p.m., they ran into a Target across from the city's Third Precinct police station and started looting. Within hours, the shelves were empty and rioters were destroying everything in sight. A group of men in black masks broke glass and tore down shelves with crowbars.[1]

Another group broke into the cash registers and destroyed displays at the front of the store. The mob also broke into a local pawn shop and an AutoZone, lighting the buildings on fire and allowing the fires to spread.

In full retreat mode, the mayor ordered cops to abandon the Third Precinct station, which was right across from the Target store. The sight of the police officers leaving made the crowd grow bigger and angrier. They broke windows and threw Molotov cocktails into the first floor of the station. The skeleton crew of cops who remained inside the precinct ran up the stairs to the roof. The fire climbed almost as quickly.

Police officers had to be rescued from the roof by helicopter.

YouTube videos and news footage of the precinct fully engulfed in flames went viral. It was nothing less than a national disgrace. Fear gripped the city. Minneapolis cops were totally humiliated—at least a dozen have resigned or are in the process of resigning from the department. For domestic terrorist organizations like Antifa, however, it was a victory of monumental proportions.

Emboldened by its triumph in Minneapolis, the radical Left brought its brand of terror across the country. The protests spread like a virus. Twenty-three states had to call in the National Guard. Dangerous and violent protests erupted in 350 American cities,[2] many of them reminiscent of some futuristic movie like *Escape from New York,* where the government lets a city filled with criminals govern themselves—where lawlessness and anarchy thrive. Law-abiding citizens watched in horror as looters ransacked and torched buildings, stores, and even churches—all, allegedly, in the name of George Floyd.

Democrat mayors and governors watched their cities burn and did nothing. In fact, they did worse than nothing. They tried to appease the mob. Around noon on June 7, Mayor Jacob Frey walked into a group of protestors in the middle of Minneapolis, a city that was still smoldering from weeks of violent riots. Rather than letting them know that this behavior would no longer be tolerated, Mayor Frey apologized to *them*. When the mob asked him to renounce his white privilege, he agreed. When they asked him to kneel before them, he did it—literally. Like many Democrat mayors, he assumed that the mob, at its core, was reasonable, that they could be convinced to stand down when their demands were met.

He was wrong.

That afternoon, Mayor Frey stood among a crowd of angry protestors, all of whom had their fists raised, and took questions from a woman who had been leading the protests. Speaking into a microphone, she said, "Jacob Frey, we have a yes or no question. Yes or no, will you commit to defunding the Minneapolis Police Department?"

When the mayor tried to answer, she kept going.

"We don't want no mo' police—we don't want people with guns toting around in our community, shooting us down. Do you have an answer? It is a yes or a no. Will you defund the Minneapolis Police Department? Quiet down, y'all, it's important that we hear this. Because if y'all don't know, he's up for reelection next year. And if he says no, guess what the fuck we gonna do next year?"

When the cheering died down, the mayor tried to answer, shaking his head no. In a cell phone video of the incident, you can hear him try to strike a reasonable tone, saying that he doesn't support *completely* defunding the department, but . . .

"Alright," said the woman with the microphone. "Get the fuck out of here! Bye! Go home, Jacob. Go home!"[3]

That morning, members of the Minneapolis City Council had announced their intention to vote on a bill that would completely abolish the city's police department, replacing it with "a new model of public safety."[4] Later that month, it would pass. Representative Ilhan Omar of Minneapolis had called the police department "rotten to the core" and demanded that it be abolished immediately.[5]

But Minneapolis was only the beginning.

In the second week of June, Antifa and other related gangs of Left-wing thugs took over a six-block section of the city of Seattle, which included the Seattle Police Department's East Precinct building. Make no mistake, this was not a peaceful protest. It was not civil disobedience. This was an armed insurrection led by Antifa and the Redneck Revolt, a militant gang of anarchists that surrounded the Arizona state capitol building on the day of Donald Trump's inauguration. They were also armed and dangerous at the Unite the Right rally in Charlottesville. But they were Democrats, so nobody cared.

These radical Leftists did nothing less than declare war on America's police, and Democrats such as Washington State governor Jay Inslee and Seattle mayor Jenny Durkan immediately surrendered.

Here's how Durkan describes the takeover: "Lawfully gathering and expressing First Amendment rights, demanding we do better as a society and demanding true equity to communities of color is not terrorism; it is patriotism." She also called it "the summer of love."

Nothing like a couple of AK-47s to heat up the passion, right?

When the protests first began to occur around the country, President Trump tweeted, "When the looting starts, the shooting starts." For this, he was decried as a racist and an authoritarian. The media attacked him from all sides, accusing him of trotting out "racist tropes" at a time of national crisis.

Well, a little less than one week after the looting started and the walls went up around the Capitol Hill Autonomous Zone, the shooting *did* start. Police, to their credit, previously chased out of their precinct, responded to the 911 calls, as the "hate America" group refused their entry. The nineteen-year-old who was shot that night died. There was no crime scene preservation, no interviewing witnesses, and no justice. Then, within forty-eight hours, there was a second round of shooting in the CHOP Zone, and then a third and a fourth. One of those shot, seeking victim status, claimed that the police didn't respond quickly enough.

Seattle police then released a video showing police and first responders being prevented by a violent crowd from getting to that victim.

Then, Schizo-Summer-of-Love Seattle mayor Jenny Durkan asked the occupants to leave. The squatters, of course, refused and threatened business owners with retaliation if they painted over their graffiti. Capitol Hill businesses and residents are now suing the city over the CHOP Zone, claiming they facilitated the actions of this radical group.

In my opinion, they should win. Of course, they'll only be able to do that if Seattle can keep its courts of law from being overrun by the mob.

Considering the way things have been going lately, I wouldn't count on it.

It comes as no surprise that the war on cops is defended and supported by the so-called elite liberal media complex, aka, the fake news. This unholy alliance of militant radicals and the press is nothing new, going as far back as the 1960s and domestic terrorist groups such as the Students for a Democrat Society (SDS) and the Weather Underground. As they did back then, major liberal news outlets today like the *New York Times* and *Washington Post* twist themselves into pretzels trying to justify a movement that amounts to mob rule.

In article after article, they wrote that defunding the police meant only the reallocation of police budgets. They insisted that term only indicated a little less funding for law enforcement and a little more for social services such as drug counseling and psychotherapy. Some of the stories wanted you to believe that defunding the police really didn't have much to do with the cops at all. They said it was more about "underlying factors" such as homelessness and poverty. One story, published on the Left-wing website *Vox,* even said that defunding the police meant a more "holistic model" of public safety.

Rather than simply reporting the various demands that groups like Antifa and Black Lives Matter were making, liberal news organizations tried to help translate their insane phrases into something that the public would be okay with. That isn't journalism. It's PR. If you ever needed proof that the liberal media has become nothing more than an arm of the Democrat Party, here it is.

On June 12, the *New York Times* allowed one of these Leftists to say the quiet part out loud, putting an end to all the contrived interpretations of the phrase with an op-ed written by Mariame Kaba. The piece is titled "Yes, We Mean Literally Abolish the Police." In it, Kaba states that police departments, presumably all eighteen thousand of them in the United States, are beyond reform, and that they should be shut down because "reform won't happen."

Well, at least they're finally starting to admit what they really mean by "defunding the police."

"There is not a single era in United States history," she wrote, "in which the police were not a force of violence against black people. . . . So, when you see a police officer pressing his knee into a black man's neck until he dies, that's the logical result of policing in America. When a police officer brutalizes a black person, he is doing what he sees as his job . . . Regardless of your view on police power, whether you want to get rid of the police or simply to make them less violent, here's an immediate demand we can all make: Cut the number of police in half and cut their budget in half. Fewer police officers equals fewer opportunities for them to brutalize and kill people."

THE BRUTALITY LIE

On the evening of Friday, June 12, the same day the *New York Times* had published an op-ed calling on cities to "literally" abolish the police, two officers in Atlanta responded to a 911 call from an employee at a Wendy's restaurant in the city. According to the call, there was a man asleep in his car in the parking lot. He was blocking cars from getting into the restaurant's drive-through lane, and he appeared to be intoxicated.

A few hours later, the man was dead—seemingly just one more Black man killed by police.

For a while, that's all we knew. The details were few and far between. We knew that there had been some kind of confrontation between the two officers and the man, and that it had involved a taser. We knew his name was Rayshard Brooks, and that he was 27 years old. We knew that one of the officers had shot Brooks, and that he had later died at a hospital.

The next day, Saturday, by the time I was getting ready for my 9 p.m. live show *Justice with Judge Jeanine*, the picture had not become much clearer. We still did not have body camera footage of the incident, and we did not know what had really happened in that parking lot in Atlanta. For a while, we all had to sit and watch the chaos unfold, listening once again to the Left's predetermined narrative about police violence—one that claims there is an epidemic of shootings against young black men in this country, based in hatred and purposeful, systemic racism, which is not true.

This is a lie.

According to the writer Heather MacDonald, writing in the *Wall Street Journal*, "A solid body of evidence finds no structural bias in the criminal justice system with regard to arrests, prosecutions or sentencing. Crime and suspect behavior, not race, determine most police actions."

The numbers, according to her years of analysis, back this up:

> In 2019 police officers fatally shot 1,004 people, most of whom were armed or otherwise dangerous. African-Americans were about a quarter of those killed by cops last year (235), a ratio that has remained stable since 2015. That share of black victims is less than what the black crime rate would predict, since police shootings are a function of how often officers encounter armed and violent suspects. In 2018, the latest year for which such data have been published, African-Americans made up 53% of known homicide offenders in the U.S. and commit about 60% of robberies, though they are 13% of the population . . . The police fatally shot nine

unarmed blacks and 19 unarmed whites in 2019, according to a *Washington Post* database, down from 38 and 32, respectively, in 2015.

Of course, nobody wants to hear those numbers. Even saying them out loud can put someone in danger of being labelled a racist. But when it comes to matters of life and death—and the careers and reputations of innocent police officers—the facts do matter.

The truth matters.

But not to the Left.

During my show that evening, I played footage of violent protests beginning in Atlanta, an eerie echo of the riots that had torn Minneapolis apart just days earlier. The show began with attorneys for Rayshard Brooks holding a press conference, one of whom said that if Rayshard Brooks had been "a white kid," there would have been a polite discussion about getting home.

"If this officer today," he said, "had been a little more empathetic, and less scared, then we probably wouldn't have a dead client, and we wouldn't be here talking to you like we are right now."

By the time the show was over, rioters had gathered in the parking lot of the Wendy's restaurant where Brooks had been shot. A white woman, who would later turn out to be Brooks' "girlfriend," set the building on fire, and the riots spread outward from there.

The next day, Atlanta police named the officers involved and released body camera footage of the incident. Thanks to that footage, we knew that the officers, Garrett Rolfe and Devin

Brosnan, had never been anything but respectful to Brooks. Based on the audio tape, we know that they had attempted to effectuate an arrest peacefully and without any sign of malice or intimidation. Then, Brooks attacked the officers. He'd grabbed Officer Brosnan's taser, run away, and pointed the taser at Officer Rolfe, leaving Rolfe no choice but to discharge his weapon.

This was a tragic event. Any needless death is tragic. But it was nothing like the death of George Floyd.

On June 17, Atlanta District Attorney Paul Howard ordered both officers who'd been involved arrested, and announced eleven charges against Officer Rolfe, one of which was felony murder. Apparently, in the DA's mind, a taser was not a "deadly weapon," and therefore Officer Rolfe was not justified in responding by firing his weapon when one was pointed and aimed at him. However, just ten days before Officer Rolfe's arrest, Paul Howard had announced that he had charged several police officers with excessive force because they used tasers. In the arrest reports for those officers, the taser is referred to as "a deadly weapon."

So, Mr. Howard, which is it? Tasers don't change based on who's holding them.

Police officers are trained that if a suspect is able to get an officer's taser and use that taser against that police officer and then incapacitate that officer, that officer is in a position to then respond with deadly physical force. New York City police officers are trained that way. Most officers in the country are trained exactly the same way.

The officer in the Rayshard Brooks case responded exactly as he was trained. A political District Attorney, under investigation himself, literally announcing what witnesses would turn evidence against the defendents, was far outside the realm of what he should and should not have been saying.

This was yet another shameless example of the Left reacting before it had all—or any—of the real facts about a case, shaping reality to fit their radical narratives and poisoning the public.

It would not be the last.

To add more lunacy to what was going on in Atlanta, Melissa Rolfe, the stepmother of Garett Rolfe, who was charged in the fatal shooting of Rayshard Brooks, lost her job as the human resources director at Equity Prime Mortgage in Atlanta. While the company has said this was due to her creating a hostile work environment, Melissa Rolfe maintains she was fired because of her relationship to her stepson. It was a political move, said Rolfe, who has firmly stood by her stepson and said the war on police must end. Melissa Rolfe has since hired famed defamation attorney Lin Wood. I suspect it will not end well for Equity Prime Mortgage in Atlanta.

A HISTORY OF VIOLENCE

The violent backlash we see today against police has played out before, with horrifying results.

On July 7, 2016, Micah Xavier Johnson drove from his hometown of Garland, Texas, to a Black Lives Matter protest in Dallas. He carried in his car a Russian-made semiautomatic rifle and a high-capacity handgun. Johnson had served in Afghanistan as an Army carpenter, but he knew how to handle the guns. In fact, according to reports, he was an excellent marksman. In his home, police would later find a stockpile of rifles and ammunition, a ballistic vest, and the ingredients to make a bomb. Johnson had planned the attack for some time. Neighbors saw him in his backyard practicing what looked like military-style maneuvers. There was also a personal journal detailing combat tactics.

Some eight hundred people had gathered for the peaceful protest, held just steps away from Dealey Plaza, where John Kennedy was assassinated in 1963. About one hundred cops guarded them. It was the cops who Johnson was interested in. His Facebook page had links to the New Black Panther Party, which the Southern Poverty Law Center describes as a "virulently racist and anti-Semitic organization" and the Black Riders Liberation Party, which, no doubt, takes its name from the Black Liberation Army. During the 1970s, the BLA killed thirteen cops, including four NYPD officers in 1971–1972.

Johnson killed three officers as soon as he arrived at the protest. He killed and injured others as they responded to the sounds of the gunshots. He shot and killed one cop point-blank in the back. In all, he murdered five police officers, and injured nine others. It was the single deadliest day for law enforcement since the 9/11 terrorist attack.

Police killed Johnson during a standoff that night. Before he died, he told cops that the reason he went on the murderous rampage was because "he was upset with white people."

When the shooting finally stopped in Dallas, anti-cop violence erupted across the country. In the days that followed, angry gunmen shot cops in Georgia, Tennessee, and Missouri.

Eleven days after Johnson murdered and maimed police, Gavin Long, a black separatist, tried his best to emulate him. On the morning of July 17, 2016, Long went hunting cops with a semiautomatic rifle. He killed three and injured three more. One of the cops was killed while he was trying to administer aid to his partner, whom Long had shot. Long finished the job on the injured police officer by standing over him and pumping bullets into his body.

East Baton Rouge Parish District Attorney Hillar Moore III later would say that Long killed because he "believes that protests are worthless."

The murderous anger toward cops continued in the aftermath of the Dallas massacre. Less than a year after the Dallas cop murders, a thirty-four-year-old ex-con named Alexander Bonds out on parole snuck up to the passenger-side window of a police van parked in the Bronx. Police officer Miosotis Familia sat inside the vehicle. Bonds had threatened to kill cops on Facebook; his girlfriend had called 911 that same day to warn police that he was acting in a manic way. The ex-con calmly pointed a silver pistol and shot the young mother of four in the head, killing her. Even the *New York Times* admitted Miosotis was "murdered for her uniform."

* * *

The truth is they've been defunding the police for years. Do you know what the starting salary for a New York City cop is today? Around $45,000. That works out to about $600 a week take-home pay. You want to try to start a family on six hundred a week in New York City? You can't afford to move out of your parents' basement with six hundred a week. And what do you get for that princely sum? You get to put on a blue uniform that might as well have a target sign painted on the back of it. According to the FBI, eighty-nine law enforcement officers were killed in line-of-duty incidents in 2019. Of those, forty-eight officers were murdered. These heroic cops came from Jersey City; Houston; Huntsville, Savannah; Detroit; Sacramento; and many more places. They were men and women, rookie cops and others near retirement. They were mothers, fathers, uncles, and aunts.

They were brown, black, and white, but the reason they were killed was simply because they were wearing blue.

ATTACKS

Now, here we are in 2020, and the blue bloodlust is happening all over again.

At this writing, as many as ten police officers have been killed as a result of the recent riots and protests, according to one law enforcement website.

During the protests in New York City, they tried to blow cops up. On the evening of May 30, 2020, a twenty-seven-year-old woman from upstate New York named Samantha Shader threw a Molotov cocktail at an NYPD van occupied by four cops. It was only by the grace of God that the bomb didn't go off. When Shader was taken into custody later, she bit the leg of one of the arresting officers. Around the same time, two Brooklyn lawyers, a man and woman in their early thirties, allegedly threw a Molotov cocktail at another cop car during the same protest.

What the newspapers call protestors are actually murderous lowlifes and losers. As I mentioned earlier, in St. Louis, looters shot and killed David Dorn, a black retired St. Louis police captain, as he helped guard his friend's store. As with George Floyd, Dorn's murder is captured on video, though only a tiny percentage of people have viewed it compared to the video of George Floyd.

The violent protests that have scorched our nation and the hateful rhetoric directed toward our police only mean more cops are going to be targeted.

Because of the timid reaction toward the protestors by Democrat leaders and the blatant support of these killers by the media, every time cops put on their uniform, they confront a fortified criminal element backed by a powerful, untruthful narrative that gives the bad guys not only the benefit of the doubt but, in far too many cases, a license to kill.

An overwhelming majority of police officers are good, hardworking men and women who became cops because they wanted to help people, not to harm them. Plenty are heroes. Did I come across racist ones? I sure did. When I was the Westchester County DA, I prosecuted an off-duty white cop who shot and killed a black man during an argument over a parking space. The cop went to jail for twenty years. There are bad people who wear badges, and they need to be weeded out. But what we don't need is to cripple or remove law enforcement protection. And we certainly don't want to send unarmed, unprepared people into violent or potentially violent situations.

Imagine you're a woman who's a victim of domestic violence. Your husband had already severely beaten you numerous times. He's threatened to shoot you, and you know he has a gun. Now, he's coming at you again, and you find the courage to call for help. But when help comes it's a social worker on your front doorstep. Is that going to make you feel safe? Maybe you can just make some tea and the three of you can sit around and just talk things through? You know what would happen if they sent some Ivy League–trained social worker instead of a cop into the type of domestic violence situation I prosecuted? You'd have two people dead on the floor, the wife and the social worker.

It's the police who stop drug dealers from selling to your children. It's the police who remove the child chained to a radiator in a basement. It's the police who find the knife used to stab a battered wife. It's the police you call when there's no one else to help you. If think we don't need police, the next time you hear someone breaking into your house, call a therapist and see what happens.

MEDIA MADNESS

Police officers are trained in de-escalation and non-violence. They learn that deadly force is an option that should be used only to protect innocent lives, including the lives of police officers. Defunding the police will mean less training, not more. It's the antithesis of a solution to the problems in policing today.

By the middle of last June, the pressure on the president to cave to the radical movement embraced by Democrats became so intense even the liberal press began to report that he would turn his back on cops. Right up to the time he stood in front of a microphone in the Rose Garden outside the West Wing, talking heads from the Left were predicting that Donald Trump would not stay true to the law-and-order stance he has held dear his entire life.

Fat chance.

What they got was the same Donald Trump who stood in front of millions of Americans at rallies across the country. The same Donald Trump who told them, face-to-face, that he would keep them safe, and promised that he would do all in his power to help cops fight crime. At a rally in Milwaukee in August 2016 after a cop shot and killed a black man, candidate Trump had this to say: "Those peddling the narrative of cops as a racist force in our society, a narrative supported with a nod by my opponent, shared directly in the responsibility for the unrest in

Milwaukee and many other places within our country." Though he was talking about Hillary Clinton then, he might as well have been talking about Joe Biden and the other Democrat leaders who care only about forwarding their own political agendas.

"Without cops, there's chaos," he said in the Rose Garden.

He reminded us that racist cops make up a tiny percentage of our police and that the overwhelming majority of cops do their jobs heroically with little thanks. He reminded us of the cops on 9/11 who ran into the World Trade Center while most people ran for their lives in the other direction. One of the cops was a sergeant in the elite Emergency Service Unit. John G. Coughlin was tough ex-Marine, a tender husband, and a father of three girls. The oldest was just sixteen then. He was a volunteer firefighter and donated his time to Toys for Tots and helping older veterans and members of the police service facing crisis situations in their personal lives. Sergeant Coughlin didn't give a damn if you were white or black. He certainly didn't care as he ran up the stairs of the South Tower that fateful day. He did what he joined the police department to do—help people.

Let's also remember police officer Steven McDonald, a cop who was shot and severely injured when he questioned some teens about a bicycle theft. The injuries from the bullets left Steven breathing through a ventilator for the rest of his shortened life. Yet, he would meet and forgive the young man who shot him.

There are no protests for cops like McDonald and Coughlin, only wives without husbands and children without fathers.

Those are the cops the president was talking about. Those and all the others are the ones he would never turn his back on.

The executive order he signed that day ensured that police departments across the country met the highest professional standards. It promised to speed up the research and development of less-lethal weapons. It allocated millions of dollars for the training of social workers to assist police in interactions with the homeless, mentally ill, and drug addicted. What the order didn't do was defund one cent from police departments. It didn't in any way inhibit cops from doing the job that has driven crime statistics to their lowest level since the 1970s.

TRUMP vs. BIDEN

While Donald Trump was standing up for police, hypocrite Joe Biden continued to deny the truth about himself. The paint wasn't dry on his parking spot outside the Senate Office Building in 1973 when he already had chummy relationships with powerful Democrat segregationists.

In fact, as recently as 2010, Biden has said that Robert Byrd, who once held the title of "Exalted Cyclops" in the Ku Klux Klan, was a "mentor," "a friend," and "a guide to him."

Apparently, young Biden picked up some of Senator Byrd's ideas.

In 1989, when President George H. W. Bush wanted to fight the illegal drug scourge in America by increasing the federal law enforcement budget by $1.5 billion, a huge investment at the time, Biden went on national TV and told America that Bush's expenditure against drugs didn't include "enough prison cells to put *them* away for a long time." If you're wondering who the "them" is, you're not paying attention.

Sleepy Joe would get his chance to do exactly what he'd said in that national address five years later. Though it was called "the Clinton crime bill," Biden was the main author of it, and he was happy to take all the credit for it. Remember what the

Biden crime bill did? Allow me to refresh your memory. For one, it incarcerated a generation of young black men and women. It added the death penalty to sixty new crimes, and it also added years to sentencing for others.

That's what Joe Biden did for black people in America.

So, what has President Trump done for African Americans?

Let me count the ways for you.

In December 2018, the president signed into law the First Step Act, a landmark criminal justice reform bill. Because of the president, thousands of people who were unfairly convicted of crimes have been released from prison. Thousands more have had unfair sentences reduced. Tanesha Bannister was one of the many who walked out of jail a free woman, thanks to President Trump. In 2004, Tanesha was sentenced to life in prison for selling crack cocaine. She was a single mother of two young children at the time. Today, she cares for elderly and disabled people. President Trump pardoned Alice Marie Johnson, who was sentenced to life without the possibility of parole for a nonviolent drug offense. The sixty-five-year-old grandmother is now a criminal justice reform advocate. The list goes on.

Before the coronavirus, the president built an economy that pushed black and other minority unemployment to the lowest levels ever. He embraced Senator Tim Scott's Opportunity Zones legislation which has created nine thousand opportunity zones in neglected neighborhoods around the country that are being developed and are funded by the private sector to the tune of seventy billion dollars.

And the list goes on.

While Joe Biden does his Crime Bill two-step, trying to explain why he called a whole generation of young blacks "predators," history tells us he has one hand on their backs, pushing them into a jail cell.

President Trump, on the other hand, is working to make black lives better. Maybe that's what the protestors should be writing on the streets.

As for those of you who want to dismantle or defund police departments, you need to remember that the vast majority of them put their lives on the line every day. It's worth saying again: It's the police officer you call when you are in trouble and dial 911. It's the police officer who makes the arrest and consoles the family when there's been a killing. It's the police officer who arrests and stops the drug dealer from selling to your kid, the police officer who removes the child who's tied to a radiator in the basement; who takes the rape victim to the emergency room; who finds the knife used to stab the battered woman; who finds the thief who stole your jewelry; who consoles the child who watched his father kill his mother while hiding his own tears; who searches for evidence in the cold case that went unsolved; who arrives on the scene when there is a fire, a vehicular accident, a bombing, and, yes, protests, looting, and arson. It is the police officer who never gives up keeping you safe.

Yet "woke America" now seeks to destroy, dismantle, and defund these police.

So, yes, zero tolerance for monsters like Chauvin, but don't destroy the thin blue line that protects us from chaos, lawlessness, and criminality.

I promise you: You won't like it.

HOW CORONAVIRUS MADE ANDREW CUOMO AMERICA'S GOVERNOR
—US News and World Report, March 23, 2020
LIE
Chris Cuomo says brother, NY Gov. Andrew Cuomo, is the 'best politician in the country
—USA Today, June 25, 2020
LIE
Two Coasts. One Virus. How New York Suffered Nearly 10 Times the Number of Deaths as California
—ProPublica, May 16, 2020
Cuomo says New York followed federal guidelines when sending coronavirus patients to nursing homes
—CNN, May 24, 2020
LIE

Chapter Eight

ESCAPE FROM NEW YORK

During the first days of quarantine, we all had our guilty pleasures, especially when it came to television. Some of us spent our days binge-watching every episode of *Tiger King*, an eight-part documentary about a man in Oklahoma who kept exotic animals chained up in his yard and hired a hit man to take out one of his rival animal keepers. Others preferred the comfort of reality television, watching the Kardashians or the Real Housewives get into tightly scripted scrapes with one another. Toward the end of spring, there was even a new show about an aging presidential candidate who sits in his basement trying to figure out how a webcam works. Sadly, that one has been renewed for a second season, and we'll be watching it all the way through to November.

For liberals, however, there was nothing better than sitting down in the late morning sunshine, frothy lattes and vegan protein shakes in hand, to watch Governor Andrew Cuomo of New York deliver his strange, rambling monologue of the day. Like a B-list soap opera actor who has long since passed his prime, Governor Cuomo was everywhere you looked during those first few months of the pandemic, always happy to launch into a dramatic, self-congratulatory speech. If you happened to be sheltering in place in New York or its surrounding areas during the pandemic, as I was for many months, Governor Cuomo was almost harder to avoid than the deadly coronavirus itself.

Was he really a great leader during that time? Not by a longshot. But he did get pretty good at playing one on television.

During a long-winded speech at the Javits Center on March 30, for instance, Cuomo launched into a long, well-rehearsed riff on a famous speech from William Shakespeare's *Henry V*, no doubt getting a few lonely liberal housewives all hot and bothered as they watched from home.

"This is a moment that is going to change this nation," he said, pausing for effect like he was expecting the dramatic music to begin at any second. "This is a moment that forges character, forges people, changes people, makes them stronger, makes them weaker . . . Ten years from now, you'll be talking about today to your children or your grandchildren, and you will shed a tear because you will remember the lives lost. You'll remember the faces, and you'll remember the names, and you'll remember how hard we worked and that we still lost loved ones."[1]

Did you hear the swelling music? Feel the tears beginning to roll down your cheeks?

Yeah, me neither.

Maybe it's because this speech, like so much of what Governor Cuomo has been doing since the day he gave his first briefing on the coronavirus—or, as the governor self-righteously insisted on calling it for a while, the "European virus"—was nothing more than a well-staged piece of political theater.[2] I wouldn't be surprised if Adam "lying sack of" Schiff, the failed screenwriter turned congressional witch hunter in chief, helped him workshop the script.

From the beginning, these briefings were all flash, style, and flourish, full of nothing but lies and fun set pieces.

If you don't believe me, consider the fact that almost none of the dire predictions that Governor Cuomo made during the pandemic actually came true. For instance, all those beds and medical curtains the governor was sitting in front of that morning—the ones he had begged President Trump to build, claiming that failing to do so would result in overflowing hospitals, hundreds of thousands of deaths, and bodies in the streets—ended up being nothing more than elaborate, expensive props.

Even on April 8, the day that hospitals in the state of New York got as close to "overwhelmed" as they ever would, the makeshift field hospital at the Javits Center hadn't ever been more than 10 percent full. In the end, only 225 of the 2,500 beds inside were ever used. At the beginning of April, doctors at major hospitals in New York told *Business Insider* that even if they had wanted to use the Javits Center getting patients transferred there was "close to impossible." The facility, according to their reports, didn't even have the equipment or ICU beds needed to handle coronavirus patients.[3] The same goes for the USNS *Comfort*, the hospital ship that Governor Cuomo had begged President Trump to send. By the time that ship sailed out of New York Harbor on April 30, it had treated only 179 patients for the coronavirus.[4] In the end, this ship did very little to help New Yorkers who were infected with coronavirus, but, much like the field hospital at the Javits Center, it did look *stunning* in the background of the governor's briefing.

On March 22, in another touching moment, Governor Cuomo announced the details of an executive order called New York State on PAUSE, which put strict limits on what New Yorkers were allowed to do during the pandemic. One piece of the order, named after the governor's mother, was a series of guidelines for protecting the elderly in New York. Keeping our senior citizens safe, according to Cuomo, would be our most important job moving forward.

"I call it Matilda's law," he said. "My mother's name is Matilda. Everybody's mother, father, sister, friend in a vulnerable population. This is about protecting them. What you do is highly—it highly affects their health and well-being . . . Be smart."[5]

And . . . scene!

It was a nice idea. But much like the Javits Center, the USNS *Comfort*, and the big stacks of ventilators that would end up getting shipped to New York State despite zero need for them, this bill was nothing more than a prop.

As always, the real story is what happened behind the scenes, while the cameras weren't rolling and the eyes of the nation were elsewhere.

That is when Governor Cuomo showed how much he really cares about the elderly.

"A FIRE THROUGH DRY GRASS"

On March 22, at the very moment that Governor Cuomo was announcing Matilda's Law, public health officials on the other end of the country were horrified. For weeks, they had been investigating a series of deaths that had occurred at the Life Care Center nursing home in Kirkland, Washington, which had become the site of the nation's first major outbreak of the Wuhan Coronavirus.

By the morning of Governor Cuomo's address, twenty-six people had died in that nursing home, thirteen of whom had tested positive for coronavirus. As far as medical investigators could tell, the outbreak had begun when someone who'd contracted the virus abroad came into the facility to visit an elderly relative. By the time anyone noticed that the infected resident was beginning to show symptoms, it was too late.

The virus had already spread.

In the days before the virus slipped through its doors, the Life Care Center was home to 120 people. By the beginning of March, there were only fifty. The rest had been transferred out to other facilities for fear that the virus would infect them, too.

For governors all over the country, what happened at the Life Care Center should have been a dire warning: protect nursing homes and the vulnerable populations inside, or suffer deadly consequences.

They all heard the warning, but only some chose to heed it.

Today, thanks to reporting by the nonprofit journalism outlet ProPublica, we know that Governor Cuomo and his public health commissioner Howard Zucker knew all about the deaths that had occurred at the Life Care Center. In fact, according to the report, they had gone over the data together several times in early March.[6] Governor Cuomo knew that once the virus infiltrated a nursing home, the result would be mass death. He knew, to use a direct quote from the governor, that the virus could spread through nursing homes like "a fire through dry grass."[7]

As the governor would put it in mid-April, "The only question is how many people will die."

He knew. He just didn't care.

On March 25, Governor Cuomo signed an executive order that required all nursing homes in New York State to accept patients who'd tested positive for the virus from local hospitals. At the time, the governor was still going along with the blatant lie that more than two million people in the United States were going to die from Covid. He had also just received a model from the University of Washington that predicted New York would run out of hospital space in about two weeks.[8] His solution—which was either stupid or evil, or both—was to take the sickest people from those hospitals and ship them to nursing homes. Bear in mind that he did this even when he knew that an enormous field hospital at the Javits Center was just five days away from being completed, and that the USNS *Comfort* was just a few days from New York Harbor.

But the governor couldn't wait.

The order stated: "No resident shall be denied readmission to the NH [nursing home] solely based on a confirmed or suspected diagnosis of coronavirus. NHs [Nursing homes] are prohibited from requiring a hospitalized resident who is determined medically stable to be tested for coronavirus prior to admission or readmission."[9]

So, not only were nursing homes forced to admit patients they knew were infected with coronavirus, but they were also prohibited from testing any incoming patients for the virus. This turned these facilities, many of which were accepting dozens of new patients a week, into death traps. The staffs at these facilities had no way of knowing which of the patients they were interacting with might be infected, and they were prohibited from testing them to find out. When he was asked in April whether the nursing homes were being given proper personal protective equipment, or PPE, Governor Cuomo said it was "not his job."[10]

Further down in the order, Governor Cuomo also prohibited the families of nursing home residents from visiting their elderly relatives, even if the person they wanted to visit was healthy and quarantined and took proper precautions. Thanks to this measure, anyone who caught the virus in a nursing home and died was forced to suffer alone, many dying without the comfort of their friends or family.

According to the state's official count, it's estimated that Governor Cuomo's order resulted in more than 6,400 deaths in nursing homes, a number that accounts for more than one-tenth of all reported deaths in similar facilities across the country.[11]

Of course, we know that number is a lie.

Between April 28 and May 3, according to a report by the Daily Caller News Foundation, the health department in New York State quietly changed the way it reported nursing home deaths, and they did it at the order of the governor.

"Until at least April 28," the report says, "the health department was disclosing coronavirus deaths of all nursing home and adult care facility residents, regardless of whether the patient died at their long-term care facility or at a hospital . . . The agency now only discloses coronavirus deaths of long-term care patients who died while physically present at their facility."[12]

So, if a nursing home resident catches coronavirus in a long-term care facility in New York, goes to the hospital, and then dies as soon as they get there, that death isn't counted toward the official tally of nursing home deaths in the state. According to the Daily Caller, New York is "the only state with a major outbreak in nursing homes to report those fatalities that way."[13]

Betsy McCaughey, a constitutional scholar and healthcare expert, estimates that the real number of people who've died in nursing homes is probably closer to ten or eleven thousand, nearly double the state's official numbers.[14]

"It's hard to know what's worse," she said, speaking about the state's decision to artificially lower the death count, "the dying or the lying."[15]

THE COVER-UP

Well, Betsy, I'd have to say it's a toss-up. Although, at least the dying seems to have stopped for now.

The lying, unfortunately, has not.

From the beginning, the governor and his handpicked team of experts lied to us about what they had done. The governor, who once said "blame me" if anything goes wrong, was quick to sidestep matters of his own culpability once there was a real accusation of wrongdoing.

On April 28, when he was asked about the nursing homes order during one of his press conferences, Governor Cuomo lied and said, "It's a good question. I don't know." During that same press conference, he blamed the global health organizations for getting it wrong, saying, "Governors don't do global pandemics."[16] In the weeks that followed, the Cuomo administration quietly amended the order on nursing homes, going so far as to remove the only existing digital copy from the internet. Today, if you go looking for it, you'll find a blank page and a note: *We're sorry,* it reads, *the page you're looking for is not found.*[17]

After a few weeks at the drawing board, the governor and his team finally figured out a way to pin the whole thing on President Trump—which, admittedly, is longer than I thought it would take. During a press conference on May 20, he said that his administration had only forced sick people into nursing homes because the federal government required it.

"I'm not going to go into politics back and forth," he said. "But anyone who wants to ask, 'Why did the state do that with Covid patients in nursing homes?' It's because the state followed the CDC's guidance of President Trump."

Lies.

First of all, the CDC's guidance did *not* require nursing homes to accept people who'd tested positive for coronavirus. Governor Cuomo's executive order did. The CDC's guidance also made sure to specify that patients should only be transferred if they were "medically ready for discharge to a long-term care facility" and the facility was "able to safely care for a patient recovering from the virus."[18] The governor's order did not. Even PolitiFact, an organization run by the left-leaning Poynter Institute, rated the governor's claim "mostly false."[19]

Did he accept blame for it? Of course not.

In fact, in the weeks that followed, there aren't many people in the world that the governor *didn't* blame. On June 23, he said that his order hadn't been a mistake, and then said it was the nursing home staff that was responsible because they weren't taking proper safety precautions. A few minutes later, he said that the deaths could also be blamed on "an air-conditioning repairman [or a] delivery person."[20]

He blamed everyone but the people responsible. In some cases, he *protected* those responsible. In his state budget, released in March, shortly after he signed the original order, the governor inserted an obscure passage that provided a liability shield for corporate officials who ran New York's hospitals, nursing homes, and other healthcare facilities. This meant that the families of the people who'd died needlessly as a result of the governor's directive would have no legal recourse. It shouldn't surprise you to learn that this provision was intensely advocated for by the Greater New York Hospital Association, a lobbying group with ties to the Cuomo administration. According to reporting in the *Guardian,* when Cuomo was running in New York's 2018 Democrat primary, this group poured more than $1 million into a Democrat committee backing his campaign.[21]

The idea that Andrew Cuomo was looking out for anyone other than himself during this pandemic was a lie.

Of course, the Left would never call him out on it.

During the early days of the pandemic, the radical Left was on the lookout for a hero, and "Bunker Boy" Joe Biden wasn't cutting it. So, they fixated on the first liberal they saw and then built him up. For months, as the death count in New York soared into the thousands, driven largely by preventable deaths in the state's nursing homes, so did the ratings for the *Andrew Cuomo Variety Hour,* a daily show that involved the governor's daughter, mother, brother, daughter's boyfriend, and a whole other zany cast of characters. During the final week of March, when the show premiered to rave reviews from the liberal media, nearly five million people were tuning in via their televisions, Facebook accounts, and Twitter feeds every day.[22]

THE BROTHERS CUOMO

Over the course of about six months, whenever Governor Cuomo got the itch to address the people of New York, and the nation, nearly every liberal news station in the country—from CNN and MSNBC to local affiliates in every time zone—would break into their normal programming and carry his press conferences live. Every day of the week, including Saturday, the heads of these networks would allow the governor to speak live for as long as he wanted, never breaking in for commentary or commercials, and when it was over, their anchors would offer nothing but effusive praise for his calm demeanor, sense of humor, and wonderful leadership skills.

Please.

If you ever needed proof that the mainstream media is blatantly, hopelessly, and shamelessly in the tank for the Democrats, there you have it. I don't think the liberal media's love for this man could have been any more obvious if they'd stood behind him with I ❤ ANDY T-shirts and giant foam fingers. No matter how many bad jokes, long stories, or boring PowerPoint slides the governor wanted to include in his press conferences, the networks were all happy to play along. When he went off on directionless tangents about his daughter, his mother, and his daughter's boyfriend, they kept their cameras fixated on him.

When he trotted out old quotes from the venerable statesman A. J. Parkinson II—a fictional character created by Governor Cuomo's father, former governor Mario Cuomo—they aired every last one without a single snarky note in the chyron.[23] Can you imagine President Trump, who is routinely "fact-checked" in real time by CNN and MSNBC, receiving similar treatment?

Of course not.

In fact, on April 13, as President Trump was right in the middle of responding to a reporter who'd accused him of "ignoring early warnings" about the coronavirus, CNN cut away from the president's daily briefing. In the minutes before the screen went blank, President Trump had been preparing to show a video that detailed every step he took to respond to the coronavirus pandemic. Apparently, CNN didn't think it was worthwhile for the American people to see. Instead, they cut back to the anchor desk, where John King was waiting.

"He has every right to defend himself," King said, speaking with a Cuomo-like flair for the dramatic as soon as the camera landed on him. "He has every right to challenge things that are factually not true. But that was just plain propaganda. And to play a propaganda video at taxpayer expense in the White House briefing room is a new—you can insert your favorite word here—in this administration."

Well, I don't know, John. It doesn't look to me like you gave President Trump a chance to defend himself against *anything,* let alone things that are "factually not true." You let one of your reporters level an accusation at him from the stands of the briefing room, and then you cut away before he had a chance to say anything in his own defense. Then, as you were ranting about him from your cozy studio in New York City, the chyron below your face had the headline ANGRY TRUMP TURNS BRIEFING INTO PROPAGANDA SESSION. Then, a few minutes later, as you were discussing the events of that day, the headline changed to TRUMP MELTS DOWN IN ANGRY RESPONSE TO REPORTS HE IGNORED VIRUS WARNINGS. Was it really important that you cut away from the President of the United States so you could bash him on live television—*again*? Couldn't you have done that in the *other* twenty-three hours your network is on the air?

Call me old-fashioned, but I believe that if you're a news network—meaning CNN, MSNBC, Fox News, and the rest—you have an obligation to keep the American people informed. Obviously, your points of view can differ, and you can broadcast as much opinion content as you want. But when the President of the United States gets up on the stage of the White House briefing room to speak, those networks had better carry it live, in full, and without any interruptions. I don't care if he wants to fire up the monitors in the briefing room and show reruns of *Little House on the Prairie* for two hours. He is the President of the United States, and the American people are entitled to hear what he has to say, especially at a time when people were petrified, unemployed, sheltered in place, and not sure what tomorrow would bring.

Now, you might be wondering whether what the president had to say that day really *did* qualify as a waste of time. Maybe you think CNN was right. Maybe they really *were* adhering to their own rigid standards, which state that silly nonsense and so-called propaganda have no place on their stations.

Well, consider this: Just a few days after CNN cut away from President Trump's daily briefing for the first time—which happened on March 18, as the president was addressing the nation from the Rose Garden—they aired yet another press conference from Andrew Cuomo.

Only this time, the show included a special guest: his brother, CNN anchor Chris Cuomo. Late in March, the younger Cuomo brother had been infected with the coronavirus, and he'd been "self-quarantining" in his basement ever since. He had been working as an anchor at CNN for seven years, and during that whole time, the network's standards and practices department had forbidden him from interviewing his brother on the air. (Yes, there really *is* a standards and practices department at CNN; I'm as surprised as you are.)

But during the first days of the coronavirus pandemic, with one brother running a vaudeville act for the country every day and the other one sick with the virus, the network changed its tune. After noticing that Andrew Cuomo had become, in the words of a CNN article from May 1, "the single most popular politician in America right now," the top brass at the network decided to allow the Brothers Cuomo to do a New York two-step, a pandemic tango, if you will, together on air. The result was the best TV crossover event since Mork and Mindy met the Fonz on *Happy Days.*

On March 18, these two had a cute little argument about which one was their mother's favorite.[24] At the time, sixteen people had died from coronavirus in New York.

About two weeks after that, they argued back and forth about which one makes their mother's spaghetti sauce better, calling each other "meatballs" and laughing like idiots through the whole interview.[25]

On that day, 1,150 people had died.[26]

On Easter Sunday, still during the period he was supposed to be quarantined in the basement, Chris Cuomo decided to take a walk through his neighborhood in the Hamptons. Along the way, he was recognized by a man on a bicycle who pointed out that he wasn't wearing a mask. Rather than moving on and wishing this man—who hadn't broken any laws or, according to his account of the matter, come within ten feet of Cuomo—a happy Easter, Cuomo screamed, "Who the hell are you?! I can do what I want! I'll find out who you are. This is not the end of this. You'll deal with this later. We will meet again!"[27] According to an interview with the man, the argument almost got physical.

How nice.

That story, as you probably could have guessed, did *not* air on CNN. Neither did Chris Cuomo's tirade.

Here is something that did, though: On April 2, during an episode of the *Andrew Cuomo Variety Hour*, things between the brothers got a little strange. Speaking from his basement in the Hamptons, where he had supposedly been locked for weeks, the younger Cuomo started going off on a tangent about . . . well, *this*: "You came to me in a dream," said Chris Cuomo to his brother. "You had on a very interesting ballet outfit, and you were dancing in the dream, and you were waving a wand and saying, 'I wish I could wave my wand and make this go away.'"

Now, here's a question. Do you think there was any discussion in the CNN control room about cutting away from whatever the hell *that* was? Do you think anyone had any reservations about airing one hour straight of these two bozos joking back and forth at each other while the city burned around them?

Of course not.

Even though that entire press conference—and every episode of Andrew Cuomo's television show—amounted to little more than an ad for what is sure to be a *very* interesting Cuomo/Ocasio-Cortez 2024 presidential campaign, the liberal media was fine with carrying the whole thing in full. When it comes to Democrats, there is no such thing as bias. The media allows them to act with impunity, carrying water for them no matter how corrupt, backward, or radical they become.

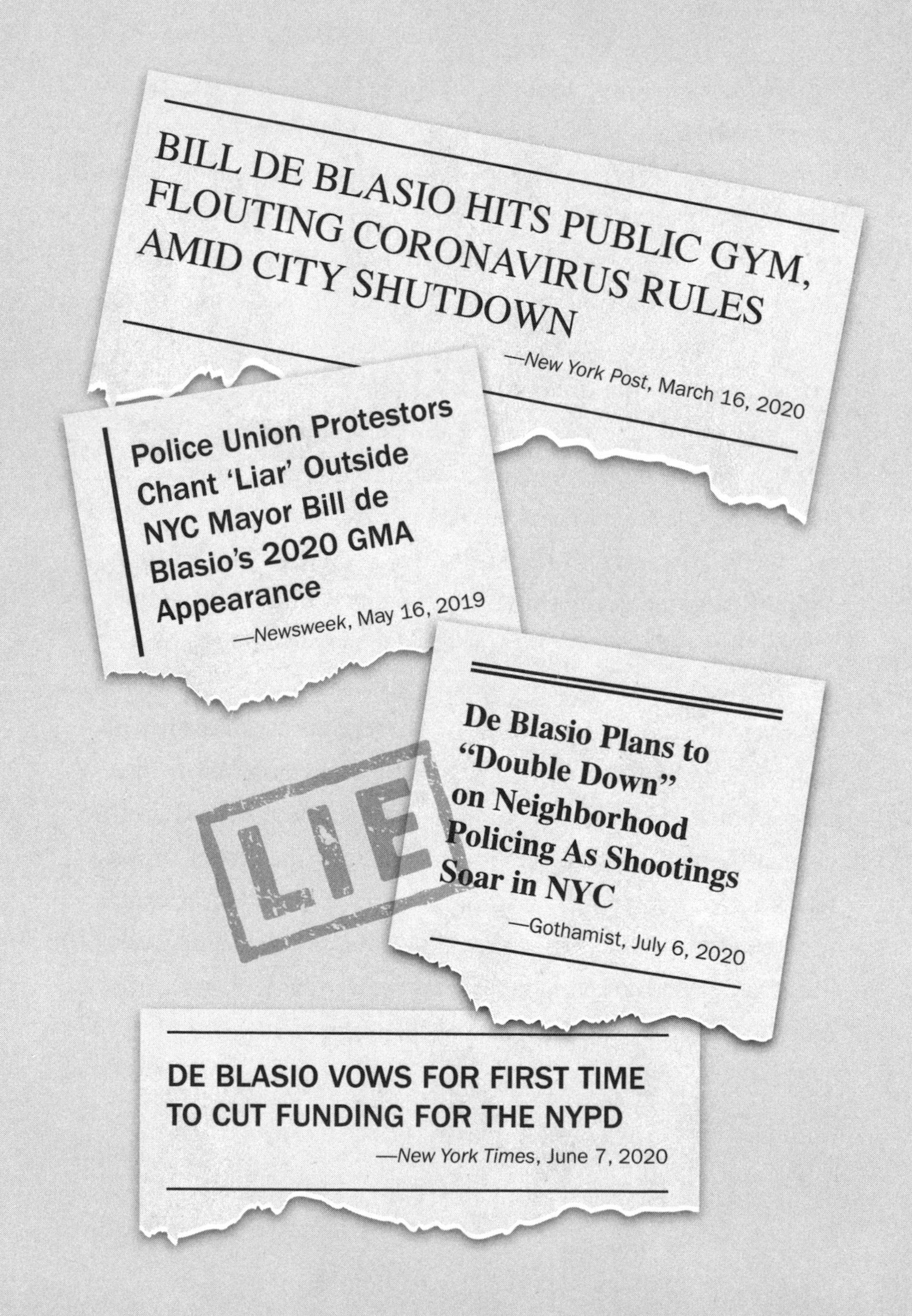
BILL DE BLASIO HITS PUBLIC GYM, FLOUTING CORONAVIRUS RULES AMID CITY SHUTDOWN

—*New York Post*, March 16, 2020

Police Union Protestors Chant 'Liar' Outside NYC Mayor Bill de Blasio's 2020 GMA Appearance

—Newsweek, May 16, 2019

De Blasio Plans to "Double Down" on Neighborhood Policing As Shootings Soar in NYC

—Gothamist, July 6, 2020

DE BLASIO VOWS FOR FIRST TIME TO CUT FUNDING FOR THE NYPD

—*New York Times*, June 7, 2020

Chapter Nine

BOZO DE BLASIO

Everyone knows that a television program is nothing without a compelling villain. In the animated series *The Simpsons*, it was Mr. Burns; in the loveable *101 Dalmations*, it was Cruella De Vil. During the pandemic, though, the *Andrew Cuomo Variety Hour* had them all beat.

On that show, we encountered one of the great villains of all time: Warren Wilhelm Jr., the sad, embattled mayor of New York City.

Of course, you probably know him by a different name. Back in 1983, when he was a young man studying Karl Marx and Spanish poetry, he changed his name to Warren de Blasio-Wilhelm to honor his mother, he says, whose maiden name was de Blasio.[1] Then, years later, in 2002, probably wanting to sound a little more Italian for a New York audience, he changed it again, choosing the one that strikes terror into all our hearts today: Bill de Blasio.

When the pandemic hit, the mayor had just finished his stint as the least impressive and strangest clown in the whole

Democrat Clown Car. During his brief run for the White House, he had managed to engender hate from all areas of the political spectrum. The Left hated him. The Right hated him. Everyone in between hated him, too. They hated him so much, in fact, that when he failed to qualify for the third clown show of the Democrat primary, he had nothing left to do but pack his bags, head out to the middle of the Nevada desert, and take long hikes through the sand for days. In the videos he posted to social media, you can see that only three or four unfortunate souls had to go on these hikes with him, which is about three or four more people than would have voted for him if he'd decided to keep up the presidential run.

After the hikes, sadly, he came back to New York.

During the coronavirus pandemic, while Governor Cuomo was gracing the screens of just about every television in the country, Mayor Wilhelm—who, in the late 1990s, had worked directly under the governor when they both served in Bill Clinton's Department of Housing and Urban Development—could always be counted on to make a little trouble offscreen. Like Wile E. Coyote to the governor's Roadrunner, Bozo de Blasio was constantly scheming in the wings. He set traps, he dropped anvils, and he blew himself up with his own Acme rockets. It seemed that every time he tried to take action, the governor would smack him around.

For a while, he was the bad guy we all loved to hate.

On the morning after he announced a complete and total shutdown of the city, for instance, de Blasio dragged his whole staff all the way from Gracie Mansion, where he lives, to the Prospect Park YMCA in Brooklyn. Despite having told us the night before that we had to adopt "a wartime posture" in response to the coronavirus, the mayor spent the morning strolling around, doing a two-hour workout, and then driving all the way back to the office, where he arrived a little after ten o'clock in the morning. Now, I'm all for staying in shape, but *two hours*? With his staff? What the hell is he doing in there? Training for the Asshole Olympics?

As anyone who lives in New York City knows, this is the same daily ritual that the mayor has maintained since he first took office in 2014. There's a thirty-minute drive to the gym, two hours at the gym, then a break for coffee, then a thirty-minute ride back, all in a big, black, gas-guzzling SUV. (Please remember this the next time he gets on his high horse about how we have to impose "strict standards in New York City" to stop global warming.) Between the gym visits and his reported penchant for long middle-of-the-day naps—usually taken, according to people who've worked for him, right after the morning workout with that day's newspaper spread over his face—you can almost understand how he's gotten so little done during his time in office.[2]

Anyone who thought he might take the pandemic as an opportunity to shape up was sorely disappointed. During the crisis, no longer able to hit the gym every morning, the mayor would still take long drives from his home to Prospect Park in Brooklyn, then walk around for an hour or two among the trees. No surprise there. I'm sure if the airports had been running, he would have flown his whole staff back out to the deserts of Arizona every day and taken his daily walks there.

With him, as always, was his wife, Chirlane McCray, the woman he placed in charge of the city's "coronavirus racial inequality task force." You might remember Chirlane because the *last* time she was placed in a position of government power—the city's ThriveNYC program, which was supposed to fix mental health issues in the city (or whatever)—she blew $1.8 billion in taxpayer money on . . . well, no one's really sure *what* she spent it on. As of this writing, she hasn't told us. Since the beginning of the crisis, she and the mayor have been more focused on imagining a New York City without police—a fantasy Chirlane described as "nirvana."

On April 26, as the First Couple of New York were strolling along in the park, one of de Blasio's critics from the far Left followed him for a few miles, saying, "This is selfish behavior . . . You call yourself a progressive, but you chauffer yourself to Brooklyn. You force people to drive you."[3] Then he posted the video on Twitter, ending the mayor's walks in the park for good. Then, without the walks, he got cranky—especially when it came to a certain group of people.

On April 28, de Blasio learned that a group of Orthodox Jews was holding a funeral in the streets of Williamsburg, Brooklyn. The funeral was for Rabbi Chaim Mertz, a prominent figure in the Jewish community who'd died of coronavirus a few days earlier. For the first time in weeks, de Blasio decided to take action and break up the funeral. Today, you can see video of police descending on the mourners, all of whom were quiet and peaceful, and dispersing the crowd in a matter of minutes.

A few hours later, the mayor posted this tweet:

> @NYCMayor: Something absolutely unacceptable happened in Williamsburg tonite: a large funeral gathering in the middle of a pandemic. When I heard, I went there myself to ensure the crowd was dispersed. And what I

> saw WILL NOT be tolerated so long as we are fighting the Coronavirus.

Huh.

You know, when he describes that "large gathering in the middle of a pandemic," I'm almost reminded of something; I just can't put my finger on what. Maybe it's some other event that's occurred recently? One where people came together for a common purpose in defiance of the state, marched together, and stood very close together in crowds? One that the mayor also attended personally?

Oh well, I'm sure it'll come to me.

The morning after he broke up the funeral, Bozo de Blasio followed his initial tweet up with this one, apparently noticing that he'd forgotten to single out the Jewish community by name.

> @NYCMayor: My message to the Jewish community, and all communities, is this simple: the time for warnings has passed. I have instructed the NYPD to proceed immediately to summons or even arrest those who gather in large groups. This is about stopping the disease and saving lives. Period.[4]

You know, I may be overreacting here. After all, if you've studied history, you'll know that this kind of thing happens all the time. We all know that once people in power start making explicit threats to the Jewish people, saying they're going to arrest large groups of them for the crime of being outside, things usually turn out just fine.

Right?

In response, several prominent Jewish activists were outraged—and rightly so. In the past year, anti-Semitic hate crimes in New York City had risen a startling 83 percent, particularly in the Orthodox community. Jews had been beaten in the streets, shot in their places of worship, and heckled for the crime of wearing the garments of their religion. As the founder of a hate crimes unit, I know that this is something that shouldn't be tolderated. I remember as DA, when Jews were targeted in Westchester County, I had to take a strong stance. The appearance of swastikas and anti-Semitic behavior throughout the county was something that was beginning to rise. I made the decision to prosecute to the full extent of the law, because hate is hate, hate leads to violence, violence leads to retaliation, and, ultimately, leads to community unrest.

A few minutes after the mayor's tweet, a Jewish writer named Seth Mandel tweeted, "You lowlife cretinous bobblehead. There's only one community you would address this way. And it's the one that just went through a pogrom on your watch, as you let it happen."[5]

I couldn't have said it better myself.

But it wasn't just the Jews who felt the wrath of de Blasio. It was all of us. As the pandemic wore on, he started lashing out at business owners, children, and . . . well, really anyone who tried to have any fun at all. A few days before Memorial Day weekend in May, for instance, he said that anyone who tried to go to the beach and swim would be "pulled right out of the water." At the end of March, he ordered city workers to take down all the basketball hoops in the city so kids wouldn't be tempted to play. He also warned that if Christian churches and Jewish synagogues didn't heed his warnings about social distancing, he would "take additional action up to the point of fines and potentially closing the building permanently."[6]

That's right, folks, move along, nothing to see here—just an angry, Marxist mayor threatening to board up churches forever if people go inside.

Everything is fine!

The crowning achievement, however, came on April 18, when Comrade de Blasio set up his now infamous "social distancing tip line." Using this phone number, New Yorkers could report people and businesses who failed to follow the city's strict social distancing guidelines. If, during the early days of the pandemic, they caught a barber trying to cut hair, a group of friends standing too close together, or—the horror!—children *playing basketball*, all they had to do was call the number, rat them out, and the "authorities" would be there in a jiffy.

Here's the mayor describing the whole thing:

> We understand there are still some people who need to get the message. And that means sometimes making sure the enforcement is there to educate people and make clear we've got to have social distancing. So, now it is easier than ever. When you see a crowd, when you see a line that is not distanced, when you see a store that is not distanced . . . now, it's as simple as taking a photo. All you've gotta do is take the photo and put the location with it and *bang*. We will make sure that enforcement comes right away.[7]

Fortunately, some of my fellow New Yorkers were happy to take the mayor up on his request. Within hours of the number going live, de Blasio's snitch line was flooded with thousands of messages—though they probably weren't the kind he was hoping for. These "tips," obtained by the *New York Post*, included, in no particular order, an image of de Blasio with a Hitler moustache, smartphone photographs of male genitalia, and messages about "snitches."[8] There were also photographs of extended middle fingers, the mayor at the gym, the mayor walking in Prospect Park, the mayor dropping a groundhog (who later died) during a ceremony in 2014, and a bowl of gummy candies in the shape of male genitalia with the message "eat a bag of dicks."[9]

From there, if you can believe it, things only get more obscene.

Throughout the pandemic, it seemed that poor old Wilhelm couldn't get anything right. First, he told us not to worry about the virus, even encouraging some New Yorkers to go out and see a movie at Lincoln Center. Then, he tried to crack down *way* too hard, channeling his inner Nicaraguan dictator to surveil us, control us, and, ultimately, drive us all absolutely insane.

There was no one, however, who hated de Blasio more than his old buddy Andrew Cuomo.

TURNSTILE JUSTICE

Now, if you've lived in New York for any length of time, you probably know that Cuomo and de Blasio have always hated each other—and I think I speak for most sane New Yorkers when I say *we get it*. These are two of the nuttiest people ever to hold public office, and, as a New Yorker myself, I can only imagine what kind of ancient curse on this land gave us both at the same time.

For years, these two have chased each other around the state like a cartoon cat and mouse, taking swipes at one another in the press, getting into silly arguments in public, and engaging in pissing contests for all the world to see. All we want is safety, security, and civil tranquility; what we get is two (allegedly) Italian men fighting over who has the bigger . . . well, let's say nose.

In 2017, Governor Cuomo told the press that unlike the mayor, he has never been a napper. In 2015, he shut down the New York City subway during a snowstorm without telling de Blasio's office. That summer, in a grim foreshadowing of what would happen during the coronavirus pandemic, these two bozos fought like hell over what to do about an outbreak of Legionnaire's disease in the South Bronx. After de Blasio failed to act, Governor Cuomo declared that his office was "taking matters into [their] own hands."[10] In the end, after a lack of coordination on testing, ten people died and just over one hundred were infected.[11]

In December 2016, they had what might be their most infamous feud, this one over a wayward deer that had appeared in Jackie Robinson Park in Harlem, drawing crowds from all over the state. Mayor de Blasio, citing a "threat to public safety," wanted to have it euthanized immediately (which, even for everyone's favorite villain, is a little over the top, don't you think?). A few days later, seeing an opportunity to smack the mayor around in public, Governor Cuomo said his office was working to find a new home for the poor little guy. This went back and forth for weeks, with the two clowns fighting it out in the press, talking through spokespeople, and finally deciding to take the deer to a new home where it could live happily away from humans.

In the end, the deer died "of stress."

With those two deciding his fate, I can believe it.

As bad as the governor and the mayor have been when they were feuding, they've been even worse on the rare occasions that they've come together to try to get things done.

Take criminal justice as an example.

Toward the end of 2019, they both supported a policy known as "bail reform," an obvious attempt by the governor to appease the most radical, de Blasio–loving wing of his party. For months, those on the radical Left had been yelling about how the imposition of bail was "unconstitutional," "unfair," and—surprise, surprise—racist.

These were all lies.

Nowhere in the Constitution does it say that the imposition of bail is unconstitutional. What it says, right there in the Eighth Amendment, is this:

> Excessive bail shall not be required, nor excessive fines imposed, nor cruel and unusual punishments inflicted.

Obviously, though, neither of these idiots had paid much attention to the Constitution in school, so they managed to pass bail reform easily. At first, this might sound great. In reality, it's the cruelest and most unusual policy around. In effect, bail reform makes certain crimes perfectly legal. As soon as it became law, word went out to criminals on the street that if you committed robbery, assault, or drug dealing, all you had to do was spend a few hours in a police station and then you'd be able to walk free.

Call it turnstile justice.

In the months that followed, crime in New York City began an upward trajectory that would continue for months, through the pandemic, riots, and beyond. Criminals who'd committed robberies, assaults, and hate crimes were allowed to walk free as soon as the police finished the paperwork, saved by the radical wing of the Democrat Party. A bank robber in Manhattan who'd been accused of robbing a bank was allowed to stroll right out of a police precinct after his arrest. Almost immediately, he robbed two more banks.[12] A career criminal with 138 arrests, many of which were for robbing people on subway platforms, was allowed to go free and rob many more people.[13] In a video taken by reporters, he screamed, "It's the Democrats! The Democrats know me, and the Republicans fear me. You can't touch me! I can't be stopped!"[14]

Sadly, he was correct.

Both of these people should have been in jail pending trial. These were public safety emergencies. The purpose of bail is to ensure that defendants return to court. No bail when someone is a serial offender and a danger to the community sends a message: *Go for it! You are free to go out and reoffend!* Should serial pedophiles who prefer to have sex with children be let out on bail to reoffend?

I think not.

Criminal justice issues like bail reform highlight the radical difference between the Right and the Left and how they view your safety. The Left have a history of allowing crime to run rampant. Just look at these ten cities with the highest violent crime rates, on average, per 100,000 people per year in the country.

1. Detroit, Michigan (1,988.63)
2. Memphis, Tennessee (1,740.51)
3. Oakland, California (1,685.39)
4. St. Louis, Missouri (1,678.73)
5. Milwaukee, Wisconsin (1,476.41)
6. Baltimore, Maryland (1,338.54)
7. Cleveland, Ohio (1,334.35)
8. Stockton, California (1,331.47)
9. Indianapolis, Indiana (1,254.66)
10. Kansas City, Missouri (1,251.45)

They are all run by Democrat mayors. Coincidence? I think not.

Now take a look at this chart with the ten cities with the highest number of homicides (per 100,000 people per year) in the country. Every one of them, too, has a Democrat as a mayor.

1. St. Louis, Missouri (49.91)
2. Detroit, Michigan (43.52)
3. New Orleans, Louisiana (38.75)
4. Baltimore, Maryland (33.84)
5. Newark, New Jersey (33.32)
6. Buffalo, New York (23.22)
7. Pittsburgh, Pennsylvania (22.43)
8. Memphis, Tennessee (21.38)
9. Atlanta, Georgia (20.47)
10. Cincinnati, Ohio (20.16)

In many cases, the pandemic has only made things worse. In Chicago during the Fourth of July weekend in 2020, there were eighty-four shootings and seventeen deaths from gun violence.[15] During one of these incidents, a stray bullet went straight through the window of a house, striking and killing a ten-year-old girl in her living room.[16] She died three days later. In Philadelphia during the same weekend, seven people were shot in a span of three hours.[17] In Milwaukee, the homicide rate jumped 95 percent.[18]

Sadly, that is only the very beginning.

Make no mistake: New York City does not appear on any lists of the most deadly cities today—thanks largely to about two decades of solid Republican leadership—but if we keep the same radical liberals at the helm of this city, it will be number one soon enough. Mayor Rudy Giuliani cleaned up the city, Mayor Mike Bloomberg managed not to screw it up, and then Bozo de Blasio destroyed it. And if you think that these radicals will be swayed by the evidence—if you think *for a second* that images of dead children or bodies in the streets will have any effect on their agenda—think again.

In February, when the crime rates were beginning to soar, Alexandria Ocasio-Cortez, one of Joe Biden's newest advisors, said we should "slow down" on talking about rolling back bail reform.

"What I would say is that we should just give this time," she said. "It's been five minutes."[19]

This is the same woman who says that when we say defund the police, we *really mean* defund the police—the same woman who, shortly before the shooting of a one-year-old in a park in Brooklyn, said that the pandemic was to blame for the spike in violence in New York City.

Has it been long enough for you now, Ms. Cortez? How many people need to die before you actually step up and do something?

She wasn't alone.

Radical liberal Cyrus Vance Jr., the district attorney of Manhattan who had been seeking access to President Trump's tax returns like a dog after a bone for years, also thinks bail reform is a great idea. He's said so himself. While the unrest was beginning and criminals were beginning to fill up the streets of New York City again, Vance wrote an op-ed in the *New York Times* with a few other DAs, which said not only that bail reform was a good idea, but that it hadn't gone far enough.

"We believe bail reform was necessary," they wrote. "No one should be held in custody awaiting trial simply because of an inability to pay bail when others accused of the same crime and with similar histories are freed . . . But we don't think the current bail reforms went far enough. Cash bail should be eliminated for all offenses, with judges given the discretion to detain the small number of individuals whose behavior poses a threat to public safety or who have demonstrated that they are unwilling to show up in court in serious cases."[20]

So, if these radical liberal DAs get their way, *all* offenses—including some of the most heinous crimes—will be outside the consideration of cash bail. Of course, before that debate could continue, the Wuhan Coronavirus arrived and shocked the city.

In response, the mayor and the governor continued their dithering and bickering. When Mayor de Blasio brought a plan to deal with the virus to the governor in early March, according to ProPublica, Cuomo reacted "with derision," pointing out that "he alone had the power to order such a measure."[21] From the beginning, Governor Cuomo sought to make himself the face of the state's response. He wasn't content to sit back while the New York City Department of Health—one of the most revered public health departments not only in the country but in the world—talked to the citizens of his state. Instead, he held press conferences every day, pontificating at length about the state's response. When Mayor de Blasio ordered a citywide shutdown on March 17, Governor Cuomo overruled it with his own shelter-in-place measure the next day. When de Blasio announced that schools would remain closed for the entire academic year, Cuomo said only he had the authority to make that decision, and said the schools could either open or close depending on what he thought was best.

For months, they went back and forth, arguing like children while their city burned.

NEW YORK CITY BURNING

But it all came to a head on June 1, when the protests that had been raging all over the country finally came to lower Manhattan. This had been happening for days, growing in intensity since May 25, the day George Floyd was killed in Minneapolis. The protests, which had begun peacefully enough, were clearly becoming riots. With each passing evening, it seemed that a new city fell to the mob.

After Minneapolis, on May 27, Los Angeles and Memphis were both engulfed in violent protests, some of which became riots.[22] The next day, the National Guard was mobilized in Minnesota.[23] Anyone could have seen that New York City was a powder keg about to explode.

But nobody cared.

Early in the evening on June 1, protestors gathered in lower Manhattan. It had been three days since the first round of protests in Brooklyn and parts of Manhattan, which left several protestors and officers injured. Compared to what was coming, though, those were nothing. Within a few hours on June 1, the gathering became a riot. The curfew that Mayor Bill de Blasio had ordered for 11 p.m., well after the sun would go down, was effectively useless. As any law enforcement officer knows, the only way to stop a violent protest like this is to order a curfew at sundown, then make sure it is enforced with zero tolerance. That night, however, the protestors knew that no police were coming. They knew that they could get away with what they were about to do, so they were emboldened.

That night, Macy's flagship store in Herald Square was looted by criminals—not protestors, but criminals—breaking in with hammers and coming out with stolen goods. Arsonists and looters on Fifth Avenue hit and emptied Chanel, Gucci, and Balmain.

Dozens of other stores were looted and destroyed.

The next day, we were all asking the universal question: Where were the police? Where are the arrests? Where are the perp walks?

I'll tell you.

The police were given a stand-down order and told not to engage, and a minimal number of cops were even deployed. The upshot? As cops stand down, criminals become emboldened. And as for you, taxes will clearly go up not just for the cleanup but because businesses can no longer afford—nor would they necessarily want—to be in a city where they are not protected from crime. In fact, one high-end New York City store is suing for failure to stop the looting. The owner of that store says that after paying taxes, the city owed a duty to the store to protect it. He says that the city had intelligence and did nothing about it.

He, like many New Yorkers, believes his taxes go to the NYPD and that the police were told to stand down. But the big stores were not the only stores. Looters stormed small businesses, many minority-owned, many shuttered now for good because of the protestors.

The next day, Governor Cuomo sat down at the briefing table for another episode of his famous program, and the rivalry between him and Bozo de Blasio came to a head. This time, there were no fancy set pieces or photographs of the governor's family. This time, he was mad. Looking straight into the camera, the governor called what happened in New York City the night before—what he and the mayor had allowed to happen—"a disgrace."

Once again, of course, he tried to deflect blame from himself.

"Look at the videos," he said. "It was a disgrace. I believe that. I believe the mayor underestimates the scope of the problem. I think he underestimates the duration of the problem, and I don't think they've used enough police to address the situation, because it's inarguable that it was not addressed last night. What happened in NYC was inexcusable . . . My option is to displace the mayor of NYC and bring in the National Guard as the governor in a state of emergency and basically take over. You would have to take over the mayor's job. You would have to displace the mayor."

THE END OF NEW YORK CITY

Do *you* feel safe? I live in New York, and something has happened that is as predictable as the sun rising tomorrow morning. New York City, once the safest big city in America, one of the world's major commercial, financial, and cultural centers, will revert to the crime-ridden days of the 1980s. Not just New York, either—soon, major cities near you will return to their troubled days of lawlessness.

It will happen whether you are on the Right or the Left. Believe me.

Understand this: Lawlessness without police equals crime and murder. The safest big city is now regressing to the bygone days of graffiti, drugs, gangs, guns, murder, and mayhem. You can thank one man: Bill de Blasio. His is the face of the return of crime. This is the face of the man who, without a doubt, is the most incompetent, inefficient, and inept mayor to darken the halls of Gracie Mansion. His response to the May 25 murder of George Floyd, like everyone else's, was outrage.

But his answer to the George Floyd murder was to let New York City burn. He cut the NYPD's budget by $1 billion. He supported a so-called police reform bill that tied the hands of police with no training under these new restrictions, and he ordered stand-downs while crimes occurred across the city.

But then again, he's always had a problem with police. I said it three years ago.

Now, as New York City devolves into chaos, Mayor de Blasio turns a blind eye.

Of course, maybe he's too busy doing arts and crafts projects on the streets of New York City. In early July, he helped Black Lives Matter paint a big mural on Fifth Avenue, right in front of Trump Tower. On July 14, someone dumped a bucket of black paint on it, and de Blasio announced a full investigation to find and prosecute the people responsible. On July 18, the same thing happened, and de Blasio called for a full investigation again. Who did he ask to carry out these investigations, you ask?

That would be the New York Police Department.

They'd better get to work while there still *are* police officers in the NYPD. Since George Floyd's death, more than eight hundred police officers have retired from the NYPD, and the department is now limiting the number of how many can retire each week. Why? The police have targets on their backs, and they know it. They are being told to stand down. They are not being given any guidance on the new law passed by the city council.

A deputy inspector and precinct commander—ironically from the Forty-Sixth Precinct, known as "the Alamo"—retired because he was not given any guidance as to how his officers should respond in light of the new limitations on their ability to arrest. The irony is that the Forty-Sixth Precinct was dubbed in the 1980s as the most dangerous square mile in America.

And the new rules restrict police actions regarding arrests and what part of a defendant's body they're allowed to touch. Picture this: Thirty-five thousand police officers, each with a gun, and not one has been trained on how to effectuate an arrest under the new guidelines where you effectively cannot touch a perp. Police will face certain prosecution if they touch the perp in the wrong way. Then, the arrest is not considered to have been made properly.

Mayor de Blasio also disbanded the anti-crime undercover unit, formerly known as the street crime unit, which directs undercover officers to areas where crime occurs according to CompStat, a colorblind pinpoint screen that identifies crime concentration. CompStat helped drive down the city's crime rate and literally revolutionized policing around the world.

Now, there is no more stop, question, and frisk; no more police concentration in those crime-ridden areas. The ones most afraid are the minority communities in the inner cities who live with crime day and night. Ask the black and Hispanic clergy. They are terrified of what is to come. The cops protecting them are gone. They've been told to stand down. They can't engage. They can't touch suspects. I've been told that if a suspect resists arrest, the cops would mosly likely let them go because they haven't been trained what to do in that circumstance. The rookie school has been canceled, morale is down, and for many, the exit from the police department can't come soon enough.

But it gets worse. Democrat de Blasio and his ilk are now working together to defeat law enforcement. Governor Andrew Cuomo, who forced nursing homes to take coronavirus-infected patients, thus leading to the deaths of the highest number of seniors in this country and then signing a bill giving everyone involved immunity, both civil and criminal, pushed for so-called bail reform, as a result of which most defendants are released as soon as the paperwork is done.

In July, just weeks after the protests that shook New York City to its core, DA Cyrus Vance Jr. sent an internal memo to his office called "Police Misconduct and Protest Related Cases," which outlined several proactive steps that he was taking to "report incidents of police misconduct and excessive force." Rather than focusing on the looters and rioters, Vance decided to make sure his office had "issued social media posts across Twitter, Facebook, and Instagram notifying the public that they may use our website to report any incidents of [police misconduct]."[24]

He also said his office was "declining to prosecute Unlawful Assembly and Disorderly Conduct protests arrests in the interests of justice."

So, as New York City burned, a sitting district attorney—in spite of the fact that businesses have been looted, many of them minority owned, many of them closed forever because of the pandemic—sent a memo out to his staff saying, as it relates to the protestors, *Go easy; dismiss them; we're not worried about that*. But we *do* want proactive investigations into possible police misconduct.

They're turning New York City into a bank for those arrested. Once someone says "I've been a victim of police brutality or police misconduct," you know some kind of brutality is going to be alleged, and the city is going to end up paying. Of course, the city won't pay for the businesses that have been looted or destroyed, but they *will* pay protestors who say they've been abused by cops.

This is the politicization of the criminal justice system.

These three Democrats create a recipe for a return of New York City to the crime-ridden 1980s, when the headlines looked like this:

HEADLESS BODY IN TOPLESS BAR
—*New York Post*, April 15, 1983

IN SUBWAY CRIME, N.Y. STILL LEADS THE WORLD
—*Los Angeles Times*, March 17, 1985

NEW YORK CITY MURDER TOLL HIGHEST IN HISTORY, POLICE SAY
—Reuters, December 25, 1988

MURDERS IN NEW YORK SET RECORDS IN 1989
—Reuters, March 31, 1990

Consider this: For forty years, New York City's education and social services budget was more than half of the total budget. The NYPD, previously at 8 percent, is now at 5 percent. The correlation of defunding police and increase in homicides has skyrocketed. There has been a 206 percent increase in shootings between this year and last year.

In July, Mayor de Blasio, speaking about the protests, told Wolf Blitzer that this was a historic moment of change, saying, "the kinds of gatherings we're used to, the parades, the fairs, we just can't have that while we're focusing on health right now."

Okay, but de Blasio exempted Black Lives Matter marches. He says they can continue despite the ban he put on all large events because "this is a historic moment of change."

Are you stupid?

The rest of us can't work, we can't enjoy sports, we can't be with our friends because of coronavirus, but anyone marching for Black Lives Matter can protest in hordes? Is that because the virus won't affect them? I thought the black community was particularly vulnerable to the virus. And what about all you guilt bullies? Telling us that if we go out we're going to infect grandma. So is it okay for protestors to get grandma sick, but the rest of us can't?

So, Bill, you've decided to take away my safety, my protection, my security, my business, and now my liberty. I've got news for you: You don't have that right. You took an oath to support the Constitution, and the first order of government is the protection of its citizens. As a public official, you don't have the right to tell police to stand down and to violate the oath that they took. You don't have the right to tell cops who want to go out and protect and defend us that they are not allowed to exercise their authority, and I don't care what your Marxist, Leftist, socialist comrades tell you. This is the United States of America, and in the United States of America, we outlaw crime and we pay police to support law and order. You, Mr. de Blasio, by not supporting law and order, are a menace to the law-abiding citizens of New York City. You are so out of sync with the rest of us and so far from the fundamental values upon which this country was founded that the best thing that can happen to you is that you be impeached and crawl back into your Marxist, Leftist hole.

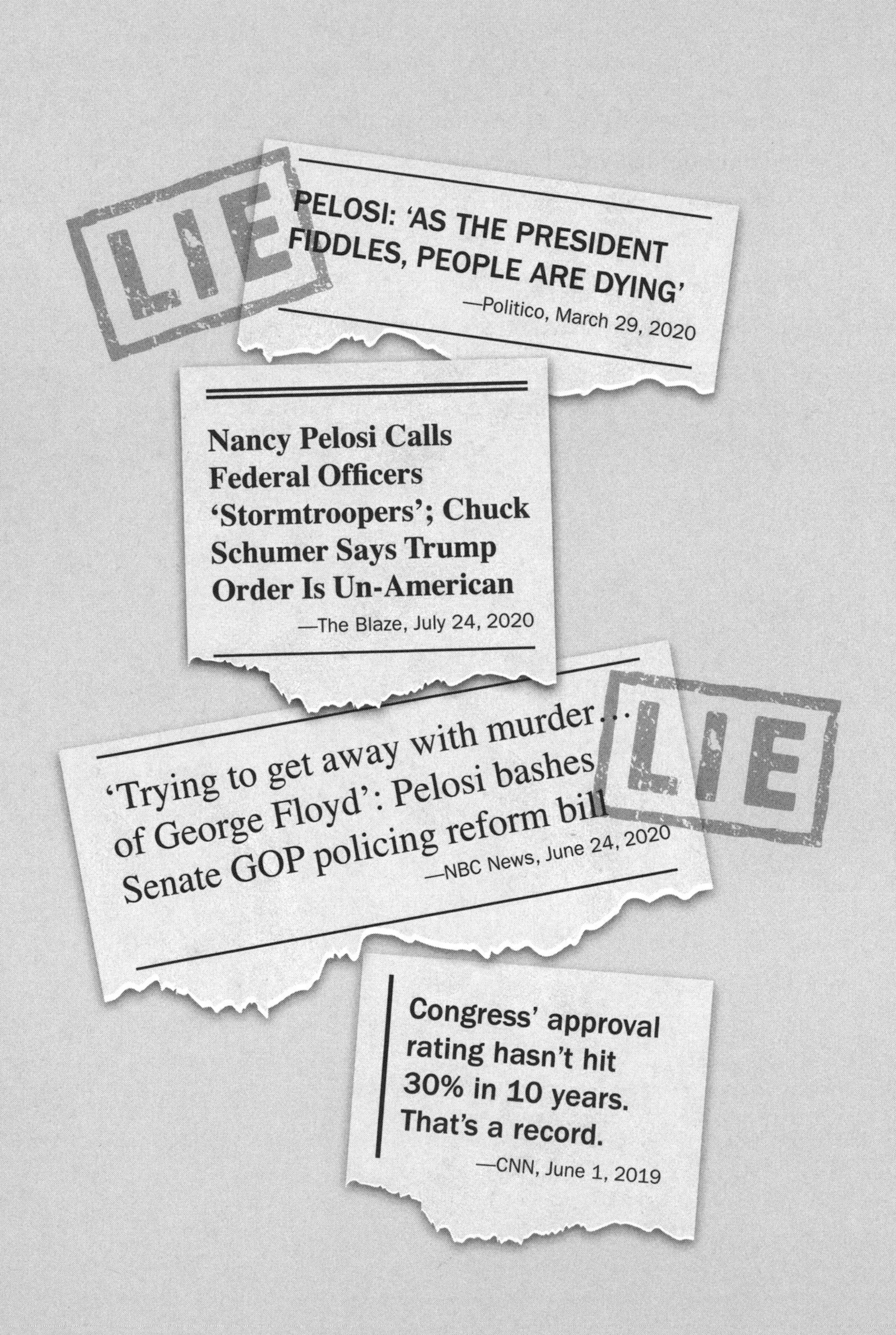
LIE
PELOSI: 'AS THE PRESIDENT FIDDLES, PEOPLE ARE DYING'
—Politico, March 29, 2020
Nancy Pelosi Calls Federal Officers 'Stormtroopers'; Chuck Schumer Says Trump Order Is Un-American
—The Blaze, July 24, 2020
'Trying to get away with murder… of George Floyd': Pelosi bashes Senate GOP policing reform bill
—NBC News, June 24, 2020
LIE
Congress' approval rating hasn't hit 30% in 10 years. That's a record.
—CNN, June 1, 2019

Chapter Ten

CONGRESS DOESN'T C.A.R.E. ABOUT YOU

During the month of June, the calls to reform our country's police departments were loud and clear. In the aftermath of the murder of George Floyd, there were peaceful protests nearly every day calling for an end to police brutality. Even before these protests devolved into rioting and looting—which, thanks to violent elements of the radical Left, happened almost immediately—these calls for action were impossible to ignore.

The cries were so loud, in fact, that even Congress couldn't ignore them.

The Democrats, of course, got to work first, slapping together a sloppy package of radical "reforms" that came straight out of the Bernie Sanders/AOC playbook. I wouldn't be surprised if it contained an amendment requiring police to wear literal targets on their backs. In the end, this bill was an empty gesture that had no hope of passing in the Senate, and the Democrats knew it.

But they announced it anyway.

Of course, they didn't *just* announce it. Rather than simply stating that they had finished writing the bill from a podium somewhere, showing respect both for the dead and the dozens of cities that were literally on fire at the time, Nancy Pelosi led her gang of angry Democrats into the lobby of the Capitol Building wearing brightly colored stoles made of African kente cloth, often worn during celebrations in West Africa. Then, after a speech for the cameras—no surprise there—she instructed the members of her party to kneel for a full eight minutes and forty-six seconds right there near the front door.

What followed was one of the strangest examples of political theater that I have ever seen—at least outside of Andrew Cuomo's rambling daytime monologues. For the first few seconds Chuck Schumer glanced around the room. Then he spent a few seconds reading a piece of paper in his hand. Jerrold Nadler, whose kente cloth nearly touched the floor, remained standing the whole time. Then, when the allotted time had elapsed and Queen Nancy Pelosi had given the signal that it was time to rise, she realized that she couldn't get up. Giggling like a child, she reached out for an assistant, who helped her get up so she could go and announce the bill.

In the middle of her announcement speech, Nancy told a story about a heartfelt conversation she'd had with the brother of George Floyd, who she says was intimately involved in drafting the Democrats' bill.

"Before he testified, he said, 'Madame Speaker, do you think I can tell George's daughter that his name will be always remembered because you'll name the bill for him?' And I said, 'Well, I'll recommend that to the Judiciary Committee and to the Congressional Black Caucus, who have shaped the bill. But I only will do that if you tell me that this legislation is worthy of George Kirby's name.'"[1]

Well, Nancy, I'd say your plan to make sure his name "will always be remembered" has not gotten off to a great start. You couldn't even remember it for ten minutes!

Neither, apparently, could *any* of the high-ranking Democrats in Congress.

A few weeks later, speaking on the floor of the Senate, Nancy Pelosi's crazy counterpart Chuck Schumer said that the Republicans' police reform bill, drafted by Senator Tim Scott and supported by fifty-six other senators, did not deserve to pass because it was opposed by the lawyer representing "Floyd Taylor . . . uh, George Taylor."[2] This came just days after Nancy Pelosi said that Senator Scott—a man who, unlike Nancy, had actually experienced discrimination throughout his life and knew what he was talking about—was trying to "get away with murder, specifically the murder of George Floyd" with their bill.

Over the next few days, Republicans in the Senate would make dozens of attempts to reach out to Democrats in order to get substantive police reform passed, but the Democrats would have none of it. In the end, they announced that they were ready to wait until next year, when they believe Joe Biden will be in the White House and the country will be ready to swallow their entire radical agenda whole.

This was not the first time they dithered while Americans suffered, and I'm sure it won't be the last.

WHO CARES?

When the economic shutdown began, Congress's approval rating was just 20 percent, proving not only how little Americans think of their elected representatives in Washington but also how broken the system really is.

While most Americans were told to shelter in place, essential workers were out working—doctors, nurses, healthcare workers, police, firefighters, first responders, truckers, delivery workers, postal workers, fast-food workers, public works workers, journalists, radio and television staff, but not Congress! Oh, no. They were sheltered in place like prima donnas, lounging around in their homes *and* getting paid!

Truth be told, most of the so-called essential workers would have preferred to be working—taking care of their families, having some control over what the future might hold for them, eliminating the financial and emotional toll of being without a paycheck.

So, what did Congress do? They passed one funding bill after another, including the so-called CARES Act, which was proof positive who cares about you. The intent of the act was to help the Americans still reeling from the worst economic collapse since the Great Depression. The end result was much different.

In spite of the dire situations Americans found themselves in, there was the typical Democrat obstruction during this process—the same obstruction that would prevent Congress from reaching a deal on police reform months later. The most unprecedented obstruction, no surprise, was in the House of Representatives, where Nancy Pelosi would begin the Democrat effort to use coronavirus as a cover to get in whatever they needed to promote their progressive socialist agenda.

The intent was to provide immediate cash to individuals or families who made less than $75,000, and an additional $500 for each child. But Nancy Pelosi, not surprisingly, not sensitive to the financial needs of ordinary Americans, was more interested in the Kennedy Center, which was already supported by billionaire philanthropists, and other cultural institutions in the United States instead of feeding Americans and getting money for them.

Imperious Nancy wasn't about to rush for ordinary Americans. The $2.2 trillion CARES Act, which included the payroll protection plan, was held up by Nancy for an additional seven days after there was already an agreement. She wanted money added beyond the payroll protection program for Planned Parenthood and the Green New Deal, and changes to our election laws.

She got $25 million for the Kennedy Center, where she is a board member, and $150 million for the National Endowment for the Arts and Humanities, none of which had anything to do with Americans out of work and not getting coronavirus or a paycheck.

During her delaying tactics, 1.6 million businesses got money to save 30 million jobs—but Republicans knew they would need to replenish money and wanted to do so by consent. Nancy would have none of it. So, another 4.4 million Americans filed for unemployment because of her delay.

Why?

House majority whip James Clyburn said it all in a phone call with his Democrat colleagues, reportedly telling them that the virus "was a tremendous opportunity to restructure things to fit our vision." So, you could see coronavirus was being used as a cover to fund liberal progressive programs.

Yet Nancy has time to show her freezer full of ice cream and concomitant tone-deaf brain freeze as she goes from *The Late Late Show with James Corden* to *The Late Show with Stephen Colbert* to *Real Time with Bill Maher.*

Maher finally put the ultimate question to her. "Really," he said. "Funding the Kennedy Center is a matter of life and death?"

The Left is not in tune with America. Last year, during the partial shutdown when 800,000 Americans were not receiving pay, Pelosi, Schiff, and her chosen vacation travelers—being paid, of course—were off to Afghanistan and Brussels after Nancy prevented the president from delivering his State of the Union Address, suggesting he send it in writing—and after *this* year's State of the Union, we know what she does with the speeches she gets in writing.

For years, Congress has gone from one thing to another, each side high-fiving one another after they think they've scored: three long years without proof of Russia collusion, destroying a Supreme Court justice nominee with rules that wouldn't get past a third grade government class, an attempt to impeach a president over a phone call.

Now, as we begin to see the light at the end of the Covid tunnel, the issue will turn to China and how they've harmed us.

Look at what they've done to us. Look at how we've been harmed. The sickness, death, the inability to attend funerals, battered women and abused children suffering in silence, the resurgence of alcoholism and drug abuse, the permanent damage to our economy, depression, and devastation coming out of this. The Chinese Communist government brought us to our knees with this virus. They let it out of China, allegedly out of a lab. They knew full well the danger. They analyzed it, understood it, and moved on it, which is why no flights were allowed out of Wuhan into Beijing or any other part of China. Yet they freely allowed flights to go to Europe and throughout the world.

Will Congress do more than pay lip service on behalf of all of us so damaged by these bad actors? Or will Congress just keep working for themselves, forgetting whom they're answerable to, and prove my point, which is that the system is broken.

With Nancy Pelosi and her gang of angry Democrats in charge, I wouldn't count on any progress anytime soon.

For anyone who doesn't remember what they *have* done this year, let's go all the way back to the beginning.

THE IMPEACHMENT DISTRACTION

At eight o'clock in the morning on January 15, Nancy Pelosi led her gang of angry Democrats out of the House chamber and through the halls of the Capitol Building, smiling for the cameras as she went. Striding behind her were Adam Schiff, the man who'd insisted repeatedly that he had seen proof of Russia collusion during the Mueller investigation; Maxine Waters, who once said President Trump should be imprisoned in "solitary confinement" for the crime of hurting her feelings; and Jerrold Nadler, who, at the time, was struggling, with the rest of them, to get his face on television.[3]

In her hand, Nancy carried two articles of impeachment against President Trump.

The first article, as you may or may not remember, was a charge connected to a phone call with the President of Ukraine. The first article of impeachment charged that President Trump had committed "abuse of power" when he delayed giving aid to Ukraine, even though the aid was given to Ukraine within the allotted time with no delay.

The other article—get this—contained the charge that President Trump had tried to defend himself against the charges laid out in the first article. According to the insane logic of liberals in Congress, this one was called "obstruction of the House." The claim of obstruction was absurd on its face given the fact that the Democrats resented that the president asserted executive privilege as opposed to litigating the issue in the separate third branch of government, the judiciary. They chose to make up a crime and charge him with a second article of impeachment.

These charges were ridiculous from the start, and there was no hope that either one would stick. Any good lawyer might have told you that.

In fact, many good lawyers did tell you that. Arguing on the floor of the Senate, Harvard professor Alan Dershowitz said it was "inconceivable that the framers would have intended so politically loaded and promiscuously deployed a term as 'abuse of power' to be weaponized as a tool of impeachment."[4] The next day, White House counsel Pat Cipollone, also speaking on the floor of the Senate, called the impeachment attempt "the most massive interference in an election in American history." And yours truly—who, if I may play my own fiddle for a moment, is no slouch when it comes to matters of the law—said the investigation was a "partisan political joke" on my show, an assessment I stand by to this day.

But you didn't need an astute legal mind to know these charges were nonsensical. You barely needed a pulse. Even House Democrats knew they had no chance of convincing the Senate. They knew that even though impeachment had squeaked out of the Democrat-stuffed House by a thin margin—with even some Democrats agreeing with Republicans—there was no way it would ever hold up in the Senate. Anyone with the ability to count to sixty-seven, the number of votes needed to convict President Trump in the Senate, could have told them that.

But the futility of their mission didn't matter. Neither did the fact that this little stunt was costing American taxpayers millions of dollars, or that it was distracting from much more pressing issues, such as the pending coronavirus pandemic. All that mattered to the Democrats—all that ever matters to them—is the attention they were getting and the anger they were stoking. They only cared about attacking the president. If it was bad for Trump, it was good for them, and if it was good for Trump, it was bad for them. So, when they finally got to live out their Inauguration Day fantasy of delivering articles of impeachment to the Senate, they were flush with pleasure.

If you don't believe me, take a look at all the photos from that morning. Nancy Pelosi never pulls a stunt without making sure there are a few photographers nearby, ready to get her face on the front page of the next morning's newspapers.

Here's one of House Democrats signing the articles of impeachment in the Rayburn Reception Room of the US Capitol, holding up their special commemorative pens for the camera. *Click!* Here's another one of them struggling to hold on to those pens as they burst into uproarious applause, thrilled that they had finally succeeded in ripping the country apart at the seams. *Click! Click!* And here, as a finale to the whole performance, is Nancy Pelosi and the rest of the gang all lined up like contestants at a beauty pageant, trying like mad to hide their smiles as their Dear Leader announces the articles of impeachment.

"So sad," she said, that creepy whisper kicking into high gear. "So tragic for a country that the actions taken by the president to undermine our national security, to violate his oath of office and jeopardize the purity of our elections has taken us to this place. So, today, we will make history. When the managers walk down the hall, we will cross a threshold in history: delivering articles of impeachment for abuse of power and obstruction of the House."

Spare me.

The public humiliation of Nancy Pelosi and her Democrat caucus of sycophants who dared not oppose her is actually an embarrassment to watch. Her impeachment of President Trump was borne not of truth, facts, or evidence but rather of a historic, vitriolic hatred usually reserved for enemies of the state. In the end, it is her animosity and her frenetic, irrational, and baseless actions against this president that will ultimately hoist her on her own petard.

No one deserves it more.

After her announcement, she rushed the vote on impeachment because of the "urgency" involved. We cannot wait, she said. We've got to stop him. The president is at it again. The sky is falling, too.

And yet there was no case to send to the Senate, so, like a child caught in a lie, she dithered for weeks hoping something—anything—might happen to make the president look bad. But every day, he kept on working and winning. So, finally, she explained her reason for procrastinating.

She wanted to ensure a fair trial in the Senate. Isn't that sweet?

She was so caught up in her own image as the imperious Queen Nancy that she of the lower house imagined herself the doyenne of the upper house: the Senate Chamber, of which she has never—nor will she ever be—a member. In December, she threatened to hold back articles of impeachment until the Senate could hold a fair trial.

Fair?

The woman whose historic hate played out for all to see wants to ensure a fair trial? The mistress of the star chamber, intent on taking down our leader in the subbasement of the Capitol Building away from the eyes and ears of the public and most of Congress, leaking through her minion Adam Schiff (himself a jester in her court), acting out a false, slanderous, untrue, libelous reading of the transcript of the president's Ukraine call?

Nancy, you said the president was welcome to come and exonerate himself—of what or why no one knows, since the transcript itself exonerates him. But in your chamber, you upend the constitution, putting centuries-old jurisprudence on its head and shifting the burden of proof to the accused without even advising him of the charges.

Folks, it has never been about truth or justice for these radicals. The House Democrats simply want to take out the most successful president Americans have put in the Oval Office—the one who's made the economy soar; who speaks our language; who actually wants us to succeed; who took out two of the world's most dangerous savages, Abu Bakr al-Baghdadi and Quds Force general Qassem Soleimani, with no civilian losses and no boots on the ground—the same president who has made the world safer and brought Iran, the world's largest state sponsor of terrorism, to her knees. That's why he's so successful and why Americans love him.

But you didn't care, Nancy. His success offended you. You should be smarter than that, Nancy. But I guess you hate him because Donald J. Trump changed the planned political establishment legacy order where you guys, irrespective of party, scratch each other's backs.

When you commandeered the meaningless War Powers Resolution after the Soleimani drone strike was over, trying to limit the president's ability to fight our enemy, you again showed your hypocrisy. When your pal Obama in 2011 decided to bomb Libya, where no American lives were lost, you said he did not need congressional authority. So, what did you learn by passing that partisan War Powers Resolution, sending that little love letter to the ayatollah, other than to seemingly say: *do what you must; we will hold him back?*

Have you no shame?

In the end, Nancy, your investigation was a joke about how to manipulate the truth and then swear to it. And after all the urgency, what did your dithering gain in your unprecedented refusal to forward the articles of impeachment to the senate?

Did you gain a political advantage?

What did you get out of waiting. other than losing votes to the Republican Party? Admit it: You caved after Mitch McConnell gave you a deadline to either send over the articles of impeachment or simply watch the Senate move forward without them. That's right. You simply caved. That's what happens when there is no case.

Of course, no one has alleged that you are smart.

While you and your fellow Democrats were clapping that morning in the Rayburn Reception Room, the deadly coronavirus was spreading, particularly through the streets of New York City that Jerrold Nadler is supposed to represent.

For weeks after that day, not a single member of the congressional leadership mentioned the virus. In fact, the first time it was mentioned on the floor of the House of Representatives was well into February, almost a month after President Trump had shut down flights from China. All they could think about, it seemed, was getting the president out of office, even while he was working day and night to shore up our borders against the deadliest enemy we had ever known.

By the time they took their eye off impeachment and started actually trying to stop the virus, it would be far too late.

NANCY PELOSI AND THE DEMOCRAT STRING ENSEMBLE

On a Sunday morning at the end of March, with millions of Americans still reeling from the worst economic collapse since the Great Depression, Nancy Pelosi appeared on CNN's *State of the Union* for a victory lap. Two days earlier, despite unprecedented obstruction by Democrats in the House, Congress had finally managed to pass a $2.2 trillion aid package for American workers.

Although it came far too late, this package included several key provisions that were instrumental in sustaining our economy. It provided tax breaks for small businesses, bailouts for the airline and hospitality industries, and the promise of $1,200 checks to Americans who made less than $75,000. In its final, watered-down form, this bill—which was called the CARES Act—was severely lacking in many important ways. It didn't do nearly enough to alleviate the suffering that many Americans were feeling. It certainly didn't do enough for the millions of Americans who'd lost their jobs that month, or the millions more who'd found themselves with less than half the income they'd had just a few months before.

Not surprisingly, Jake Tapper did *not* mention the fact that in the eleventh hour, Pelosi and her band of Democrat thugs had attempted to hijack the stimulus bill with a shotgun, using our national crisis as an opportunity to get some of their craziest legislative ideas passed under cover of darkness. He didn't mention the random—and completely *insane*—provisions on fossil fuels, corporate diversity, and abortion that they had attempted to stuff into the fine print of this already half-baked bill, or how Republicans had fought valiantly to get each and every one cut right back out.

Instead, Tapper allowed Nancy Pelosi to end the interview with this lie-filled whopper of a monologue, delivered in her signature wavering, half-insane whisper: "What the president, his denial at the beginning, uh, was deadly," she said. "His delaying of getting equipment, uh, to where it continues his delaying—to where it's needed, is deadly . . . We have to have testing, testing, testing. That's what we said from the start . . . I don't know what the scientists are saying to him. I don't know what the scientists are saying—what did the president know about this? What did the president know and when did he know it? That's for an after-action review. But as the president fiddles, people are dying."

I'm sorry, Nancy, did you say *fiddles*? Is *that* what you call what the president was doing at the beginning of this crisis? Leaving aside your cheap (and unsuccessful) attempt to invoke the shadowy language of the Nixon impeachment—"What did the president know and when did he know it?"—let me catch you up on what President Trump was *actually* doing while you and your fellow radicals were screwing around with our nation's only economic lifeline.

I'm sure you were too busy scheming in the basement of the Capitol Building to notice.

On March 19, the day the Republicans put forth their first version of this bill, he met with the Coronavirus Task Force at 9:00 a.m., planning out a strategy for the weekend ahead. At 11:00 a.m., he held a press conference in the Brady Press Briefing

Room—despite unbelievable opposition from the hostile White House press corps—and assured the country that the task force was hard at work. At 12:15, he received his daily intelligence briefing, dealing with the dozens of other problems going on around the world that most people won't even read about. Later that day, he visited the headquarters of our Federal Emergency Management Agency and got on a conference call with governors to "prepare, mitigate, and respond to coronavirus." During this call, he dealt with dozens of requests for ventilators, hospital beds, and other medical equipment, most of which would turn out to be completely unnecessary by the end of the crisis. By 3:30, he was back at the White House, where he met *again* with the Coronavirus Task Force and made calls from the Oval Office until late into the night.[5]

That was just one day. The ones that came after were even busier. According to Mark Meadows, who took over as White House chief of staff in April, the president would often make "five dozen work-related calls a day during the pandemic," working so hard that he often went whole days without eating.[6] Today, thanks to their efforts, the United States has one of the most robust testing programs for coronavirus in the world. Even though President Trump knows that this will drive up the positivity rate, giving the appearance of more cases, he has done it to keep Americans safe.

As you can probably see, Nancy, our executive branch sprung right into action when this crisis hit. President Trump assembled the best experts on infectious disease in the world and started fighting to contain the spread of this virus, corralling the medical deep state so it worked for him. Even in the face of unprecedented incompetence at federal agencies like the CDC, the FDA, and the NIH, he managed to lead a forceful and quick response to the virus. Today, he is still moving at warp speed to get rid of this disease for good. On July 22, the federal government entered into a contract with the Pfizer pharmaceutical company to create 100 million doses of a vaccine, which will be given out for free. You, on the other hand, moved at the speed of molasses. You were so concerned about impeachment, your liberal agenda, and your interviews on CNN that you didn't even *mention* the coronavirus in the House until late February. And once you *did* start doing your job, you took breaks every few days for partisan speeches and long interviews on cable news. If anyone was "fiddling" during this crucial period in American history, Nancy, it was you and your fellow Democrat members of Congress.

Over a period of two months, these people failed repeatedly to pass simple legislation in a timely manner. They bickered, they argued, and they engaged in cheap PR stunts to boost their own public profiles. Some, as I'm sure you remember, even used private information about the severity of this crisis—information that was not available to the American public—to make illegal stock market maneuvers, resulting in millions of dollars' worth of ill-gotten financial gains. Others tried to grab headlines by grandstanding or making craven, sanctimonious speeches whenever they managed to find a camera.

If President Trump was "fiddling" during this crisis—a trope that became popular within liberal social media circles—then Nancy Pelosi and her fellow liberal lawmakers were conducting entire symphonies. As the president worked to bring this country back from the brink, foregoing sleep and most meals to get the job done, they danced around the Capitol Building with their fiddles, trombones, and saxophones in hand, drowning out all the chaos and cries for help that were coming in from the outside. If it hadn't been for the immense pressure that President Trump put on these people to get their deals done quickly, they might never have acted at all.

In fact, at the very moment President Trump was overseeing the shipment of thousands of ventilators to New York City—many of which would never be used—these morons were fighting to include $25 million for the Kennedy Center for the Arts, the government-owned venue in Washington, DC, that holds plays, concerts, and orchestra recitals for the elite in the stimulus bill.

As you can see, while President Trump was trying to keep people from dying in the streets, these people were *literally* more worried about fiddling!

Clearly, if anyone is to blame for the economic collapse that will certainly follow this disastrous pandemic, it's them, not the man who is fighting daily to get us back to work, get our schools open, and kickstart the economy again.

THE GREAT CONGRESSIONAL SELL-OFF

Of course, I'm not saying that members of Congress did *nothing* during the first days of the coronavirus pandemic. Plenty of them got right to work, but not in the way we might have hoped.

On January 24, for instance, as the Senate was hearing arguments from the House managers about the impeachment of President Trump, several United States senators were allowed to take a break to hear a closed-door presentation about the threat posed by the coronavirus. At the behest of President Trump, several public health experts gave a closed-door briefing about the threat posed by the coronavirus that was open to all senators.

One senator who was present was Kelly Loeffler, a Republican from Georgia who'd been in Congress for twenty days. She'd been given her seat when its previous occupant, Senator Johnny Isakson, had been forced to retire for health reasons. President Trump had suggested that Representative Doug Collins, a well-known freedom fighter, be appointed senator. Governor Brian Kemp had chosen Loeffler instead.

Nobody involved in giving her a Senate seat seemed to care that she had absolutely no experience representing the people of Georgia, or that her husband, Jeffrey Sprecher, was the chairman of the New York Stock Exchange. Having gone right from her previous job as the CEO of a company in the financial services industry to the United States Senate, she had an easier time slipping into that seat than Hunter Biden did during his interview at Burisma Holdings—and *that's* saying something.

Whatever Governor Kemp's reason for appointing her, she showed little allegiance to Georgia, the governor, or anyone other than her own pocketbook—probably Hermès.

Just a few hours after that briefing, Senator Loeffler and her husband began unloading about $20 million worth of stock in companies that would soon lose hundreds of thousands of dollars in value, a move that no average American investor would have made without advance knowledge of the crisis.[8] First, they sold all their shares in a company called Resideo Technologies—stock that was valued between $50,000 and $100,000. Then, they sold off a few other small technology stocks, many of which would lose more than half their value in the days to come.[9]

Throughout February and March, she and her husband continued dumping stocks that would effectively become trash in the days ahead, making fifty-six different transactions.[10] She also purchased stock in companies that were sure to do well during a global pandemic--companies like DuPont, which manufactures personal protective equipment, or Citrix, a company that does teleconferencing. In January and February, Loeffler and her husband bought between $450,000 and $1 million worth of stock in those companies. The heist culminated in the sale of just over $18.7 million in Intercontinental Exchange stock in three separate deals dated January 24 and February 14.

One thing is for sure: Nobody who was buying all this stock from her had any idea what was about to happen to the United States in the days ahead. But Loeffler did. In effect, she had tossed them a bomb that only she knew was going to go off and pretended it was just a bowling ball with a funny string attached. These people hadn't heard a special briefing from public health officials about how the economy was on the verge of collapse. They didn't know that what they were buying was effectively worthless. In the months since she was caught for this little scheme, Loeffler has blamed everything and everyone—the Democrats, the media, even socialism. She's said she had absolutely no idea that the trades were even being made, claiming that a third party did it all for her.

Now, I don't usually get into the business of campaigning for congressional candidates. But in the case of this one particular down-ballot race, I have a message for my readers in Georgia: Make sure that the next time Kelly Loeffler is up for reelection, which happens to be this November, she is out on the curb the next morning.

De Blasio Defends NYC's Sanctuary City Police After Trump's State of the Union Address

—Gothamist, February 5, 2020

LIE

Sanctuary Cities Are Safer

—NPR, January 29, 2017

BIDEN ON UNIVISION: DEPORTING 3 MILLION 'WAS A BIG MISTAKE'

—The Hill, February 15, 2020

LIE

State Dems thumbing noses at rule of law with illegal immigrant licenses

—*New York Post*, June 17, 2020

Chapter Eleven

THE OPEN BORDERS LIE

When the Democrat Clown Car finally emptied out, leaving Joe Biden to sit by himself behind the wheel, many of us believed that the most radical phase of the 2020 election was over. We thought that the days of hearing about open borders, Medicare for All, and the evil, structural racism of the United States were behind us. After all, Biden was an establishment candidate who seemed to have nothing in common with these old radicals. We thought that all we had to do from that moment forward was sit, enjoy the debates, and wait for the results to roll in on election night, when President Trump would finally send Sleepy Joe down into the carnival dunk tank of history with ease, leaving only his aviator sunglasses and a big red nose bobbing on the surface of the water.

Sadly, we were wrong.

As the final days of this election drag on, it is clearer than ever that the extreme Left's radical agenda did not die for good when the final round of far-Left lunatics dropped out. Despite the fact that Leftist candidates like Bernie Sanders, Elizabeth Warren, and Julián Castro have long since exited the Democrat Clown Car, their ideas are still unbelievably, chillingly alive. As I write this, their warped views on structural racism, identity politics, and the evils of free speech are spreading through the country faster than any virus ever could, turning all the young liberals they touch into violent, brain-dead zombies. In the past few months alone, these roving hordes of the "woke" undead have burned down buildings, looted countless stores, and torn down statues of our most beloved historical figures. I shudder to think what might happen if their party's chosen candidate—a man who, as of this writing, has failed to condemn the riots even as our cities burn, whose campaign backers are calling every day for him to support a complete defunding of our police forces—ever wins the White House.

Already, the radicals in his own party have been able to yank Biden by his puppet strings to the left on several key issues. Shortly after they knocked Crazy Bernie Sanders out of the race in March, the Biden campaign named Alexandria Ocasio-Cortez, the far-Left radical socialist who has led the charge in Congress to abolish Immigration and Customs Enforcement (ICE) and to *completely* defund police, as a key advisor on the environment. Under her stewardship, the Biden campaign has completely swallowed the Green New Deal, including in their climate change proposal that this wacky legislation is "a crucial framework for meeting the climate challenges we face . . . the United States urgently needs to embrace greater ambition on an epic scale to meet the scope of this challenge."[1]

The prosecutor in me says that AOC wrote that all herself, and Joe Biden passively acquiesced.

And if you think that AOC is going to keep her influence over Joe Biden confined strictly to matters of the environment, you might ask yourself whether, historically, she has been the kind of person who has a problem wading into issues in which she has absolutely no experience. Remember, this is the same person who showed up to her first day in Congress unable to correctly name the three branches of government and the same person who said before she got there that she couldn't wait to start signing bills into law.

Make no mistake: The radical Left is coming for the Biden campaign. There are still plenty of puppet strings up for grabs. On many issues, the takeover has already begun.

RUNNING FROM THE LEFT

All hopes of Joe Biden being an establishment candidate were dispelled when he took a hard left on immigration. During the first Democrat debate in July 2019, Biden was one of only three candidates—out of ten on the stage—who didn't raise his hand when asked if he would support Julián Castro's proposal to make crossing the United States border without papers perfectly legal. (Of course, there's a part of me that suspects he just didn't understand the question.) During a debate that was held a few months later, he separated himself from just about every other Democrat in the country by saying that crossing the border between the United States and Mexico illegally was "a crime."

Sadly, this was a radical statement in today's political climate, and Biden paid dearly for it. During a later debate in September, Biden was interrupted several times during one of his long, rambling answers to a question by protestors who screamed *"Three million deportations!"* from the stands.[2]

They were referencing the fact—which I'm sure most Democrats will conveniently forget by Election Day—that during their eight years in the White House, President Barack Obama and his sidekick Mexico Joe successfully carried out the deportations of about three million illegal immigrants. In fact, during the first three years of their administration, Obama and Biden set a high score for deportations per year that *still* hasn't been beaten—even by the so-called racist who's in the White House now. According to ICE, during Obama's first term, Biden and Obama deported more than 385,000 people each year in fiscal years 2009 through 2011.

Then, in 2012, deportations reached a record high of 409,849.[3]

When these two took office, rates of illegal immigration were soaring to the highest they had been in decades. Something needed to be done, and there was no radical Left obsessed with identity politics to stop them. Part of being the commander in chief was keeping the United States safe from harm, and for a while, President Obama did that by allowing the men and women of ICE to do their jobs. Back then, he didn't see anything wrong with it.

After all, Barack Obama and Joe Biden had both grown up in a Democrat Party that at least pretended to respect the rule of law. Under President Bill Clinton, their party had led the charge on curbing the flow of illegal immigrants into the United States, making it a key component of his reelection strategy. In his 1996 State of the Union address, President Clinton said, "After years of neglect, this administration has taken a strong stand to stiffen the protection of our borders."[4] That same year, Clinton signed into law the Illegal Immigration Reform and Immigrant

Responsibility Act of 1996, and made immigration reform one of the Democrat Party's key issues.

Here is a paragraph from the Democrat Party's platform for that year:

> Today's Democratic Party also believes we must remain a nation of laws. We cannot tolerate illegal immigration and we must stop it. For years before Bill Clinton became President, Washington talked tough, but failed to act. In 1992, our borders might as well not have existed. The border was under-patrolled, and what patrols there were, were under-equipped. Drugs flowed freely. Illegal immigration was rampant. Criminal immigrants, deported after committing crimes in America, returned the very next day to commit crimes again.

Can you imagine what would happen to a Democrat candidate who wrote those words in the year 2020? If Joe Biden tried, he'd be thrown into woke jail so fast that his puppet head would pop off.

According to NPR—among the most liberal news sources in the country—64 percent of Democrats used to believe that illegal immigrants put an unfair burden on our country because they take jobs, housing, and healthcare that Americans had to pay for. As of February 2019, that number was only 11 percent, and you don't need to be a genius to know that it hasn't gone back up since then.[5]

It wasn't only the 1990s. As recently as 2006, as Peter Beinart has written in *The Atlantic*, it was perfectly acceptable for left-leaning figures like Paul Krugman to write that "immigration reduces the wages of domestic workers who compete with immigrants," concluding that we needed to "reduce the flow of low-skill immigrants."[6] That same year, it was also acceptable for a Democrat senator to write this sentence in his bestselling coming-of-age memoir without anyone calling him a racist or a bigot: "When I see Mexican flags waved at pro-immigration demonstrations, I sometimes feel a flush of patriotic resentment. When I'm forced to use a translator to communicate with the guy fixing my car, I feel a certain frustration."[7]

That senator, by the way, was named Barack Obama, and the book was called *The Audacity of Hope.*

In the next few lines, Obama goes on to talk about why we need to make sure everyone who enters the United States learns English, stating that "a common language makes us stronger." I have no idea what would happen if he tried to say the same thing today.

Six years after that book came out, its author was running for his second term as President of the United States and there were massive protests beginning to occur at some of his major campaign stops. For the most part, they centered on his immigration policy. You see, after Obama was elected for the first time in 2008, the Democrats realized that courting the votes of illegal immigrants was a great way to stay in power, and they were finding it very difficult to do that while the head of the party was deporting illegal aliens in droves.

So, they demanded that he stop immediately.

One of these protest groups was called #Not1MoreDeportation, and it was led by a woman named Marisa Franco. In a press release, this group demanded not only that the Obama administration stop deportations, but also that they pass a law declaring that illegal immigration was not a crime.[8] It worked—at least in part. For the next few years, the Obama administration drastically reduced the number of deportations it carried out, caving to pressure from the radical Left, just as Joe Biden would do in the years ahead.

In May 2020, Joe Biden reached out to Marisa Franco and asked her to be one of the lead members on his "immigration unity task force." In the years since, she had written articles about how Obama and Biden had built a "massive deportation machine, all gassed up and ready for Trump to take over." [9] Over the past few months, Biden has apologized profusely for his role in deporting illegal immigrants, many of whom had committed violent felonies during their stays in the United States.

There was no apology to the victims of those crimes.

In February, he said that the deportations were "a big mistake," saying "we took too long to get it right. The point is that there was too many. [sic] I saw the pain in the eyes of so many people who saw their families being deported. I know what it's like to lose family members. It was painful. It wasn't until 2012 that we began to get it right with the DACA program and trying very much in 2014 to expand that and moving in the right direction."

When Biden released his plan for immigration earlier this year, the fingerprints of the radical Left were all over it. In the first few pages, the Biden campaign promises to grant amnesty to all eleven million undocumented immigrants in the United States.[10] It also states that during the first one hundred days of the Biden administration—should there ever be one—nobody would be deported for anything, not even felonies. Here are some of the other gems according to Breitbart.com:

- Releasing all border crossers into the US interior
- Restarting welfare-dependent legal immigration to the US
- Cracking down on ICE agents
- Ending President Trump's National Emergency Declaration at the southern border
- Ending a travel ban from foreign countries that sponsor terrorism
- Providing amnesty to 3.5 million DACA-enrolled and DACA-eligible illegal aliens
- Providing federal student loans and free community college to DACA illegal aliens [11]

Amazing. The Left's emphasis is now to allow illegal aliens into the country, to stop the deportation of criminals, and to place American citizens in harm's way in sanctuary cities developed for illegal criminals, all the while tying the hands of ICE agents.

Make no mistake: Even with most of the far-Left radicals out of the running for president, you are *still* looking at the most extreme Leftist agenda America has ever witnessed.

You need to start worrying. In fact, you need to be afraid.

These people don't care about you or law and order. I'll say it again. These people don't care about you, your safety, civil tranquility, innocent Americans or law and order. Because if they did, they would support the police, law enforcement, ICE, Border Patrol, the military, and all agencies designed to protect the safety of the America citizenry. But no. These Leftists openly defy the law and protect those who are guilty of violating it. As a result, areas of crime are being created that endanger innocent Americans in sanctuary cities and sanctuary states. We are now seeing once again how the Left's reliance on identity politics, which focuses on race, gender, class, and sexual orientation, supersedes issues of guilt or innocence and instead seeks to protect the guilty and punish the innocent.

These liberal politicians don't care about the danger in which they are placing American citizens every day by encouraging untold numbers of illegal aliens to pour into this country every year, then housing and protecting them in sanctuary cities. If the coronavirus pandemic has taught us anything, it should be that a country without borders is doomed.

The door is open for the victimization of the American citizen.

A PREVENTABLE CRIME

Maria Fuertes was thirty years old when she left the Dominican Republic to come to the United States. She thought she was leaving violence behind for good. In her home city of Santo Domingo, death and savagery were commonplace.

So, she came to the United States, the land of freedom and opportunity, where she believed the justice system would ensure her safety and security, as it did for all citizens. She did everything she was supposed to. She came here legally, got a job, raised her three children—and later grandchildren—in a small neighborhood in Queens called Richmond Park.

According to her granddaughter Daria, she was a woman "who dedicated her time to taking care of others," and never complained when things got tough.[12]

Clearly, Maria Fuertes was a shining example of what this country can provide for people who come legally, work hard, and follow the rules.

But a few miles from Maria's apartment in Queens, a group of illegal immigrants moved in, bringing with them the violence she had come to America to escape. One of them was a twenty-one-year-old man named Reeaz Khan, a skinny Guyanese national with a propensity for violence and a sick, twisted mind.

One night in November 2019, Khan shattered a ceramic mug and used the sharp edges to stab his father in the chest and arms. By the time police arrived, Khan had drawn large amounts of blood. The police arrested Khan and kept him in a New York City jail for a few days,[13] eventually charging him with assault and possession of a weapon. They also learned that he was in the United States illegally, but they took no action because of Bill de Blasio and his sanctuary city policy. According to this policy, they were not permitted to ask about his citizenship status.

While he was in jail, officers at ICE learned that Khan was an illegal immigrant and took action, as they are supposed to. Shortly after he was arrested, ICE sent a fax to the New York Police Department, requesting a hold on Khan under what is called a detainer request. These requests are a common tool for ICE, and they are extremely useful in apprehending violent dirtbags like Reeaz Khan. When a detainer request is issued, the police department is supposed to hold a suspect for forty-eight hours, giving federal authorities enough time to come by, pick him up, and remove him for deportation proceedings.

However, these requests are only useful if they're honored.[14] And in a sanctuary city like New York City, where the rights of illegal immigrants matter more than the rights of their victims, these requests are rarely honored—and that's putting it mildly. According to the *New York Times*, "out of more than 7,500 detainer requests lodged by the ICE New York Bureau field office [in 2019], local authorities honored about 10."[15]

That's right. Ten. Not ten *percent*, but ten requests out of 7,500. At this point, ICE might as well just print out all these detainer requests and leave them around the weight machines at the Prospect Park YMCA. At least then Bill de Blasio would see them.

When the fax came in from ICE with the detainer request for Reeaz Khan, the NYPD followed their bogus "sanctuary city" guidelines and ignored it. Later, officers would lie and claim that the fax had never come in at all, a fact that was clearly disputed by the evidence.

In other words, that was a lie.

Then, in November, just a few days after he was arrested, Reeaz Khan was arraigned for assault and criminal possession of a weapon, and the judge in his case ordered him to appear back in court on January 13. Because no one ever told the judge that a detainer request had come from ICE,[16] all he could do was bang his gavel, set a court date, and hope that Khan—who had not exactly shown himself to have a good head on his shoulders—did as he was told and showed up to court. This was never going to go anywhere good. But no one could have imagined what would happen.

On the evening of January 6, just under a week before Khan was set to stand trial for assault, he went out to meet his cousins—also illegal aliens—at a hookah bar in Richmond Park. When he couldn't find them where they were supposed to meet, he walked home angry.[17]

It was around this time of the evening that Maria, known to her neighbors as "cat lady" or *abuelita*, was returning from her daily trip to the grocery store to turn in her bottles and cans. Khan spotted Maria from a few blocks away and came up behind her. He shoved her down to the concrete. He beat her with his fists. He sexually assaulted her. Then he left her to die behind a parked car in the street. Because of her old age and the extreme hunch in her back, Maria never had any chance to fight back or escape. It was hours before someone found her and alerted her son Ray, who happened to be in a nearby deli when he heard the news. He accompanied his mother to the hospital, assuming she'd fallen off the curb and would recover quickly.

She didn't.

Maria Fuertes died on the morning of January 7, 2020, leaving behind a loving family and two wonderful granddaughters. At the time, her killer was still at large. And if it hadn't been for video footage of the attack, he might never have been found. Luckily, police asked the community for help, and Khan's brother convinced the sick punk to turn himself in. As of this writing, he has tried to explain his actions by claiming that his "pants were down, and he slipped and fell into her," giving the court a sob story about his own grandmother and how he could never, *ever* do something like that to an innocent old lady.

Please. If my experience has taught me anything, it's that sick animals like this are always cowards.

When it comes time to admit what they did, they will lie every time.

Shortly after the attack, members of Maria's family were right to blame Bill de Blasio and his dangerous sanctuary city policies for her death, pointing out, correctly, that if it hadn't been for these absurd laws, Reeaz Khan would have been deported the *first* time he committed a violent act. Top officials in the Trump administration, shocked and angered by the senseless killing, also spoke out against New York City and its sanctuary city policies. The president even invited Maria's granddaughter Daria to the White House to speak.

Just a few days after the murder, Matthew Albence, then the acting director of ICE, put it bluntly: "A phone call," he said. "One simple phone call, and Ms. Fuertes would be alive today."

But I guess that's too much to ask of a Leftist or a liberal.[18]

LIARS

That same day, in response, Mayor de Blasio, through a spokesperson, said it was "shameful that the Trump administration is politicizing this tragedy," and went on to lie about how he and his administration were cooperating with federal law enforcement. Then, his spokesperson tried to change the subject.[19]

Oh really, Bill? Which part was shameful? The part when President Trump and his administration protected an illegal alien criminal instead of allowing federal law enforcement to do its job? The part when they *lied* about it to save face?

I despise liars with every ounce of energy—with every bone in my body. They are scum of the earth. It's one thing to have these sanctuary city policies in the first place, which do nothing for American citizens and protect illegal aliens. But it's another thing when politicians like Bill de Blasio continue to lie about the hand they had in causing that horrible death.

Oh, and one other thing, Bill. You can't *politicize* a tragedy that only happened because of your own bad politics. From the moment you and your ultra-liberal administration allowed

Reeaz Khan to walk out of that courthouse in New York City, not caring one iota about the damage he might inflict on innocent, hardworking immigrants like Maria Fuertes, this was political. By denying the men and women of law enforcement and ICE, who have a keener sense of danger than you, you are substituting your idiocy, your political pandering, and your hate for law enforcement, which was exhibited almost immediately upon taking office. Now you seek to tie their hands and not let them pursue suspects?

Who the hell are you?

You can't hide behind the tragic nature of this crime now, ask that nobody talk about why it happened in the first place, and then accuse anyone of politicizing it.

If you ever needed proof that Democrats like Bill de Blasio care more about their political agenda than immigrants or people in general, here it is. These people would rather risk it all to defend illegal immigrants than crack down on real criminals and protect American citizens, even naturalized citizens who go through the trouble of swearing allegiance to this country, understanding our history, and working hard to pass their citizenship tests.

These political whores don't care that Americans overwhelmingly support enforcement of the law. So why wouldn't the Left care? It's simple. Their goal is power. They get that power when illegal aliens vote, because they know they've lost the vote of law-abiding Americans—the ones who support the Constitution, the foundation of our laws. The Leftists, on the other hand, prefer to subjugate the laws of the land, even if it means sacrificing the rest of us at their altar of political correctness and identity politics.

For professional politicians, these things are never personal. Everything is about power, and anyone who can't help them get that power is expendable—including law-abiding immigrants like Maria Fuertes.

TAKE HIM TO COURT AND SUE

As I said in my first book, *To Punish and Protect*, written when I was district attorney, we don't take crime personally enough. When you get into law enforcement, you often hear that you should be "detached and objective." Question: How can any human being remain objective about an elderly woman being raped and beaten by some animal, right in the middle of the street in the very country that he stole his way into?

That is what these professional politicians, the vast majority of whom have absolutely no experience in law enforcement, will never understand. To them, it's all about numbers and collecting votes. They don't feel a victim's pain the way they should, nor do they understand that that pain extends beyond the victim to family, friends, and the community.

To President Trump, however, crimes like the one that was committed against Maria Fuertes *are* personal. Offenses against common decency, especially when they involve children, always are. Less than a month after Maria Fuertes was killed, President Trump honored her by mentioning her in his third State of the Union address, one of the most touching and well-written addresses ever delivered by an American president.

"Tragically," said the president, "there are many cities in America where radical politicians have chosen to provide sanctuary for these criminal illegal aliens. In sanctuary cities, local officials order police to release dangerous criminal aliens to prey upon the public, instead of handing them over to ICE to be safely removed." Then he delivered the facts of the case in an objective yet compassionate manner that perfectly conveyed the seriousness of the problem. "Just twenty-nine days ago," he said, "a criminal alien freed by the sanctuary city of New York was charged with the brutal rape and murder of a ninety-two-year-old woman. The killer had been previously arrested for assault, but under New York's sanctuary policies, he was set free. If the city had honored ICE's detainer request, his victim would be alive today."[20]

This was certainly an unusual and shocking thing to hear during a State of the Union Address—but a discussion, nonetheless, that was necessary. I know from experience that when you dance around issues, trying to protect everybody's feelings and ignoring how serious the situation really is, it only leads to more misery. President Trump knows this, too. That's why he interrupted what was otherwise a jubilant, optimistic speech with such horrifying language. He knew that if regular Americans didn't feel at least some modicum of the pain felt by families whose relatives are victimized by illegal aliens, they might just allow Democrats to keep ignoring the issue while innocent people suffer. No other president would have had the good sense—or the courage—to do it.

But Maria Fuertes wasn't the only innocent victim honored during that speech. President Trump also told the story of Rocky Jones, a giant of a man who was tragically killed by an illegal immigrant on a shooting spree. The president had Rocky's brother, Jody, stand up while the whole chamber applauded, and made a series of promises to reform our broken immigration system. I don't know anyone who could have heard that section of

President Trump's speech and not been moved beyond all words by what they had just heard.

Oh, wait. Yes I do.

As soon as the speech ended, Nancy Pelosi, the ice cream queen, couldn't stand not being in the spotlight. She put on a smug face, grabbed her pre-ripped copy of the speech, and then tore pages right in half as she turned to make sure the cameras caught her doing so. I wonder, Nancy, whether you managed to tear right through the names of some of those victims you and your fellow Democrats abandoned? Or did your little crease go right through the part of the speech where President Trump warned us about the coronavirus?

Was it not enough that you refused to meet with the families of Nisa Mickens, Kayla Cuevas, and Brandon Mendoza when they waited outside your office in 2019? The ones who called themselves angel moms because their sons and daughters had been murdered by illegal immigrants?

Right now, as I write this, there is a bill before the United States Congress that would allow the families of people who've been victimized by criminal illegal immigrants to sue the sanctuary cities that harbored their assailants. If it were to become law—and it should—these families would be entitled to compensation from those who protected the criminal and not the victim. These are people that our justice system has failed. We will never be able to make up for the fact that the selfish pandering of politicians pimping themselves for votes caused them incalculable and unnecessary misery. So, the least we can do is give them some sense of justice.

Until we have a Congress that is willing to step up and do its job, which is probably a long way away given that they have a 25 percent approval rating, and get in sync with the American people, President Trump and his administration will have to keep putting the pressure on the Left in other ways.[21]

DRASTIC MEASURES

They say that desperate times call for desperate measures, and that's never been truer than it is for our immigration crisis. Having exhausted all viable diplomatic approaches, President Trump has now been forced to resort to desperate measures—and the results have been astounding.

Take, for example, his recent spat with Governor Andrew Cuomo over New York State's decision not to share information about illegal immigrants with ICE—a class in pressure and negotiation by one of the best dealmakers in the world.

In December 2019, the Democrat-run legislature of New York passed a law that would finally, after years of back-and-forth bickering in the state legislature, allow the Department of Motor Vehicles to issue driver's licenses to illegal immigrants. These lawmakers decided that granting further rights to people who had already broken our laws was an issue of paramount importance.[22]

Are you wondering why?

Well, don't. The explanation is as simple as it is stupid. In the state of New York, as in most states, voter registration is done through the Department of Motor Vehicles. Anyone who can get a license, provided they're not a felon, can also register to vote. And historically, when only American citizens are allowed to vote, liberal politicians don't do so well. So, they've expended massive amounts of energy in the past few years making it easier for illegal aliens to vote, hoping this will win them the support of the illegal immigrant population forever. When the state of New York passed its Green Light Law in 2019, it cleared the way for illegal aliens to get driver's licenses, and those driver's licenses gave them the right to vote, giving liberals a die-hard group of Democrat-for-life voters.

Of course, New York isn't the only state to give illegal immigrants driver's licenses. Fifteen other states, as well as the District of Columbia and Puerto Rico, do that. The issue came when President Trump, whose main priority is the safety and security of American citizens, asked the Department of Motor Vehicles in New York to share information about the illegal aliens to whom it'd be giving licenses with the federal government. The president did not demand that the program be stopped or that any illegal aliens be deported. He only asked for information so that federal authorities could keep track of who these people were, where they lived, and whether they might pose a danger to their communities. It's the same information the federal government can access about any American citizen at any given time.

But Andrew Cuomo, once again pandering to the illegal immigrant community, refused. He knew that the media, eager as it is at all times to paint Trump as a racist, dictatorial maniac, would pick the story up and paint him as a brave defender of the weak. Remember, this was long before the series premiere of the *Andrew Cuomo Variety Hour*, so the governor was still desperate for as much media attention as he could get. Very few people outside of the state of New York even knew who he was.

So, Governor Cuomo instructed the Department of Motor Vehicles not to share any information about illegal immigrants who are granted driver's licenses with ICE. He did it because he knew his radical Leftist base would riot if he didn't, and he did it because he didn't think that President Trump would fight back.

He was wrong.

In early February, much to the dismay of travelers everywhere (myself included), President Trump announced that New Yorkers would no longer qualify for Global Entry, the system that allows preapproved travelers to bypass some security protocols in airports.[23] This was an unprecedented move by a president who knows how to apply pressure and hit second-rate politicians like Cuomo and de Blasio where it hurts. I know, because as someone who travels often, I was distraught by the lack of access to Global Entry. I was distraught by the fact that I could no longer go through the lines that I previously could, cutting my wait time by thirty to forty-five minutes. Thousands of travelers around New York State felt the same way. Within a few days, airport lines stalled, calls to the governor's office came in by the hundreds, and an enormous number of people were inconvenienced.

If you're the governor of New York, this is a nightmare scenario. At least we *thought* it was. Remember, this was back before the days of 408,000 cases of coronavirus, riots in lower Manhattan, and more than eleven thousand people dead in nursing homes.

But for President Trump, the pain was exactly the point. Since he's been in office, hundreds of people have suffered at the hands of illegal immigrants who could have been stopped if we only had adequate information about them. Those families have been forced to feel unimaginable pain twice over—once at the loss of their loved ones, then again at the thought that these senseless crimes could have been prevented. It was clear during President Trump's State of the Union address that he feels this pain, and he wants the rest of the country to feel it, too. His decision to suspend the Global Entry program, like his graphic recounting of the crimes committed by illegal immigrants during the State of the Union, was a small way to shake American citizens out of our complacency about this issue. It was a tiny reminder of the danger we are placing ourselves in every day that we allow people to enter this country unaccounted for and then disappear into our communities without getting any identifying information about them.

President Trump and his administration knew that every New Yorker who was refused Global Entry over those few months would have no choice but to start thinking about the danger posed by illegal immigrants. And if they got a little angry with him in the process, then so be it.

This was a decision that only President Trump, a president who'll damn the torpedoes for the American people irrespective of political consequences or anything else, could have made. Since day one of his administration, this man has fought to do what he thought was right no matter how unpopular or hated that made him in the press. Compared to all that, a little fight with Andrew Cuomo was nothing. I have no doubt that when he's elected again this November, he'll keep fighting for what he believes is right.

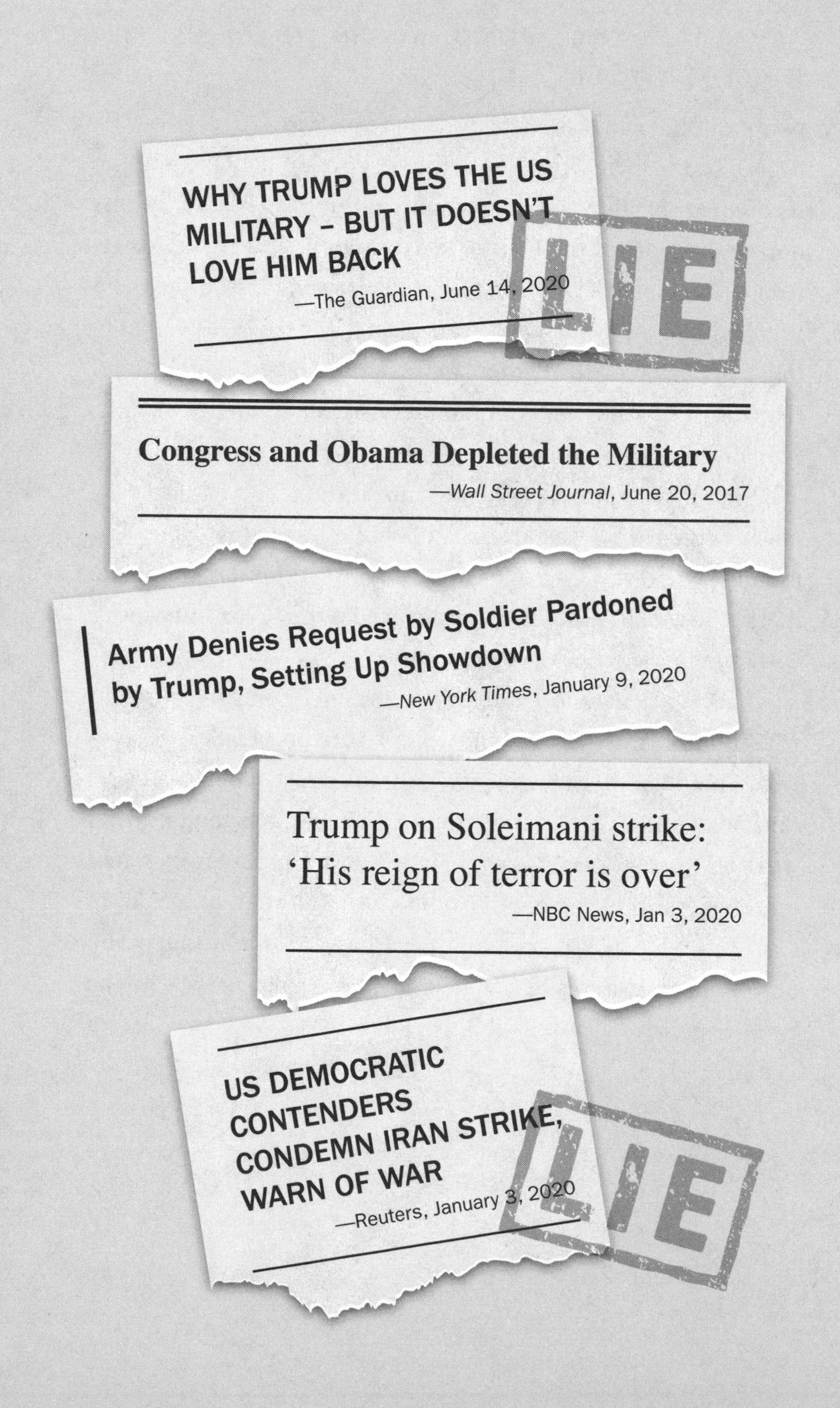
WHY TRUMP LOVES THE US MILITARY – BUT IT DOESN'T LOVE HIM BACK
—The Guardian, June 14, 2020
LIE
Congress and Obama Depleted the Military
—Wall Street Journal, June 20, 2017
Army Denies Request by Soldier Pardoned by Trump, Setting Up Showdown
—New York Times, January 9, 2020
Trump on Soleimani strike: 'His reign of terror is over'
—NBC News, Jan 3, 2020
US DEMOCRATIC CONTENDERS CONDEMN IRAN STRIKE, WARN OF WAR
—Reuters, January 3, 2020
LIE

Chapter Twelve

COMMANDER IN CHIEF

During my career in law enforcement, I've encountered more than my fair share of sick individuals. I've investigated, prosecuted, and sentenced career criminals, murderers, rapists, child molesters. During that time, I've learned that not all evil dirtbags are created equal. Some of them murder because of passion; others do it for hire; still others do it because they're clinically insane. For the most part, these people belong in jails or mental institutions.

Sometimes, though, you'll come across a cold, calculating monster—someone who's got his wits about him and all his mental faculties intact, but nonetheless chooses to spend his life inflicting pain and torture on his fellow man. These people are evil, and no amount of bloodshed is ever enough for them. They plan the kill, enjoy it, savor it, and keep memorabilia so they can enjoy it yet again.

This, folks, is the kind of animal Iranian terrorist general Qassem Soleimani was. It is why, one way or another, he needed to die—no ifs, ands, or buts, and no investigation, prosecution, or trial. Just eliminate him from the face of the earth. We shouldn't have had to breathe the same air he did.

As it happened, someone with a little more pull than me felt the same way about Soleimani.

THE STRIKE

In case you haven't noticed—and I don't know how you couldn't—President Trump doesn't like America's enemies. He doesn't like them one bit. Out of all of our enemies, the one he perhaps liked the least was Soleimani. If you're wondering how the Iranian terrorist got to the top of Donald Trump's shit list, let me give you a rundown of his qualifications.

Soleimani was radicalized by Muslim clerics as a young man and participated in a violent overthrow of the Iranian government in 1979.[1] You might remember the Iranian hostage crisis, which marked the lowest point in America's military reputation until Barack Obama became commander in chief. During that crisis, a group of Iranian college students who were supportive of the Iranian Revolution took over the US embassy in Tehran and held fifty-two American diplomats and citizens hostage for 444 days. For months, President Jimmy Carter—who displayed *almost* as much military ineptitude as President Obama during this crisis—tried in vain to get the hostages back. His attempts at diplomacy failed. When he finally did order a rescue mission called Operation Eagle Claw on April 12, 1980, it failed miserably when one of the helicopters being used crashed into a transport aircraft, leaving eight American servicemen dead.[2] In response to this colossal blunder, secretary of state Cyrus Vance—whose son, Cyrus Vance Jr., would later make an even bigger fool of himself than his father during his shameful tenure as DA in Manhattan—resigned from his position.[3]

Only when President Ronald Reagan was sworn into office did the thugs in Iran get the message that the United States would not be trifled with. They knew that they wouldn't be able to bully Ronald Reagan the way they had Jimmy Carter. So, on Inauguration Day in 1980, just a few minutes after Reagan was sworn in on the steps of the Capitol Building, the hostages were released.

Still, the 1979 revolt had brought about major changes in Iran. It had replaced secular rulers with Ayatollah Khomeini, a ruthless Islamic zealot who hated America about as much as he hated Israel. Although Khomeini died over thirty years ago, his legacy and the hatred he held toward the United States are what still drives the Iranian government. Today, Ali Khamenei, the current leader of Iran, still routinely refers to the United States as "the Great Satan" and makes violent threats against our country. He also posts tweets calling for the elimination of Israel, referring to those in the West as a "usurping, evil, wolf-like entity."[4] Oh, and by the way, he's allowed to say those things via his own Twitter account—which, to this day, has never been "fact-checked" by the company the way that President Trump's tweets are.

But back to Soleimani.

At the age of fourteen, he joined Iran's Revolutionary Guard, and he would eventually become the head of an elite unit of the Guard called the Quds Force. Part military intelligence, part terrorist cell, the Quds Force is sort of like a roving recruitment center for the world's lowlifes. While leading the bloody unit, Soleimani established Shiite militias in Iraq, Syria, and Afghanistan while joining other terrorist organizations such as Hezbollah and Hamas.[5]

To Soleimani, all those who didn't believe in the rigid doctrines of radical Islam—particularly those in Israel, one of the strongest allies of the United States in the region—were considered infidels. To them, of course, the term *infidels* includes everyone who isn't a radical believer in Islamic fundamentalism. To them, we're all infidels. He believed Jews were "evil usurpers" and Americans were "imperialist monsters," all of whom deserved to die for their crimes against Allah.[6] Anyone who died trying to destroy the enemies of Islam, according to the warped worldview of Soleimani and his band of thugs, were "martyrs" to the cause of radical Islam.[7]

Among his fellow terrorists, Soleimani was famous for his brutality and savagery, often ordering his followers to assassinate rivals, kidnap soldiers, and supply arms to terror groups. According to intelligence gathered by the Central Intelligence Agency, he personally directed the terror groups that killed thousands of Americans during the Iraq War.[8] And he killed them in the most cowardly, despicable way possible.

In 2011, the bloodthirsty Iranian helped to invent and manufacture devices called EFPs, short for "explosively formed projectiles," which could be hidden under rocks along broken roads in the desert. Once activated, these devices would fire molten copper slugs into the air, where they could penetrate armor, destroy tanks, and rip through the bodies of American soldiers like tissue paper. For anyone unfortunate enough to be caught in the path of one of these sadistic torture devices, the pain was excruciating and recovery was unlikely. The hot copper projectiles could crush bone, rip muscle, and melt the skin right off a young soldier's body.

According to the official statistics of the United States military, EFPs were responsible for just over 20 percent of all U.S.

combat deaths, and about 30 percent of all injuries.[9] Chances are if you see an American vet missing limbs or body parts, you can blame Soleimani. In previous wars, they would have died. But because of advances in medicine, they have been able to survive.

These devices were invented not simply to kill, but to maim, torture, and wound.

It's just inconceivable that we let him get away with murder for so long. Both George W. Bush and Barack Obama had shots at taking Soleimani out, but neither had the balls to pull the trigger on the operation. In the years after those missed opportunities, Qassem Soleimani went on to kill hundreds of American men and women—not to mention the thousands whose lives he ruined by injuring and maiming them. He ramped up production of his infamous roadside bombs and caused unspeakable carnage to soldiers and civilians from all over the world, from Syria and Iraq to Yemen, Israel, and Lebanon. There was virtually no country in the world untouched by this man's cruelty and appetite for carnage.

Because of Bush's and Obama's inaction—whether brought on by fear or indifference—he moved through the world with impunity, seemingly unafraid that he'd be attacked or arrested for his crimes. During that time, world leaders and diplomats from all over the globe were asking—practically begging—the United States to intervene and kill Soleimani.

One memorable plea came in 2011, after Soleimani and his Quds Force tried to hire a Mexican drug cartel to blow up a Saudi ambassador to the United States while he sat having lunch a few blocks from the White House. The plot failed when the head of the drug cartel that Soleimani approached turned out to be an informant for the United States Drug Enforcement

Administration, who reported the request immediately, sending the Quds Force scattering like the rats they are.[10] Due to a lack of action by the Obama administration, no one involved in this little scheme was ever brought to justice. But in the aftermath of this assassination attempt, two former American officials sat before Congress and told two different committees, on two separate occasions, that Soleimani needed to go—immediately.

"Soleimani travels a lot," said one of them, practically laying out the roadmap for a targeted killing. "He's all over the place. Go get him. Either try to capture him or kill him."[11]

Eventually that plea reached the White House, and nothing happened. Apparently, Obama and his cabal of lying liberals didn't want to treat Iran like the aggressive, dictatorial regime that it was; they wanted to sit down at the negotiating table and talk things out, as if the whole thing were just a schoolyard skirmish. They wanted to play nice and shake hands and send them over $1.5 billion in cash on pallets, as they later did as part of the disastrous Iran nuclear deal.[12] What's interesting, of course, is that President Obama could easily have wired this money. There was no good reason to send it all over in cash on pallets the way he did.

Many have wondered why over one billion dollars in cash was sent to Iran. The excuse the Obama administration initially gave was that we didn't have a banking relationship with them, as if they weren't a country with a budget and a government and a military operation. Some have suggested the cash was nothing more than a ransom to free three Americans held by Tehran. But the Obama administration denied that, saying the money was owed to Iran because of a long-standing dispute tied to a failed arms deal from the 1970s. So, we paid them almost fifty years later for arms after they held American hostages for 444 days. It certainly sounds like something Obama would do!

So, it's no wonder that when the warning came from these two brave government officials that Qassem Soleimani should be assassinated, President Obama and his administration took a hard pass.

Luckily, Donald Trump has the balls that Barack Obama does not.

Like a rat out of a hole, Soleimani showed his head two days after Christmas 2019. His elite unit fired missiles into army bases in Iraq and killed an American military contractor. American intelligence then warned the president that the Quds Force leader wasn't going to stop there. He was planning to bomb an American embassy in Baghdad and assassinate American diplomats and personnel throughout the region.

President Trump put his military brass on notice. Find this scum, and find him fast.

A week later, in the middle of a cold night in early January, President Donald Trump walked into the White House Situation Room. There waiting for him were some of his most trusted advisors. Secretary of State Mike Pompeo, Secretary of Defense Mark T. Esper, and Vice President Mike Pence.[13] The president sat at the conference table and in front of a screen the size of a laptop computer. The AMX audio and video control panel would allow him to watch the strike in real time. Just minutes after the president arrived, a voice emanated from the comms device at the center of the conference room table. The drone's pursuit of Soleimani's convoy had begun.[14]

According to reports, General Soleimani was famous among his fellow terrorists for giving long, tearful speeches to mercenaries and suicide bombers he'd send out into battle to kill Americans.

He used to weep with them, apologizing profusely, saying he only wished he could be "martyred" in battle instead of them.

President Trump was about to grant Soleimani his wish. Less than two minutes after the voice notified the room that pursuit had begun, the drone fired its missiles at Soleimani's motorcade. In the car with him was Abu Mahdi al-Muhandis, the commander of the Kata'ib Hezbollah militia, one of the groups that was responsible for the attack on the US embassy in Baghdad on New Year's Eve.

When the kill was confirmed, President Trump thanked everyone in the room and returned to the residence in the White House. For nearly fifty years, Soleimani conducted a reign of terror that killed and maimed Americans and our allies as previous United States presidents either looked the other way or didn't have the stomach or the determination to rid the world of such heinous terrorists. In less than five minutes, Donald Trump had him removed from the face of the earth—piece by piece.

THE LYING, LEAKING OBAMA YEARS

In Obama's White House, image was all that mattered. Military decisions were scrutinized by a bunch of twentysomething Ivy League Lefties in basement offices, then poll-tested and focus-grouped to death. If anyone actually managed to reach a decision, the battlefield opportunity would have passed, and the situation would have gotten much worse. There was no central leadership and certainly no expertise in warfare. Instead of battle-tested warriors making calls, you had people like Ben Rhodes, a young, liberal bozo whose only qualification for the job was a degree in fiction writing from New York University. Instead of American heroes like Michael Flynn, you had Susan

Rice, a woman who had sought to subvert a presidential election in 2016 and then lied about it. In the words of one general who worked with him, President Obama and his team "didn't seem interested in getting to know the military."[15]

From their first day, Obama and his band of liberal losers decided that America's posture on the world's stage would be meek and apologetic. Instead of a proud military that had historically struck fear in the hearts of every miscreant on the planet, Obama wanted his soldiers "seen but not heard." What kind of a commander in chief issues an order like that? I'll tell you what kind: one who was an embarrassment to the men and women who served under him. President Obama promised to "finish the job" in Afghanistan when he knew full well it was impossible. He set a red line in Syria that he had no intention of upholding but never expected that he'd be called upon to actually deliver on his promise.[16]

Worse even than the spineless way Obama commanded his armed forces was the way he gutted it. In his first term, he promised his defense secretary, Robert Gates, that the cuts he proposed to the military would be minimal, just one dollar for every ten he cut from domestic spending.

That was a lie.

What he did was demand that half of the proposed cuts come out of the military budget. Obama didn't care that many of our B-52 bombers were built more than fifty years earlier, when Kennedy was president. He didn't care that many of our tanks, infantry carriers, and artillery have been around since Ronald Reagan. He didn't care that our nuclear arsenal was atrophied and outdated. By the end of his second term, he announced he was cutting our troops by forty thousand, a step toward a proposed eventual reduction of almost half a million. In 2014, he had Defense Secretary Chuck Hagel announce that the Obama administration would be shrinking the size of the military down to "pre–World War II" levels, eliminating an entire class of Air Force attack jets and jettisoning other key pieces of military equipment—and they said that like it was a good thing.[17]

President Obama's actions indicated not only that did he not care about the military, but that his intention was to reduce and make the military impotent on the world stage. As Russia and China were advancing their military arsenal and their technology, Obama was intentionally moving it back decades.

As if that weren't bad enough, he stopped training the soldiers that he kept.[18] I'm not kidding. According to an op-ed in the *Washington Post* written by retired Major General Robert Scales, under Obama fewer than one-third of combat brigades were ready for combat.[19]

Obama's sin against our military was biblical in proportion. During his reign of ineptitude, the morale of our men and women in uniform sunk to its lowest level. A general who worked for his administration said he and his fellow members of this military were "embarrassed to be associated with the amateurism of the Obama administration's attempts to craft a plan that makes strategic sense."[20]

By the time he left office, only about 30 percent of our troops approved of his leadership as commander in chief.

Is anyone really surprised by this? I wasn't. When he arrived in the Oval Office, President Obama had no experience making decisions or handling matters of life and death. He'd been a community organizer, then a professor, then a professional politician, always looking for the next job. He had no interest in trying to understand how the military worked or what was necessary to keep it going. More importantly, he had no interest in having America be number one on the world stage, whether it be militarily, economically, or in any other way—as evidenced by the fact that he apologized for America within weeks of taking the Oval Office.

So, one is left to ask: Why on earth did the man take the job if one of his first acts was to apologize to the world for letting America be America and then starting to tear it down militarily?

A REAL LEADER

When President Trump became the commander in chief, on the other hand, you could see the chests of our military leaders swell. Finally, there was someone in the Oval Office who would take the shackles off and allow our fighting men and women to once again be the envy of the world.

He turned his attention right away to rebuilding our military. He signed the National Defense Authorization Act, which approved $738 billion in defense spending.[21] The money went to investing in combat aircraft like the F-35, F/A-18, and F-15EX and Black Hawk and Chinook helicopters. It went to buy new or update existing submarines, destroyers, and guided missile frigates. It raised soldiers' pay and provided for education and childcare improvements. It provided the funds not only to train all of our combat brigades and make them ready to fight, but to find ways to make the decision-making process in the Pentagon more efficient.

Then there were the battlefield decisions. Instead of a war of attrition against ISIS, as Obama fought, President Trump gave his commanders the green light to fight a war of annihilation, which included telling General Mattis that his experience in terms of fighting a war was sufficient to make decisions regarding that war. He untied their hands, allowing generals to do what generals do, leaving out the pollsters, the fiction writers, the finger-to-the-wind people, which was his strength, as evidenced by the fact that he rid the Middle East of the caliphate. Trump let the generals be generals. He did not insert himself in a way that interfered with their experience so that he could make political points, as Obama did.

This war of annihilation also included taking out ISIS leader Abu Bakr al-Baghdadi.

I was in the Oval Office when the president met with the Special Forces who took out al-Baghdadi, including the four-legged hero called Conan who risked his life to help kill the ISIS leader.

When they chased al-Baghdadi into a dead-end tunnel, the Delta Force team sent the beautiful Belgian Malinois in first because they believed the coward was wearing a suicide vest. They were right. On seeing the dog, al-Baghdadi detonated the vest, killing himself and the three children he'd brought with him as shields. The blast collapsed the tunnel on Conan, who was severely injured.

I remember that when the press alerted the world that al-Baghdadi was dead, I felt terrible about the three children he had brought with him as shields. How disgusting! But I was fascinated by the story of the dog who had chased this terrorist into the tunnel. I've always been a dog lover, and I had heard that Conan had been injured in the attack as well. I knew I wanted to meet him.

Within a few days, I was on the phone with President Trump. I asked him if he had any plans to bring Conan the hero dog to the United States.

He asked why that would be necessary. So, I told him.

"Mr. President," I said, "America loves a dog, especially a hero dog. You've *got* to bring him to America."

After several phone calls, I learned that the dog was injured, that he was still working, and that his handlers were still working. Finally, because of my persistence, after many weeks, I got some good news.

The president's personal secretary called to tell me that Conan the hero dog was finally coming to the Oval Office. I intended to go see him with Lara Trump, who rescues animals all the time. In the end, Lara couldn't attend because of a prior commitment, and Conan had no plans to be there for more than one day.

But nothing was going to stop me.

On November 25, I went by myself to the White House. I sat in the West Wing waiting, and finally the president called me in. I remember entering the Oval Office and seeing a crowd of tall men in dark suits all over the place. They were against the wall like wallpaper wrapped around the office. I saw the White House chief of staff, Vice President Mike Pence, many generals surrounding the president, and six of the Special Forces soldiers who'd carried out the strike. President Trump was sitting behind the Resolute Desk, and there, in front of the desk, facing him along with the Special Forces, was Conan! For a second, I had the urge to just run over and pet him on the head, and then I remembered: *This is a killer dog. This is the Oval Office. This is the president.* So, I stood against the wall as the president introduced me to everyone. I said hi. But there was only one thing on my mind.

"Mr. President," I said, "can I approach the dog?"

Everybody looked at me like I was nuts. But slowly, without waiting for an answer, I approached Conan, made eye contact with his handler, who nodded, and I put my head right up to his face while I rubbed his head. Then I grabbed the leash and started walking around the Oval Office with him. Within a few minutes, he was my new best friend!

To this day, Vice President Mike Pence tells a story about that day.

"Everybody loves Judge Jeanine," he says. "But nobody knows how tough she is. In a room full of generals, she goes up to the killer dog and rubs his ears in and says, 'You're so cute!' We were all waiting for the dog to maul her."

I was sad to give the leash back when Conan was to be introduced to the press and the nation.

That afternoon, I stood on the Colonnade and watched as the president, along with the First Lady and vice president, introduced Conan to the press. As usual, the press couldn't let the feel-good moment just happen. Instead, they began berating President Trump with mean-spirited questions. At one point, only half joking, the president told a reporter he was lucky that Conan was in a good mood.

"He's trained to attack," the president said.

Though I might have played a role in his honoring Conan, President Trump needed no such coaxing to personally thank our fighting men and women in uniform. His colloquy to make those Special Forces men comfortable and at ease was really something to witness. These are men who kill for a living, who aren't accustomed to being in suits, who are standing within a couple feet of the President of the United States. You could tell that a shirt and tie were not the most comfortable attire for them to be in. Their biceps were bulging out of their jackets. But they were in awe of his humor and his down-to-earth manner. He was a regular guy cracking jokes, making sure they were comfortable. He told them how proud he was of them. How grateful the country was, how impressed he was. Tremendous respect was given to these men on that day. I doubt they would have gotten the same respect from the president before President Trump. He took pictures with them and gave them gifts, little memorabilia for them to take. The First Lady came in, gracious and beautiful as always. They see the combative Donald Trump. If the public could only see moments like that—this is a guy that blue-collar America loves. This is a guy who's not haughty, not condescending, doesn't think he's better because he's the President of the United States. This is a guy who's got one vision—and that vision is for a strong America and a strong military protecting this country, including a dog, and everyone in that room knew it.

And in the end, I made a friend. It's the best picture in my whole library, and you can see it on the back cover of this book.

HATERS

Recently there's a lot of talk of friction between the president and his military leaders. The media has reported that some of the top brass of the military establishment doesn't get along with Donald Trump—at least not after they've left his administration and entered the world of political commentary, book deals, and Left-leaning think tanks.

No surprise there.

In my opinion, they should all be ashamed of themselves. Rather than trying to cash in on their time working with President Trump, telling lies about him for money like political whores, they should be thankful. If you're *ever* in a position to work with President Trump, you should thank your lucky stars that he asked you, and thank your lucky stars that you had the opportunity to work in the White House in the first place. Instead, these people want to go out and cheapen the commander in chief for a few bucks.

It makes me sick.

Here's what I know: President Trump has always had tremendous respect for law enforcement and the military. He also understands that force is what's needed to gain respect, and sometimes weak people don't like that.

Yet for all his billions, Donald Trump is a regular guy. I knew it when I used to walk down the streets of New York City with him. He would always stop to talk to cops, construction workers, and street vendors who were so excited even to meet him. When he was in restaurants that he owned, he would always go into the kitchens to talk to the line cooks. The idea that he doesn't connect with people or that he isn't the man to lead this nation is hogwash.

If you want proof, just look at his relationship with the soldiers of the US military. I've watched President Trump greet the men and women who protect us. His gratitude and admiration for them is remarkable. It's also a private matter for him. Yes, I really mean private. As everyone knows, President Trump never shies away from the spotlight. When he meets with our troops, however, there's a Donald Trump you literally rarely see. When he travels to a war zone, he spends most of his time with the soldiers, not in some safe corner with the generals. Last Thanksgiving, he served the troops turkey and stuffing. He and the First Lady spent much of his time there taking photos with them. These aren't the phony photo ops his predecessors did. The same thing that made Donald Trump one of the most successful real estate titans in the world is the same thing that makes him a great commander in chief.

To him, the boots on the ground are every bit as important as any fancy four-star general—in fact, they're more so. If you need proof of this, allow me to introduce you to Army Special Forces major Mathew Golsteyn.

MERCY

At first, Major Mathew Golsteyn's story was like something out of a war movie. Then it turned into a horror show and an embarrassment for the brave men and women who fight for our freedom. It could have ended as a great American military travesty were it not for President Trump.

The story begins in Afghanistan, in February 2010. Obama had just sent thirty thousand more troops into that godforsaken country, extending the never-ending war while depleting his fighting forces. The first big battle of the so-called surge was the battle of Marjah, a town filled with Taliban warriors and the agricultural center of Afghanistan's poppy fields. But Obama's Trump-hating general in charge of the operation, Stanley McChrystal, was interested in more than just the removal of the insurgents and heroin suppliers who filled Marjah. He wanted to install his own hand-picked government.

It was a classic example of "nation building," the Democrats' favorite foreign policy, only instead of a whole country it was just a town. Hey, you gotta start somewhere, right? (Just ask John Bolton, who never met a small village he didn't want to bomb and then build back up in a few years.) McChrystal's pick to run the government he was installing was Abdul Zahir Aryan, a real beauty. Aryan spent four years in jail for stabbing his stepson, who had intervened in the beating he was giving his wife.

As is always the case in these ill-conceived politicized military schemes, the people who make the decisions sit in cushy armchairs or parade around in dress uniform while soldiers on the battlefield are injured or killed.

During the battle of Marjah, Major Golsteyn led a patrol through muddy poppy fields to locate and destroy several enemy sniper locations that were inflicting severe damage on American and Afghani soldiers. When one of the vehicles that accompanied Golsteyn's company became stuck in the mud, heavy enemy machine gun fire pinned down the patrol. In an open battlefield, Golsteyn and his company were sitting ducks. For four hours, machine guns and rifles firing tungsten steel core penetrator rounds rained bullets on them. Despite the risk, however, Golsteyn several times carried wounded soldiers under heavy fire to a medical support team and safety. He then took the matter of the machine gun nest into his own hands. Completely exposed, the major fired a shoulder-held anti-tank gun into a small structure where one of the machine gun nests was located. The direct hit disabled enemy fire long enough for him to coordinate an airstrike by F/A-18 Hornet jets. For his heroism, the Army awarded him a Silver Star.

That part was the war movie. Now comes the horror show.

Two days before Golsteyn's heroic actions won him the Silver Star, the major led a team searching for insurgents and explosives. Two members of that team, Marine sergeant Jeremy R. McQueary and Marine lance corporal Larry M. Johnson, opened a booby-trapped garage door and were blown to bits.

Sergeant McQueary was born in Columbus, Indiana. His father was a sheriff's deputy. He joined the Marines when he was just eighteen. He married his high school sweetheart. His wife, Rae, became pregnant between his second and last tour in Afghanistan. His son, Hadley, was five months old when McQueary was killed.

Lance Corporal Johnson was nineteen when he was killed. Before he joined the Marines, he lived with his parents in Scranton, Pennsylvania. When he told his older sister that he was going to enlist, she chuckled. Larry was just five foot seven and didn't look like the Marine type. His height, however, had little to do with the size of his heart. He would call his mom via a satellite phone when he was being sent on mission, even sometimes when he was not supposed to. While fighting in Afghanistan, he bought her a Crock-Pot for Christmas one year.

US troops would capture the bombmaker and a cache of explosives soon after. He'd been credibly identified by a reliable informant. Then, for reasons we might never fully know, the Army decided to let the bombmaker walk free.

To add insult to injury, Major Golsteyn and another US soldier were tasked with escorting the murderous bombmaker off base. As infuriated as the major must have been, he would later say that he decided to give the alleged murderer the benefit of the doubt. He told himself that if the bombmaker walked in any direction besides toward the battlefield and the Taliban, he would let him go free. But if he didn't, then Golsteyn would know that he was going back to make more bombs that would kill more soldiers like Jeremy McQueary and Larry Johnson.

The bombmaker walked straight toward the Taliban camp. It was several years later that Major Golsteyn admitted to killing the bombmaker while he was interviewing for a job with the CIA. He was honest. When the Army found out, they first took away his Silver Star, then took away his Special Forces insignia, and finally kicked him out of the armed services. That's how the Army treated a bona fide American hero.

It was at this point that the story goes from bad to worse.

My Fox colleague Bret Baier invited Major Golsteyn onto to his show and asked him point-blank if he'd killed the bombmaker. Golsteyn could have dodged the question. He could have lied.

However, unlike the Democrats, who lie to us all the time, Major Golsteyn told the truth. He was of the ilk who have no intention of lying, who represent a commitment to truth and honor and the best of America.

In his heart, he knew the right thing was the truth. He answered honestly.

Soon after the show, the Army reopened its case against the major and then charged him with murder.

If Obama were still president, heroes like Major Golsteyn would now be serving a life sentence at the United States Disciplinary Barracks at Fort Leavenworth or some other military prison. Obama preferred to release traitors and terrorists. His preference was not for battlefield heroes—his preference was for people like Chelsea Manning, whose sentence he commuted despite the fact that Manning was a traitor to the United States.

Donald Trump, however, is not Barack Obama. First of all, he doesn't wear a helmet when he rides his bicycle. Second of all, he doesn't pardon traitors. He pardons people who fight for this country.

On October 12, 2019, the president tweeted that he was reviewing Major Golsteyn's case. "We train our boys to be killing machines," he wrote in the tweet, "then prosecute them when they kill!"

Sensing he was going to pardon the major, senior Pentagon officials came at the president hard, lobbying for him to let the Army justice system take care of the case. Though people might think that military justice operates apart from any outside influence, that's just not the case. The Army's criminal justice system is subjected to enormous pressure by the liberal press. The Lefties in the media smelled blood, and wanted Golsteyn sacrificed. But what made the case a near travesty was that there's a whole bunch of decision-makers in the upper echelons of our armed forces who are either leftovers from the Obama years, or even worse. For those of you who don't think there is a deep state in the Pentagon, think again.

When President Trump first took office, he deferred to his generals. I had dinner with him once in his private dining room and asked about his relationship with them. He told me that when it comes to battlefield decisions, he leaves it up to the generals. They are the people, he said, who know what's going on.

But in the years since, the president realized that many of the guys in charge, some of whom had been in charge for decades, had agendas just like the entrenched administrative state within the federal government. Over years, these generals built an internal power structure that operated outside the normal military chain of command. There were elements in the Pentagon, he found out, that were part of the deep state.

If these generals had their way, Major Golsteyn would no doubt now be somewhere in a military prison serving a life sentence. President Trump, however, didn't care how many stars they wore, he wasn't going to let the generals politicize and interfere with the operation of war in a major theatre.

The following month President Trump issued the major a full pardon.

It infuriates me when people question the president's loyalty and love for the military and our heroes in uniform. From what we've seen, it's clear how much they mean to him. It's obvious that, the Left has an agenda here. They want to take a man who is beloved by most soldiers in the United States military—one who has fought tirelessly for them every day he's been in office—and make it seem like he's an enemy of the armed forces. On June 26, 2020, the *New York Times* published a story claiming that the Russians—surprise, surprise—offered bounties to Afghan militants for killing US troops.[22] They reported that President Trump knew about this arrangement and did nothing.

Hogwash.

In the days that followed, President Trump made it clear that he had never received a briefing on this information. Several members of his intelligence community also pointed out that this claim was completely unverified, making it little more than a rumor.

If the liberal lying Left wants to start making a president responsible for every allegation or rumor that is not corroborated, the presidential daily briefing would be longer than one of Joe Biden's rambling stories. Nobody would be able to read everything inside, and the only things the president should be reading in the presidential daily briefings is what has been verified.

By the way, is anyone surprised that of all the thousands of pieces of unverified intelligence that are floating around, the

New York Times just happened to settle on the one that involved Russia? The one country in the Left's years-long conspiracy theory to take down President Trump?

To the reporters who keep breaking these stories: Get over it! Snap out of it! See a therapist, whatever you need to do. But we, the American people, have had enough of it!

Here's the truth. We haven't had a commander in chief like Trump since Reagan. Period. He's not only as patriotic as Reagan, but he's even more forward-thinking.

On December 20, 2019, President Trump created the first new branch of the military since 1947. In doing so, he took a huge step in ensuring the safety of the American people for generations to come. The press scoffed. Liberal losers on late night TV had field day. If they'd bothered to remove their heads from their derrières for a minute, they might have realized how vital the protection of the thousands of our military and civilian satellites is. They provide everything from guidance systems for our ballistic missiles and surveillance of troop movements to GPS. If you think your package from Amazon is going to arrive without a satellite, you're sorely mistaken. The Space Force will not only protect our way of life; it will give us the upper hand in satellite weaponry, which both Russia and China are quickly developing.

Look, I can use the rest of the pages in this book giving you reasons why Donald Trump is the best thing to happen to our military since they stopped riding horses. But you don't have to listen to me. If you want to know what kind of a commander in chief President Trump is, ask Mathew Golsteyn's wife and family. Or ask any of the other soldiers who finally have someone in their corner.

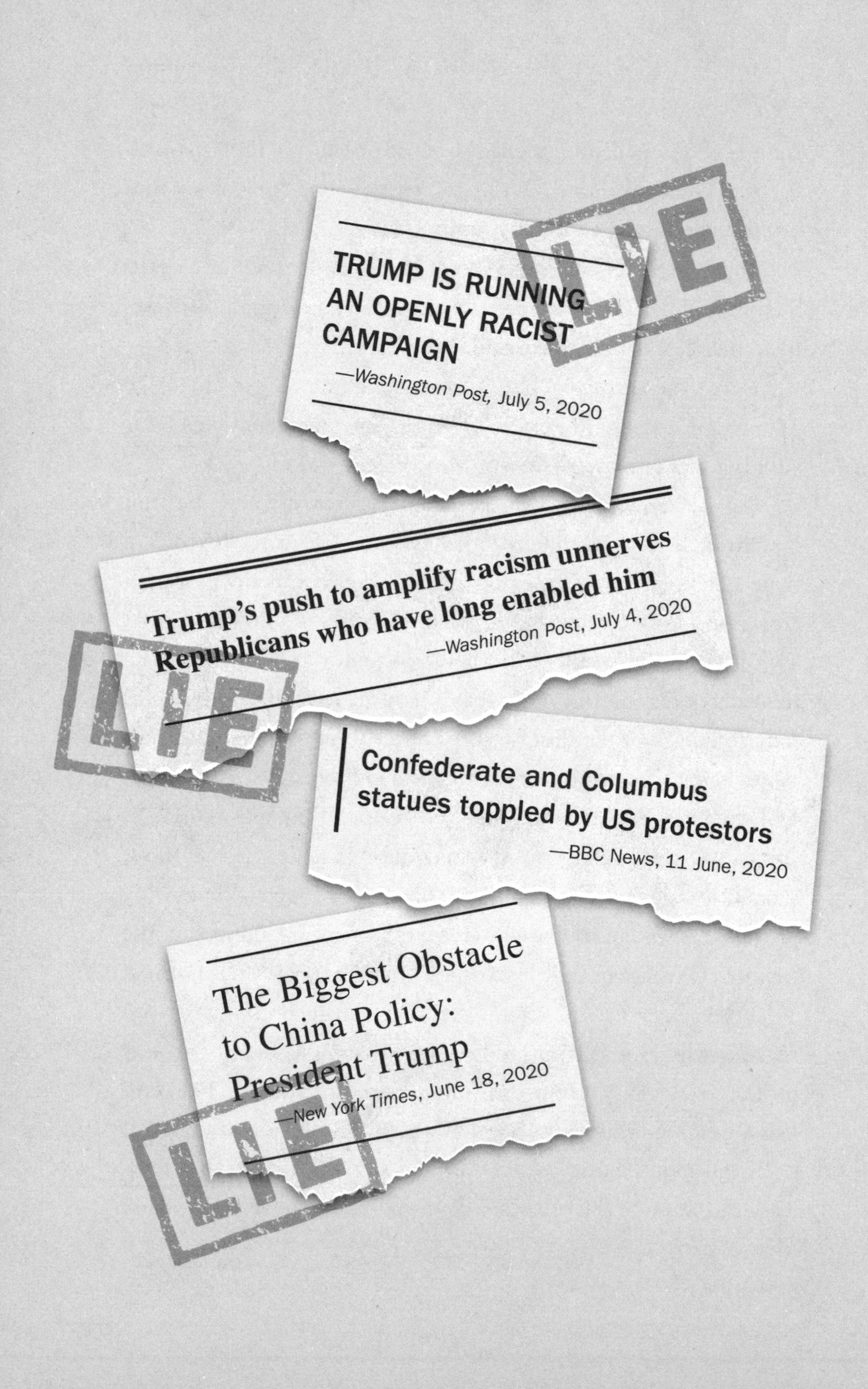
TRUMP IS RUNNING AN OPENLY RACIST CAMPAIGN
—Washington Post, July 5, 2020
LIE
Trump's push to amplify racism unnerves Republicans who have long enabled him
—Washington Post, July 4, 2020
LIE
Confederate and Columbus statues toppled by US protestors
—BBC News, 11 June, 2020
The Biggest Obstacle to China Policy: President Trump
—New York Times, June 18, 2020
LIE

Chapter Thirteen

CLOSING STATEMENT

On the day before the Fourth of July, President Donald Trump traveled to South Dakota, where he was set to give a speech in front of Mount Rushmore. The monument, according to the anchors on CNN, is "majestic" and "quite a sight."[1]

Of course, they said that a long time ago—all the way back in 2014, when President Barack Obama visited.

When President Trump announced he would be visiting the monument for a speech, the media had nothing good to say about it. Once the fake newscasters heard that President Trump would be using the monument as a location for a speech about how the Left is trying to "tear down our country's history," they started to...well, *tear down our country's history.*

Suddenly, Mount Rushmore was not an impressive monument to four of our nation's most prominent presidents. Instead, it was "a monument of two slaveowners on land wrestled away from Native Americans." Three days before President Trump's speech, the *New York Times* posted a tweet that read: "Mount Rushmore was built on land that belonged to the Lakota tribe and sculpted by a man who had strong bonds with the Ku Klux Klan. It features the faces of 2 U.S. presidents who were slave-holders."[2] Several other media organizations chimed in.

This, folks, is what happens when you negotiate with terrorists.

For months, mobs of angry Leftists had been swarming the streets of our cities, attacking our police, burning down our buildings, looting our stores, and defacing monuments to our nation's history. Their actions began a violent crime wave that continues to this day. In Chicago, Baltimore, Minneapolis, San Francisco, and New York—all cities that had the misfortune of being run by liberal Democrats when the Covid pandemic and the riots arrived—the homicide rates had increased dramatically. Shootings began occurring with alarming frequency. The percentages were up 50, 100, 200 percent. It wasn't long before law-abiding citizens became terrified to go outside and walk the streets for fear they would become victims of the violence.

By the Fourth of July, Americans felt as if they were in the middle of another revolution. Most years, Americans celebrate their independence from Great Britain with parades, barbecues, and picnics generally held on bright, sunny summer days. They celebrate the Declaration of Independence, where it is written that all men are created equal and possess certain unalienable rights, which include life, liberty, and the pursuit of happiness. When that document was written, it was agreed that the purpose of government—whose power comes from the consent of the governed—was to secure these rights.

This year, it was different. We were being tested in ways that were both unfamiliar and frightening. Dark clouds of hate and anger surrounded us as Black Lives Matter, Antifa, and anarchists who hate America tried to tell us what we should think and say, what we should believe, and what was right and wrong.

Calls for the destruction and toppling of historical statues, defunding police departments, occupying and overtaking public and private property, and not just calls but *demands* for socialism shocked our collective consciousness.

As these anarchists destroyed property, burned buildings, and looted stores, we paid for the destruction and damage and cleaned up after them with millions of our taxpayer dollars.

Yet our leaders, afraid of pressure from the "woke" mob, often gave in to their demands.

When they came for the monuments of Confederate generals, mayors and governors sat by and did nothing. They watched while statues of Robert E. Lee and other Confederates came down in Southern cities. Many of us who feel no affinity for the Confederacy were indifferent about seeing these statues removed. Then, when the mob had torn down all the Confederates and came for the Founding Fathers, only a few raised objections. On June 14, a statue of Thomas Jefferson—the man who put pen to paper and wrote our Declaration of Independence—was pulled down in Portland. So were statues of George Washington and Christopher Columbus.[3]

On June 20 in San Francisco,[4] the mob came for a statue of Ulysses S. Grant, the man who galvanized the Union Army to defeat the Confederacy. By the time *that* statue came down, the mob had scrawled slurs on it with red spray paint. The real history—which these Leftists never seem interested in—is much different. When Grant married his wife, according to his biographer Ron Chernow, he *did* inherit one slave, who'd been with his wife's family for years. Then, rather than selling that slave for an enormous profit, Grant—who was dirt poor at the time, barely able to afford clothing for himself—set that slave free.[5] In the years that followed, Grant commandeered the Union Army during the Civil War and won, effectively ending slavery. Then, he was elected President of the United States. During his time in the White House, he worked to support reconstruction in the South and to fight for equality for all people. As one of his final acts in office, he founded the Department of Justice for the sole purpose of hunting down and prosecuting members of the Ku Klux Klan.[6]

But sure, let's say he's a racist because "woke Twitter" says he is.

Who are these people who claim to be about eliminating racism yet tear down statues of great men like Ulysses S. Grant? Who are these people who destroyed the monument of an abolitionist in Boston, paid for by the first all-black regiment who fought in the Civil War? As I write this, the mob is even eyeing the Abraham Lincoln emancipation monument.

Black Entertainment Television founder Robert Johnson is slamming protestors for toppling statues—even the ones of Confederate generals—calling these protestors "borderline anarchists."[7] He questions whether black Americans even support this. And the universities where this all started? Today, Princeton University announced it will remove the name of President Woodrow Wilson from its campus, citing his "racist thinking."[8]

These protestors have burned and vandalized churches, from St. Patrick's in New York City to St. John's in Washington, DC, a historic church a short walk from the White House, where Abraham Lincoln would go to pray. Christian figures and symbols—Mother Mary, even Jesus Christ himself—have been targeted.[9]

Think about it.

In what states were you prevented from practicing your religion during coronavirus? All Democrat states. Now, think about the states where the militancy was allowed to happen during the worst of the riots. All Democrat. Are you beginning to see a pattern here? There's far less looting and burning in red states because there the Republican governors had no problem calling in the National Guard in addition to ordering police to arrest those violating the law.

So, why do they do this? Is there a method to this madness?

Not really.

These mobs behave this way because they've been fed a lie—the biggest one of them all, upon which the Left has based its entire twisted playbook for tearing down America, both literally *and* figuratively. The lie is that the United States of America is an evil country, founded on racism and genocide. Theirs is a revisionist history based on dishonest documents like the *New York Times*' 1619 Project, or the litany of bestselling books on how to deal with our evil, systemically racist society. These Leftists believe America is beyond redemption.

In their eyes, there is nothing in our history worth saving. These people would tear down a monument to George Washington as quickly as they'd toss out a used scrap of paper. If they had their way, the whole country would look like Portland, Oregon, the statues of the Founding Fathers all gone, leaving only a statue of Vladimir Lenin standing.

Make no mistake: This is an insurgency that is destabilizing our government. Where are our leaders condemning these acts? Where are our leaders, both Democrat and Republican? Where is the outrage? Are they afraid? Where is the guy running for president, Joe Biden? He's not criticizing this. He doesn't need to come out of his bunker to say the obvious. He can hide down there, but at least he needs to take a stand—or is he in favor of this? Is he in favor of this unruly lawlessness? Where is Nancy Pelosi, who can't wait to show up in front of a camera to show off her color-coordinated masks? Her only thought has been to blame Republicans for the death of George Floyd, and now to blame Donald Trump for the coronavirus. Where is Hillary Clinton? She hasn't stopped talking since she lost the election. Where is the chorus of people we elected, we campaigned for, we believed in, to stand up for law and order?

One leader we have heard from is Barack Obama.

"There is a great awakening going on in this country," he said during a digital town hall with his old sidekick Joe Biden.[10]

So, *that's* what you call it? A great awakening?

The anti-cop sentiment and rage has caused police deaths and over a thousand injured across the country. In spite of the incredible number of shootings in Chicago in one weekend, prompting President Trump to send a letter to Governor J. B. Pritzker and Mayor Lori Lightfoot calling on them to protect victims, these Democrats are at best hands-off and at worst encouraging when it comes to this lawlessness. This lawlessness creates an atmosphere of anarchy that itself invites actions. Like a homeless man sleeping on a sidewalk set on fire by firecrackers by a couple of thugs.[11] Like a man shot in cold blood in New York City simply wiping down his car.[12] Like a white employee in Macy's beaten down by a black man in the store with no one coming to help.

Now, no surprise, gun and ammunition sales are through the roof.[13] The combination of the coronavirus lockdown and the daily shock of repeated lawlessness has people on edge. They feel helpless and alone. With crime statistics increasing, gun purchases rising, police reluctant or told not to respond, including to 911 calls that may yield no response, there is destined to be trouble.

Luckily, President Trump is willing to stand up to the Left. He is the only man who has shown time and time again that he has the grit, resolve, and determination to face them down with everything in his power. He refuses to apologize for keeping Americans safe. He won't back down. In the lead-up to his Fourth of July speech, given on July 3, with the country burning down around him and the Leftist media calling what he was about to say hateful, racist, and disgusting, he had the courage to stand in front of one of our nation's greatest monuments and deliver the message anyway:

> The radical view of American history is a web of lies—all perspective is removed, every virtue is obscured, every motive is twisted, every fact is distorted, and every flaw is magnified until the history is purged and the record is disfigured beyond all recognition.
>
> This movement is openly attacking the legacies of every person on Mount Rushmore. They defile the memory of Washington, Jefferson, Lincoln, and Roosevelt. Today, we will set history and history's record straight.[14]

And he did. Throughout his Fourth of July address, President Trump reminded us of the people who made America great in the first place—the ones who sacrificed for their country, seeking to make the United States of America a better place through hard work and ingenuity, not destruction, rioting, and mayhem.

Still, the lies persist.

CHINA

As we march toward the election in November, we are sure to hear that President Trump is not doing enough to combat the threat of coronavirus.

This is a lie.

The truth?

The coronavirus, originating in Wuhan, China, has already taken 140,000 American lives, sent over 51 million Americans to the unemployment line, triggered the expenditure of trillions of dollars to avoid complete economic collapse, and tested the American spirit as never before. To win the battle against this deadly virus, we know what is required: masks, social distancing, and cleanliness. Along with those personal responsibilities, the Trump administration continues to move at warp speed to get the vaccines, therapeutics, testing, and personal protective equipment needed to fight this battle. But as we fight together, we cannot let the negative emotions directly caused by the unleashing of the virus to tear us apart.

Many are legitimately mad, angry, and depressed because they have been locked down in their homes. Many are anxious because of lost jobs or businesses that they know will ultimately fail. Many are desperate because of the inability to pay their rent, mortgages, or credit card debt. Many are even fearful of becoming infected with the virus itself. Many parents working from home, thrown into the job of teaching their own children, are frustrated as the teachers unions push back on schools reopening. Many churches and religious institutions are off-limits, while marijuana dispensaries are open as essential businesses. Many are unable to work out and blow off steam because of the refusal to allow gyms to reopen. And many grandparents are isolated as children and grandchildren are not allowed to visit for fear of infecting them.

These are all predictable and understandable reactions and emotions brought on by the virus, which has now teed up issues for Americans to deal with that in another time we might have dealt with differently—like the burning and looting of our cities because of civil unrest, and the gunning down of children in war zones like Chicago, Minneapolis, Baltimore, and now New York. There are protests devolving, literally, into a cultural revolution as statues are torn down, businesses are burnt to the ground, religious institutions are vandalized, and anarchists attempt to literally erase our history. We have seen the rise of mindless mobs that would rather burn our history books than read them.

This "cancel culture" has declared war on free expression and our First Amendment rights. This isn't just a blip in our history or Americans going a bit nuts. This is American self-immolation and self-destruction. It is the achievement of the goal of the Chinese Communist Party.

So, what now?

We cannot fight in a partisan way. A house divided against itself cannot stand. This nation is in the fight of its life with the Chinese Communist Party, which unleashed the virus on us, has ripped us off for decades. In July, Attorney General William Barr delivered one of the most powerful speeches about a rising China ever delivered by an American government official:

> China's Communist government has perfected a wide array of predatory and often unlawful tactics: currency manipulation, tariffs, quotas, state-led strategic investment and acquisition, theft and forced transfer of intellectual

> property, state subsidies, dumping, cyberattacks, and industrial espionage. About 80 percent of all federal economic espionage prosecutions allege conduct undertaken for the benefit of the Chinese state, and about 60 percent of all trade secret theft cases have been connected to China.[15]

We've heard about this for years from President Trump. Free trade and a friendly America previously allowed a mercantilist and authoritarian China to use banks and financial markets in Hong Kong to suck the jobs and capital and lifeblood out of America to the Chinese mainland. Americans made this sacrifice because we wanted to support Hong Kong's freedom and democracy. However, with the passage of a single law, the Chinese Communist Party canceled all freedom and democracy in Hong Kong. It was certainly no accident that the Chinese Communist Party used the distraction of a global pandemic to make its reprehensible move on Hong Kong. Its well-known historical MO: Turn your back on them, and their military will invade; take your eye off the ball, and they will steal whatever they can.

Attorney General Barr had it right when he said China's intent is not to trade with our companies but to simply raid them and steal the intellectual property and trade secrets that make this nation so strong and our work force so prosperous. It's time to recognize that Communist China has carried out a continuous and relentless attack upon American workers. They have been successful in part thanks to American corporate and financial interests that have effectively lobbied on their behalf. Hollywood has agreed to change characters and alter their movies to please the Chinese Communist Party. American tech companies can allow themselves to become pawns of Chinese influence, according to

Bill Barr, helping Chinese companies to build "the great firewall" of China, the world's most sophisticated system for internet surveillance and censorship. So, let us never forget, as we experience these turbulent times, that it was the Chinese Communist Party that lied and allowed this virus to spread and is now tearing this society apart. As hard as they may lobby to be recognized as a peaceful sovereign nation, during the pandemic they hoarded the masks for themselves, attempted to exploit the shortage for propaganda purposes, shipped often defective equipment, and then required foreign leaders to thank Beijing for the shipments. Let us never forget that this nation, the world's greatest superpower, will be on its knees to this regime if we don't immediately take our medical supply chain from them. China is our largest supplier of medical devices. Why? America also depends on the Chinese supply chain, especially pharmaceuticals. Should China decide to limit or restrict these supplies, we are in trouble.

Let us never forget that America, as she fights within herself, is now in the fight of her life with the Chinese Communist Party, which has ripped her off for decades and now wants to take America down for good.

THE POLICE

At home, those on the Left continue to spread the vicious lie that police officers are biased against black people. This is sure to continue throughout the 2020 election. No matter what happens, progressives on the the Left will continue to behave as if there is an epidemic of unchecked killings of young black men and women by police all over this country—as if these officers kill black people *because* they are black, just because they feel like it.

This has always been a lie—and it still is.

Why do we try so hard to convince those who supposedly care but in reality simply don't care—that *all* black lives matter. That means every black life, not just those taken by police. In reality, a minuscule percentage of all black lives lost in any given year are taken by police.

It's time we convince ourselves of what we need to do to help innocent victims of crimes. All victims are equal. None is considered more important because of who killed them. A murder is a murder. A killer is a killer. A victim is a victim.

The Left has an agenda, and it doesn't involve the silent victims of crime—the ones who go quietly unannounced and unheralded, some not even old enough to spell their own names. They are worthy of distinction. They are worthy of note. They are worthy of remembrance.

But the Left doesn't care. In July, when Alexandria Ocasio-Cortez said that the alarming rise of shootings in New York City was a result of "underemployment," a one-year-old child was shot in the middle of a park in Brooklyn. His name was Davell Gardner Jr., and he didn't need to die.[16] At the end of June in Chicago, a ten-year-old girl named Lena Marie Nunez was killed when a stray bullet entered her window. She didn't need to die, either.[17]

It's time we recognized that it's not about convincing the radicals on the Left. They are not listening. They know the truth, but theirs is a different agenda.

We are seeing in real time the impact of that agenda. Their defund-the-police movement has led to a massive increase in crime in New York City. The bozo who calls himself mayor boasts that New York City is the safest large city. Because of this man, New York City will become just another dangerous, crime-ridden city with all the implications that come from that.

JOE BIDEN

Of course, there is no bigger lie than the one Democrats push every day, either directly or passively. They want us to believe that Bunker Joe Biden, a man who is in obvious cognitive decline, is fit to become the next President of the United States.

In reality, Biden is not only unfit—he has also proven himself to be one of the most blatant, bald-faced liars in the country.

Consider this: On May 14, 2020, Joe Biden did a virtual town hall on MSNBC and was asked this simple question: "What was your involvement in the investigation of Michael Flynn and the FBI investigation?" The former vice president answered in a forceful, confident manner: "I was never a part or had any knowledge of any criminal investigation into Flynn while I was in office, period. Not one single time."[18]

Well, let's look at the facts.

The FBI opened its investigation into General Flynn in the middle of August 2016—three months before the presidential election. Code named Crossfire Razor, the probe's stated goal was, essentially, to find out if Flynn was a Russian agent. But it was also the pretext on which the crooked FBI and Justice Department based the whole phony Russian collusion delusion against the 2016 Donald J. Trump for President campaign. That investigation was called Crossfire Hurricane (they're cute with names, right?), and you remember all the lowlifes involved: British secret agent Christopher Steele and his phony dossier, Steele's connection to the US Justice Department. Bruce and Nellie Ohr. The FBI lovebirds, agents Peter Strzok and Lisa Page, and the "insurance policy":

Lisa Page text to Peter Strzok: *"He's (Trump) not going to become president, right?!"*

Strzok's text back to Page: *"No. No he won't. We'll stop him."*

You remember the manipulation of the FISA warrants.

You remember the whole clown show.

On January 4, it appeared as though the FBI had closed the case.

But on January 5, 2017, Obama convened an emergency meeting in the Oval Office. In attendance was a who's who of the top level of the anti-Trump cabal in his administration. In the room was disgraced former FBI Director James Comey, Deputy Attorney General Sally Yates, National Security Advisor Susan Rice, and old sleepy Vice President Joe Biden. The topic of discussion was the transcripts of General Flynn's phone conversations with Sergey Kislyak, a Russian diplomat.

The reason we know about the meeting is because in June 2020, Michael Sherwin, the acting United State Attorney for the District of Columbia, turned over to Michael Flynn's defense team files related to the FBI's investigation into their client. The Attorney General, William Barr, had declassified a trove of files from the FBI's investigation. Included in the material was a note written by none other than fired FBI agent Strzok that described the meeting held in the Oval Office during the last weeks of Obama's presidency.[19]

What the notes tell us is that Obama, along with his top lieutenants such as Susan Rice and Sally Yates, was about to initiate a major escalation of his criminal attack against Donald Trump. Up until then, for the most part, the crimes they'd committed were against a presidential candidate.

There was only one little problem with the plan. There was nothing to investigate. Even Comey knew that. In the Oval Office that day, he told Obama that Flynn's calls "appear legit."[20]

This is where the greatest legal mind since Clarence Darrow offered a solution. According to Strzok's notes, Vice President Joe Biden then invoked the Logan Act as a pretext for the investigation.

Don't know what the Logan Act is? You're not alone.

Before that moment, if you'd asked 99 percent of the legal profession to tell you what the Logan Act was, you would have received blank stares in return. Enacted by the United States Congress in 1799, the act forbids private citizens from engaging in unauthorized correspondence with foreign governments. Only two people in American history have been charged with violating the act. The first was in 1802, and the second in 1852.

So how is it that a man who can't remember that in our Declaration of Independence it was our "Creator" who endowed men with their unalienable rights can be able to cite a law as obscure as the Logan Act right from the top of his head? Well, Joe Biden is either Rain Man or he was previously in on the discussions that Strzok, McCabe, and the rest of the anti-Trump FBI cabal were having about how to get Flynn.

I'm going with the second scenario.

What this moment tells us is that—surprise, surprise—Biden is a liar. But it also tells us he was as dirty as any of the Obama conspirators in the plan to take down General Flynn and, ultimately, the duly elected President of the United States.

Indictments must now be issued for obstruction, fraud, knowingly providing false information to a court, tampering with official records, and more. Leaker and Unmasker Susan Rice, another vindictive one, should be charged with perjury for all her lies during her stint in the Obama administration. The FBI was created to protect us, to gather evidence against the guilty, and to exonerate and close files regarding the innocent, not to falsely implicate them for the FBI's own political vendettas.

The FBI also needs a complete overhaul. The man who was brought in to run it is as deep in the swamp as you can get. Christopher Wray knew all of what was going on. He was, like Robert Mueller, James Comey, Rod Rosenstein, and the whole lot of them, part of the swamp. Not surprisingly, Christopher Wray was Andrew Weissman's supervisor. Wray has resisted congressional requests and congressional oversight. He kept Andrew McCabe and Strzok on as FBI agents. He knew that Robert Mueller's special counsel office saw these notes and did nothing. They knew that these notes had been hidden from Michael Flynn, who was being prosecuted as a result of the FBI's hatred toward him. Christopher Wray is an establishment, institutional cover.

Mr. President, we have lost faith in the FBI, and it cannot be restored until Christopher Wray is gone. What Christopher Wray neglected to say is that the person he has hired to be counsel to the FBI is a current law partner of preeminent FBI abusers Rod Rosenstein and Sally Yates. King & Spaulding, where Jones is from, is also home to Rod Rosenstein and Sally Yates.[21]

As for Michael Flynn, there is no way to make up for the damage inflicted on this war hero. I believe in this system in which I served for thirty-two years, as a prosecutor, judge, and District Attorney.

The judge in charge of sentencing Michael Flynn refuses to dismiss the case against him, while a higher court has ordered him to do so. As this book goes to print, the charges against Michael Flynn are still pending because of a miscarriage of justice. Judge Emmett Sullivan so hates Michael Flynn that he literally accused him of crimes, including treason, having nothing to do with what Michael Flynn was brought before the court for.

Two days before he lied to the American people in the televised town hall, Biden said this about the January 5, 2020, Oval Office meeting to *Good Morning America* host George Stephanopoulos:

"I was aware that there was, that they had asked for an investigation," Biden responded, apparently referring to the FBI. "But that's all I know about it. I don't think anything else."[22]

It's common knowledge that the man running against President Trump in 2020 is in mental decline. But that's not the worst part of him being president. The worst part is that he's a liar of monumental proportions.

We cannot have a man like him in the White House. There is only one man strong enough to fight the battle facing us, and that is President Donald J. Trump.

IN CLOSING . . .

What we have seen in 2020 America is unlike anything we have seen in the past. The 2020 election will be the most important one of our lifetimes. Our freedom, our safety, and our way of life are all at stake.

In 1838, a 28-year-old lawyer named Abraham Lincoln gave a speech at the Young Men's Lyceum in Springfield, Illinois, warning about the forces that might tear the United States apart from within. His warning still rings true today.

"From whence shall we expect the approach of danger?" he asked. "Shall some trans-Atlantic military giant step the earth and crush us at a blow? Never. All the armies of Europe and Asia . . . could not by force take a drink from the Ohio River or make a track on the Blue Ridge in the trial of a thousand years. No, if destruction be our lot we must ourselves be its author and finisher. As a nation of free men, we will live forever or die by suicide."[23]

We were attacked by an invading enemy when the coronavirus arrived. There is no doubt about that. But that is not the greatest threat to the United States of America. The greatest threat to the United States remains those inside this country who would rather tear it down—the ones who spread lies about our founding fathers, our police officers, and our history.

Our job is to fight for the America that our Founding Fathers envisioned—one where you could follow your dreams and pursue your happiness. The path we were on with the greatest economy, the strongest military, and a leader who wanted America to be proud and prosperous—not the one that the Leftist progressives want to impose on us. But the America where we can say what we want to do when we want and, yes, even think what we want.

Now, America finds herself fighting the forces of darkness that are threatening our nation. There is only one way out of that—and that is by keeping the torch of truth and allowing it to light our path forward.

We have a choice. Either we choose to believe the lies of Joe Biden and the radical Left, who would have us believe that we are a nation conceived in sin and damned to a life of repentance forever, or we can believe the truth: that we are an imperfect nation, but a great one—a nation that has always tried, no matter the circumstances, to live up to the values enshrined in our founding documents.

We can make America great again. Donald Trump is the president who will take us there.

ACKNOWLEDGMENTS

As we embark on our third book together, I want to express my deep gratitude to the team at Hachette led by publisher Daisy Blackwell Hutton and marketing and sales VPs Patsy Jones and Billy Clark. I thank them and everyone in sales, marketing, publicity, and production for all their support. I am truly proud to continue to be one of your authors.

To Editorial Director Kate Hartson, whose sense of humor and calm demeanor helped guide us to the finish line. Many thanks to Sean McGowan, who has shown unending and relentless enthusiasm collaborating on this book.

Always my thanks to my lawyer Al Pirro, who I can count on to support me in every endeavor.

Finally, to my Stella and Lancelot, who, during the writing of this book and the pandemic, have sat by my side as I've worked on every page. And thank God, Stella didn't chew up the manuscript!

NOTES

CHAPTER 1: HERE'S MY OPEN

1. Leah Barkoukis. "Public Health Experts Write Open Letter Supporting Protests: 'White Supremacy...Contributes to COVID-19'." *Townhall*, June 3, 2020. https://townhall.com/tipsheet/leahbarkoukis/2020/06/03/public-health-and-disease-experts-sign-letter-supporting-protests-n2569959.
2. Mallory Simon. "Over 1,000 Health Professionals Sign a Letter Saying, Don't Shut Down Protests Using Coronavirus Concerns as an Excuse." *CNN Health*, June 5, 2020. https://www.cnn.com/2020/06/05/health/health-care-open-letter-protests-coronavirus-trnd/index.html.
3. Anthony Leonardi. "'We could have the summer of love!': Seattle mayor says she doesn't know when CHAZ occupation will conclude." *Washington Examiner,* June 11, 2020. https://www.washingtonexaminer.com/news/we-could-have-the-summer-of-love-seattle-mayor-says-she-doesnt-know-when-chaz-occupation-will-conclude
4. Yaron Steinbuch. "Chirlane McCray Says NYPD-Free New York City Would be 'Nirvana'." *New York Post*, June 11, 2020. https://nypost.com/2020/06/11/chirlane-mccray-says-nypd-free-new-york-city-would-be-nirvana/.
5. Christopher Woody. "These Were the 50 Most Violent Cities in the World in 2018." *Business Insider*, March 12, 2019. https://www.businessinsider.com/most-violent-cities-in-the-world-in-2018-2019-3.
6. Kim Kelly. "Meet the Gun Club Patrolling Seattle's Leftist Utopia." The Daily Beast, June 14, 2020. https://www.thedailybeast.com/seattles-capitol-hill-autonomous-zone-chaz-has-armed-guards
7. Ryan Saavedra. "'Summer of Love' Over: Seattle Mayor to Dismantle 'CHOP' Zone After Violence, Reports Say." *The Daily Wire*, June 22, 2020. https://www.dailywire.com/news/summer-of-love-over-seattle-mayor-to-dismantle-chop-zone-after-violence-reports-say.
8. Matthew Rosenberg. "Michael Flynn Is Harsh Judge of C.I.A.'s Role." *New York Times,* December 12, 2016. https://www.nytimes.com/2016/12/12/us/politics/donald-trump-cia-michael-flynn.html
9. Fox News. "Hasan Called Himself 'Soldier of Allah' on Business Cards." *Fox News*, November 12, 2009. https://www.foxnews.com/story/hasan-called-himself-soldier-of-allah-on-business-cards.
10. White House, Office of the Press Secretary. "Remarks by the President to the UN General Assembly." *The White House*, September 25, 2012. https://obamawhitehouse.archives.gov/the-press-office/2012/09/25/remarks-president-un-general-assembly.
11. Sharon Lerner. "2.2 MILLION PEOPLE IN THE UNITED STATES COULD DIE IF CORONAVIRUS GOES UNCHECKED." The Interceot, March 17, 2020.
12. CNN. "Cuomo Calls Out 'Fools' Breaking Social Distancing." *CNN Business*. https://www.cnn.com/videos/media/2020/05/05/closing-argument-fools-breaking-social-distancing-reopening-cpt-vpx.cnn.
13. David Remnick. "An American Uprising: Who, Really, is the Agitator Here?" *The New Yorker*, May 31, 2020. https://www.newyorker.com/news/daily-comment/an-american-uprising-george-floyd-minneapolis-protests.
14. Sam Dorman. "Black Firefighter 'Devastated' After Rioters Destroy Bar He Spent Life Savings to Build." *Fox News*, May 29, 2020. https://www.foxnews.com/us/black-firefighter-devastated-minneapolis-riots-bar.
15. Ibid.

16. Sam Dorman. "Black Firefighter 'Devastated' After Rioters Destroy Bar He Spent Life Savings to Build." *Fox News*, May 29, 2020. https://www.foxnews.com/us/black-firefighter-devastated-minneapolis-riots-bar.
17. Tim Hains. "CNN's Chris Cuomo: Who Says Protests Are Supposed to be Polite and Peaceful?" *RealClearPolitics*, June 4, 2020. https://www.realclearpolitics.com/video/2020/06/04/cnns_chris_cuomo_who_says_protests_are_supposed.html.

CHAPTER 2: A MAN FOR THIS SEASON

1. Yun Li. "This is Now the Longest US Economic Expansion in History." *CNBC*, July 2, 2019. https://www.cnbc.com/2019/07/02/this-is-now-the-longest-us-economic-expansion-in-history.html.
2. Mustafa Salim and Liz Sly. "Supporters of Iranian-Backed Militia End Siege of U.S. Embassy in Baghdad." *Washington Post*, January 1, 2020. https://www.washingtonpost.com/world/supporters-of-iranian-backed-militia-start-withdrawing-from-besieged-us-embassy-in-baghdad-following-militia-orders/2020/01/01/8280cb34-2c9e-11ea-9b60-817cc18cf173_story.html.
3. Ibid.
4. Kevin Liptak. "How the Trumps Spent Their New Year's Eve." *CNN Politics*, January 1, 2020. https://www.cnn.com/2020/01/01/politics/trump-new-years-eve-mar-a-lago-gala/index.html.
5. Sui-Lee Wee and Donald G. McNeil Jr. "China Identifies New Virus Causing Pneumonialike Illness." *New York Times*, January 21, 2020. https://www.nytimes.com/2020/01/08/health/china-pneumonia-outbreak-virus.html.
6. Steve Eder, Henry Fountain, Michael H. Keller, Muyi Xiao, and Alexandra Stevenson. "430,000 People Have Traveled From China to U.S. Since Coronavirus Surfaced." April 4, 2020. https://www.nytimes.com/2020/04/04/us/coronavirus-china-travel-restrictions.html
7. Maggie Haberman. "Trade Adviser Warned White House in January of Risks of a Pandemic." *New York Times*, April 17, 2020. https://www.nytimes.com/2020/04/06/us/politics/navarro-warning-trump-coronavirus.html.
8. Tal Axelrod. "Biden slams Trump response to coronavirus epidemic: This is no time for "fearmongering." The Hill, February 1, 2020. https://thehill.com/homenews/campaign/481028-biden-slams-trump-for-cutting-health-programs-before-coronavirus-outbreak
9. Carl M. Cannon. "Viral Identity Politics." *RealClearPolitics*, March 12, 2020. https://www.realclearpolitics.com/articles/2020/03/12/viral_identity_politics_142642.html.
10. Erin Schaff. "Full Transcript: Trump's 2020 State of the Union Address." *New York* Times, February 5, 2020. https://www.nytimes.com/2020/02/05/us/politics/state-of-union-transcript.html.
11. Tom Elliott. "Flashback: NYC 'Health Commissioner' Urged New Yorkers to Gather in Public Places." *Grabienews*, March 27, 2020. https://news.grabien.com/story-flashback-nyc-health-commissioner-urged-new-yorkers-gather-p.
12. Eric Morath and Sarah Chaney. "U.S. Employers Cut 701,000 Jobs in March." *Wall Street Journal*, April 3, 2020. ttps://www.wsj.com/articles/u-s-jobs-report-likely-to-show-start-of-record-labor-market-collapse-11585906617
13. Avie Schneider. "Dow Plunges 2,300 Points: Stocks In Meltdown As Panic Selling Continues," NPR, March 12, 2020. https://www.npr.org/2020/03/12/814853898/stocks-in-meltdown-over-trumps-coronavirus-plan
14. Rebecca Savransky. "Obama to Trump: 'What magic wand do you have?'" *The Hill,* June 1, 2016. https://thehill.com/blogs/blog-briefing-room/news/281936-obama-to-trump-what-magic-wand-do-you-have.
15. Salvador Hernandez. "NBA Stars are Helping Pay the Salaries of Stadium Workers During the Coronavirus Shutdown." *Buzzfeed News*, March 13, 2020. https://www.buzzfeednews.com/article/salvadorhernandez/zion-williamson-nba-stars-pledge-money-coronavirus.
16. Spencer Bakalar and Madeleine Carlisle. "'They Feel Like They've Been Remembered': Bus Drivers Deliver Lunches to Kids Whose Schools Have Closed Due

to Coronavirus." *Time*, March 23, 2020. https://time.com/5808475/coronavirus-school-lunches-bus-drivers/.
17. https://www.youtube.com/watch?v=L_PqJhp8HEQ
18. Elizabeth Cohen. "Vaccine for New Chinese Coronavirus in the Works." *CNN Health*, January 20, 2020. https://www.cnn.com/2020/01/20/health/coronavirus-nih-vaccine-development/index.html.
19. Dan Vergano. "The First Case of the Chinese Coronavirus Has Hit the US, CDC Reports." *Buzzfeed News*, January 21, 2020. https://www.buzzfeednews.com/article/danvergano/coronavirus-first-us-case-washington.
20. John Nolte. "Nolte: 53 Times the Establishment Media Said 'Chinese' or 'Wuhan' Virus." *Breitbart*, March 18, 2020. https://www.breitbart.com/the-media/2020/03/18/nolte-53-times-the-establishment-media-said-chinese-or-wuhan-virus/.
21. WHO. "WHO Issues Best Practices for Naming New Human Infectious Diseases." *World Health Organization*, May 8, 2015. https://www.who.int/mediacentre/news/notes/2015/naming-new-diseases/en/.
22. Tristan Justice. "17 Diseases Named After Places or People." *The Federalist*, March 13, 2020. https://thefederalist.com/2020/03/13/17-diseases-named-after-places-or-people/.
23. Katie Rogers. "Trump Now Claims He Always Knew the Coronavirus Would Be a Pandemic." *New York Times*, March 17, 2020. https://www.nytimes.com/2020/03/17/us/politics/trump-coronavirus.html.
24. Josephine Harvey. "Yes, Viruses Used to be Named After Places. Here's Why They Aren't Anymore." *Huffpost*, March 19, 2020. https://www.huffpost.com/entry/trump-coronavirus-racist-virus-names_n_5e727ecdc5b6f5b7c53d5c48.
25. Michael Cabanatuan. "Coronavirus: Asian American Groups Compile Hate Crime Reports as Trump Persists in 'Chinese Virus' Attacks." *San Francisco Chronicle*, March 19, 2020. https://www.sfchronicle.com/bayarea/article/Coronavirus-Asian-American-groups-compile-hate-15144295.php.

CHAPTER 3: BUNKER BIDEN

1. https://www.cdc.gov/coronavirus/2019-ncov/cases-updates/cases-in-us.html.
2. Gabriel Debenedetti. "Joe Biden's Plan to Look Presidential During the Coronavirus Crisis." *New York Magazine*, March 18, 2020. https://nymag.com/intelligencer/2020/03/joe-bidens-plan-to-look-presidential-in-coronavirus-crisis.html.
3. Michael M. Grynbaum. "A Drop in TV Ratings for a Democratic Debate Praised for its Substance." *New York Times,* March 16, 2020. https://www.nytimes.com/2020/03/16/business/media/cnn-debate-ratings-coronavirus.html.
4. Matt Margolis. "Joe Biden Appears to Forget What Office He's Funning for (Again) During Victory Speech." *PJ Media*, March 11, 2020. https://pjmedia.com/election/matt-margolis/2020/03/11/joe-biden-forgets-what-office-hes-running-for-again-during-victory-speech-n380459.
5. Matt Margolis. "Joe Biden Appears to Forget What Office He's Funning for (Again) During Victory Speech." *PJ Media*, March 11, 2020. https://pjmedia.com/election/matt-margolis/2020/03/11/joe-biden-forgets-what-office-hes-running-for-again-during-victory-speech-n380459.
6. Matt Margolis. "Joe Biden Defends Telling Fake War Story Because the 'Central Point' Was 'Correct'." *PJ Media*, August 30, 2019. https://pjmedia.com/news-and-politics/matt-margolis/2019/08/30/joe-biden-defends-telling-his-false-war-story-because-the-central-point-was-correct-n68452.
7. Eric Lach. "Why Joe Biden's Gaffes Matter." *The New Yorker*, August 13, 2019. https://www.newyorker.com/news/dispatch/why-joe-bidens-gaffes-matter.
8. Marc A. Thiessen. "It's Fair to Speculate Whether Biden is Mentally Fit to be President." *Washington Post*, March 12, 2020. https://www.washingtonpost.com/opinions/2020/03/12/its-fair-speculate-whether-biden-is-mentally-fit-be-president/.
9. Eric Lach. "Why Joe Biden's Gaffes Matter." *The New Yorker*, August 13, 2019. https://www.newyorker.com/news/dispatch/why-joe-bidens-gaffes-matter.
10. Marc Caputo. "Biden Plans Shadow Coronavirus Briefings." *Politico,* March 20, 2020. https://www.politico.com/news/2020/03/20/biden-coronavirus-plannings-139629.

11. Matt Flegenheimer. "Biden's First Fun for President Was a Calamity. Some Missteps Still Resonate." *New York Times*, June 3, 2019. https://www.nytimes.com/2019/06/03/us/politics/biden-1988-presidential-campaign.html.
12. Matt Flegenheimer. "Biden's First Fun for President Was a Calamity. Some Missteps Still Resonate." *New York Times*, June 3, 2019. https://www.nytimes.com/2019/06/03/us/politics/biden-1988-presidential-campaign.html.
13. Zephyr Teachout. "'Middle Class' Joe Biden Has a Corruption Problem—It Makes Him a Weak Candidate." *The Guardian*, January 20, 2020. https://www.theguardian.com/commentisfree/2020/jan/20/joe-biden-corruption-donald-trump.
14. Brian Schwartz. "Joe Biden's Campaign Chairman Rallies Wall Street Donors for a Big Fundraising Push Ahead of Primaries." *CNBC*, January 13, 2020. https://www.cnbc.com/2020/01/13/joe-biden-campaign-chairman-rallies-wall-street-donors-for-fundraising-push.html?__source=sharebar%7Ctwitter&par=sharebar.
15. Donna Brazile. "Inside Hillary Clinton's Secret Takeover of the DNC." *Politico* Magazine, November 2, 2017. https://www.politico.com/magazine/story/2017/11/02/clinton-brazile-hacks-2016-215774.
16. Biden Book
17. Edward-Isaac Dovere. "When Obama Talked Biden Out of Running for President." *The Atlantic*, April 25, 2019. https://www.theatlantic.com/politics/archive/2019/04/bidens-20202-announcement-brought-praise-obama/587989/.
18. Marc Caputo. "Biden Plans Shadow Coronavirus Briefings." *Politco,* March 20, 2020. https://www.politico.com/news/2020/03/20/biden-coronavirus-plannings-139629.
19. Ibid.
20. Gregg Re. "Hunter Biden Scandals Explained: Ukraine, China, Drug History, and More." *Fox News*, March 8, 2020. https://www.foxnews.com/politics/hunter-bidens-controversies-explained.
21. Marc Caputo. "Biden to Trump: Start Acting Like 'A Wartime President'." *Politico*, March 23, 2020. https://www.politico.com/news/2020/03/23/biden-to-trump-start-acting-like-a-wartime-president-144195.

CHAPTER 4: FAKE NEWS GOES VIRAL

1. Ashley Parker and Nick Corasaniti. "Some Donald Trump Voters Warn of Revolution if Hillary Clinton Wins." *New York Times*, October 27, 2016. https://www.nytimes.com/2016/10/28/us/politics/donald-trump-voters.html.
2. Shawn Paul Wood. "Bad News: Negative Headlines Get Much More Attention." *Adweek*, February 21, 2014. https://www.adweek.com/digital/bad-news-negative-headlines-get-much-more-attention/.
3. Gregg Re. "After Attacking Trump's Coronavirus-Related China Travel Ban as Xenophobic Dems and Media Have Changed Tune." *Fox News*, April 1, 2020. https://www.foxnews.com/politics/dems-media-change-tune-trump-attacks-coronavirus-china-travel-ban.
4. Nicole Narea. "Coronavirus is Already Here. Blocking Travelers Won't Prevent its Spread." *Vox*, March 14, 2020. https://www.vox.com/2020/3/12/21176669/travel-ban-trump-coronavirus-china-italy-europe.
5. John Nolte. "Nolte: CBS News Plays Italy Hospital Footage—Again—For Report on U.S. Coronavirus Response." *Breitbart*, April 9, 2020. https://www.breitbart.com/the-media/2020/04/09/cbs-news-caught-broadcasting-fake-hospital-footage-second-time/.
6. Joel B. Pollak. "Media Blame Donald Trump for Man's Death After Ingesting Fish Tank Cleaner." *Breitbart*, March 24, 2020. https://www.breitbart.com/the-media/2020/03/24/media-blame-donald-trump-for-mans-death-after-ingesting-fish-tank-cleaner/.
7. https://twitter.com/axios/status/1242425467438858241?ref_src=twsrc%5Etfw%7Ctwcamp%5Etweetembed%7Ctwterm%5E1242425467438858241%7Ctwgr%5E&ref_url=https%3A%2F%2Fwww.breitbart.com%2Fthe-media%2F2020%2F03%2F24%2Fmedia-blame-donald-trump-for-mans-death-after-in
8. Charles Piller and Kelly Servick. "Two Elite Medical Journals Retract Coronavirus Papers Over Data Integrity Questions." *Science* Magazine, June 4, 2020. https://www.

sciencemag.org/news/2020/06/two-elite-medical-journals-retract-coronavirus-papers-over-data-integrity-questions.
9. Jeffrey Lord. "Journalists Forget Their Own Predictions: Millions of Americans to Die." *MRCNewsBusters*, May 30, 2020. https://www.newsbusters.org/blogs/nb/jeffrey-lord/2020/05/30/journalists-forget-their-own-predictions-millions-americans-die.
10. Ibid.
11. Mark Landler and Stephen Castle. "Behind the Virus Report That Jarred the U.S. and the U.K. to Action," *New York Times,* March 17. https://www.nytimes.com/2020/03/17/world/europe/coronavirus-imperial-college-johnson.html
12. Ibid.
13. Hannah Boland and Ellie Zolfagharifard. "Coding That Led to Lockdown Was 'Totally Unreliable' and a 'Buggy Mess', Say Experts." *The Telegraph*, May 16, 2020. https://www.telegraph.co.uk/technology/2020/05/16/coding-led-lockdown-totally-unreliable-buggy-mess-say-experts/.
14. Ibid.
15. Ibid.
16. Lee Bell. "What is Moore's Law? WIRED explains the theory that defined the tech industry," August 28, 2016. https://www.wired.co.uk/article/wired-explains-moores-law
17. John Fund. "'Professor Lockdown' Modeler Resigns in Disgrace." *National Review*, May 6, 2020. https://www.nationalreview.com/corner/professor-lockdown-modeler-resigns-in-disgrace/.
18. Ibid.
19. https://www.spectator.co.uk/article/six-questions-that-neil-ferguson-should-be-asked
20. James Sturcke. "Bird flu pandemic 'could kill 150m,'" *The Guardian,* September 30, 2005. https://www.theguardian.com/world/2005/sep/30/birdflu.jamessturcke
21. John Fund. "'Professor Lockdown' Modeler Resigns in Disgrace." *National Review*, May 6, 2020. https://www.nationalreview.com/corner/professor-lockdown-modeler-resigns-in-disgrace/.
22. Ibid.
23. Ibid.
24. Imperial College COVID-19 Response Team. "Impact of Non-Pharmaceutical Interventions to Reduce COVID-19 Mortality and Healthcare Demand." *Imperial College*, March 16, 2020. https://www.imperial.ac.uk/media/imperial-college/medicine/sph/ide/gida-fellowships/Imperial-College-COVID19-NPI-modelling-16-03-2020.pdf.
25. Ibid
26. Ibid.
27. John Fund. "'Professor Lockdown' Modeler Resigns in Disgrace." *National Review*, May 6, 2020. https://www.nationalreview.com/corner/professor-lockdown-modeler-resigns-in-disgrace/.
28. https://www.cdc.gov/nchs/nvss/vsrr/covid19/index.htm
29. Ibid.
30. COVID-19-stricken TRANSCRIPT: 3/31/20, The Rachel Maddow Show. http://www.msnbc.com/transcripts/rachel-maddow-show/2020-03-31
31. David Adam. "UK Has Enough Intensive Care Units for Coronavirus, Expert Predicts." *NewScientist*, March 25, 2020. https://www.newscientist.com/article/2238578-uk-has-enough-intensive-care-units-for-coronavirus-expert-predicts/.

CHAPTER 5: THE LIBERAL LOCKDOWN

1. Kimberly Amadeo. "Current US Unemployment Rate Statistics and News: How it Compares to Other Unemployment Data." *The Balance*, July 2, 2020. https://www.thebalance.com/current-u-s-unemployment-rate-statistics-and-news-3305733.
2. George Neumayr. "The COVID Skeptics Were Right: The Cure Was Worse Than the Disease." *The American Spectator*, June 11, 2020. https://spectator.org/covid-skeptics-right-coronavirus-lockdown/.
2a. https://www.reuters.com/article/us-health-coronavirus-usa-hydroxychloroq/special-report-doctors-embrace-drug-touted-by-trump-for-covid-19-without-hard-evidence-it-works-idUSKBN21O2VO

2b. https://www.newsweek.com/dr-fauci-meet-tinder-date-if-willing-take-risk-1498317
2c. https://www.ncbi.nlm.nih.gov/pmc/articles/PMC7194665/
3. Jade Bremner. "U.S. Alcohol Sales Increase 55 Percent in One Week Amid Coronavirus Pandemic." *Newsweek*, April 1, 2020. https://www.newsweek.com/us-alcohol-sales-increase-55-percent-one-week-amid-coronavirus-pandemic-1495510.
4. Julie Bosman. "Domestic Violence Calls Mount as Restrictions Linger: 'No One Can Leave'." *New York Times*, May 15, 2020. https://www.nytimes.com/2020/05/15/us/domestic-violence-coronavirus.html.
5. https://www.un.org/News/briefings/docs/2005/050929_Nabarro.doc.htm.
6. John Fund. "'Professor Lockdown' Modeler Resigns in Disgrace." *National Review,* May 6, 2020. https://www.nationalreview.com/corner/professor-lockdown-modeler-resigns-in-disgrace/.
7. United Press International. "Virtual City Used to Study Flu Pandemic." *Medical Press*, May 9, 2006. https://medicalxpress.com/news/2006-05-virtual-city-flu-pandemic.html.
8. Jeffrey A. Tucker. "The 2006 Origins of the Lockdown Idea." *American Institute for Economic Research*, May 15, 2020. https://www.aier.org/article/the-2006-origins-of-the-lockdown-idea/
9. Eric Lipton and Jennifer Steinhauer. "The Untold Story of the Birth of Social Distancing." *New York Times*, April 22, 2020. https://www.nytimes.com/2020/04/22/us/politics/social-distancing-coronavirus.html.
10. Ibid.
11. Jeffrey A. Tucker. "The 2006 Origins of the Lockdown Idea." *American Institute for Economic Research*, May 15, 2020. https://www.aier.org/article/the-2006-origins-of-the-lockdown-idea/.
12. Ryan Saavedra. "Obama Admin Allegedly Depleted Federal Stockpile of N95 Masks, Never Replaced, Reports Say." *The Daily Wire, March 26, 2020.* https://www.dailywire.com/news/obama-admin-allegedly-depleted-federal-stockpile-of-n95-masks-never-replaced-reports-say.
13. N. Qualls, A. Levitt, N. Kanade, et al. "Community Mitigation Guidelines to Prevent Pandemic Influenza." *Centers for Disease Control and Prevention,* April 21, 2017. https://www.cdc.gov/mmwr/volumes/66/rr/rr6601a1.htm#suggestedcitation.
14. Warren Fiske. "Did Fauci tell U.S. 'Not to worry about' Coronavirus?" *Politfact*, April 29, 2020. https://www.politifact.com/factchecks/2020/apr/29/steve-bannon/did-fauci-tell-us-not-worry-about-coronavirus/.
15. Michael Axelsson. "60 Minutes Interview Dr. Anthony Fauci – 'NO reason to be walking around with a MASK'." *Bing*, June 9, 2020. https://www.bing.com/videos/search?q=anthony+fauci+60+minutes+masks&docid=608038193602366921&mid=6EAF1C54A34457454EBD6EAF1C54A34457454EBD&view=detail&FORM=VIRE.
16. Stacey Lennox. "What If I Trust Science and Don't Trust Dr. Fauci?" *PJ Media,* June 20, 2020. https://pjmedia.com/columns/stacey-lennox/2020/06/20/what-if-i-trust-science-and-dont-trust-dr-fauci-n551584.

CHAPTER 6: A SWAMP OF LIES

1. Chris Edwards. "Federal Bureaucracy Grew 70% More Under Bush than Obama." *Fee*, February 16, 2016. https://fee.org/articles/bureaucracy-grew-70-more-under-bush-than-obama/.
2. Shawn Boburg, Robert O'Harrow Jr., Neena Satija, and Amy Goldstein. "Inside the Coronavirus Testing Failure: Alarm and Dismay Among the Scientists Who Sought to Help." *Washington Post,* April 3, 2020. https://www.washingtonpost.com/investigations/2020/04/03/coronavirus-cdc-test-kits-public-health-labs/?arc404=true.
3. Ibid.
4. Ibid.
5. White House. "15 Days to Slow the Spread." White House, March 16, 2020. https://www.whitehouse.gov/articles/15-days-slow-spread/.
6. Natasha Mascarenhas. "California Governor Announces a Statewide Shelter in Place." *Tech Crunch*, March 19, 2020. https://techcrunch.com/2020/03/19/governor-of-california-announces-a-statewide-shelter-in-place/.

6a. https://justthenews.com/accountability/political-ethics/fauci-says-americans-should-trust-doctors-himself-his-career
7. Governor Phil Murphy. "Transcript: March 17th, 2020 Coronavirus Briefing Media." *Official Site of the State of New Jersey,* March 17, 2020. https://www.nj.gov/governor/news/news/562020/20200317b.shtml.
8. S. Garg, L. Kim, M. Whitaker, et al. "Hospitalization Rates and Characteristics of Patients Hospitalized with Laboratory-Confirmed Coronavirus Disease 2019." *Centers for Disease Control and Prevention*, April 17, 2020. https://www.cdc.gov/mmwr/volumes/69/wr/mm6915e3.htm#suggestedcitation.
9. Karina Zaiets and Ramon Padilla. "Coronavirus, Diabetes, Obesity, and Other Underlying Conditions: Which Patients are Most at Risk?" *USA Today*, April 15, 2020. https://www.usatoday.com/in-depth/news/2020/04/15/coronavirus-risk-90-patients-had-underlying-conditions/2962721001/.
10. Dhrumil Mehta. "Most Americans Like How Their Governor is Handling the Coronavirus Outbreak." *FiveThirtyEight*, April 10, 2020. https://fivethirtyeight.com/features/most-americans-like-how-their-governor-is-handling-the-coronavirus-outbreak/.
11. Nick Sibilla. "Michigan Bans Many Stores from Selling Seeds, Home Gardening Supplies, Calls Them 'Not Necessary'." *Forbes,* April 16, 2020. https://www.forbes.com/sites/nicksibilla/2020/04/16/michigan-bans-many-stores-from-selling-seeds-home-gardening-supplies-calls-them-not-necessary/#281ef7925f80.
12. Jeanine Pirro. "Judge Jeanine: Michigan Gov. Whitmer was taking advantage of the COVID-19 crisis until she got caught." *Fox News*, April 22, 2020. https://video.foxnews.com/v/6151190589001#sp=show-clips.
13. Ryan Saavedra. "Emails Show Democrat Gretchen Whitmer's Office Gave 'Green Light' to Give Taxpayer Money to Democrat Groups for Contact Tracing, Report Says." *The Daily Wire*, May 26, 2020. https://www.dailywire.com/news/breaking-emails-show-democrat-gretchen-whitmers-office-gave-green-light-to-give-taxpayer-money-to-democrat-groups-for-contact-tracing-report-says
14. Emily Zanotti. "Gov. Whitmer Considers Extending Michigan Lockdown to Punish Protestors." *The Daily Wire*, April 20, 2020. https://www.dailywire.com/news/gov-whitmer-considers-extending-michigan-lockdown-to-punish-protesters.
15. Kate Sheehy. "Embattled Michigan Governor in Hot Water Over Hubby's Boat Request." *New York Post,* May 25, 2020. https://nypost.com/2020/05/25/michigan-gov-gretchen-whitmer-in-hot-water-over-husbands-boat-request/.

CHAPTER 7: DE-*FEND* THE POLICE

1. Jessica McBride. "VIDEO: Minneapolis Target Looted, Autozone on Fire in George Floyd Protests." *Heavy*, May 28, 2020. https://heavy.com/news/2020/05/video-minneapolis-target-looted-autozone-on-fire-in-george-floyd-protests/.
2. Mohammed Haddad. "Mapping US Cities Where George Floyd Protests Have Erupted." *Aljazeera*, June 2, 2020. https://www.aljazeera.com/indepth/interactive/2020/06/mapping-cities-george-floyd-protests-erupted-200601081654119.html.
3. Lauren Edmonds. "Minneapolis Mayor is BOOED Out of a Black Lives Matter Protest After Refusing to Disband the City's Police – As Rep. Ilhan Omar Calls for the 'Rotten' Department to be Disbanded After George Floyd's Death." *Daily Mail*, June 6, 2020. https://www.dailymail.co.uk/news/article-8395687/Minneapolis-Mayor-BOOED-protest-refusing-defund-citys-police.html.
4. Dakin Andone, Christina Maxouris, and Josh Campbell. "Minneapolis City Council Members Intend to Defund and Dismantle City's Police Department." *CNN*, June 8, 2020. https://www.cnn.com/2020/06/07/us/george-floyd-protests-sunday/index.html.
5. Lauren Edmonds. "Minneapolis Mayor is BOOED Out of a Black Lives Matter Protest After Refusing to Disband the City's Police – As Rep. Ilhan Omar Calls for the 'Rotten' Department to be Disbanded After George Floyd's Death." *Daily Mail*, June 6, 2020. https://www.dailymail.co.uk/news/article-8395687/Minneapolis-Mayor-BOOED-protest-refusing-defund-citys-police.html.

6. Mariame Kaba. "Yes, We Mean Literally Abolish the Police." *New York Times,* June 12, 2020. https://www.nytimes.com/2020/06/12/opinion/sunday/floyd-abolish-defund-police.html.

CHAPTER 8: ESCAPE FROM NEW YORK

1. Emma Colton. "Andrew Cuomo Labels Coronavirus the 'European Virus' in Latest Press Briefing." *Washington Examiner*, May 11, 2020. https://www.washingtonexaminer.com/news/andrew-cuomo-labels-coronavirus-the-european-virus-in-latest-press-briefing.
2. Abby Narishkin, Steve Cameron, and Libertina Brandt. "Why NYC's Largest Emergency Hospital is Pretty Much Empty." *Business Insider*, April 20, 2020. https://www.businessinsider.com/why-nycs-largest-emergency-hospital-javits-center-pretty-much-empty-2020-4.
3. Ashley Collman. "The 500-Bed US Navy Hospital Ship Comfort is Leaving NYC After Treating Just 179 Patients in 3 Weeks." *Business Insider,* April 22, 2020. https://www.businessinsider.com/usns-comfort-leaving-nyc-few-coronavirus-patients-three-weeks-2020-4.
4. Governor Andrew M. Cuomo. "Governor Cuomo Signs the 'New York State on PAUSE' Executive Order." *New York State Government*, March 20, 2020. https://www.governor.ny.gov/news/governor-cuomo-signs-new-york-state-pause-executive-order.
5. Joaquin Sapien and Joe Sexton. "'Fire Through Dry Grass': Andrew Cuomo Saw COVID-19's Threat to Nursing Homes. Then He Risked Adding to It." *Propublica*, June 16, 2020. https://www.propublica.org/article/fire-through-dry-grass-andrew-cuomo-saw-covid-19-threat-to-nursing-homes-then-he-risked-adding-to-it.
6. Ibid.
7. Gregg Re. "New York Health Website Deletes Cuomo's Order Linked to Nursing Home Fatalities." *Fox News*, May 26, 2020. https://www.foxnews.com/politics/new-york-health-website-deletes-cuomos-order-on-nursing-homes.
8. Bernadette Hogan, Carl Campanile, and Bruce Golding. "Gov. Cuomo Says 'It's not our job' to Provide PPE to Nursing Homes." *New York Post*, April 22, 2020. https://nypost.com/2020/04/22/coronavirus-in-ny-cuomo-says-nursing-homes-must-supply-own-ppe/#:~:text=Andrew%20Cuomo%20insisted%20that%20%E2%80%9Cit%E2%80%99s%20not%20our%20job%E2%80%9D,than%203%2C000%20patients%20have%20lost%20their%20lives%20.
9. Luis Ferré-Sadurní and Amy Julia Harris. "Does Cuomo Share Blame for 6,200 Virus Deaths in N.Y. Nursing Homes?" *New York Times*, July 14, 2020. https://www.nytimes.com/2020/07/08/nyregion/nursing-homes-deaths-coronavirus.html.
10. Peter Hasson. "New York Started Undercounting Nursing Home Resident Deaths After Cuomo Faced Scrutiny." *Daily Caller,* May 19, 2020. https://dailycaller.com/2020/05/19/andrew-cuomo-coronavirus-new-york-undercounting-nursing-home-fatalities-timeline/.
11. Matt Margolis. "Cuomo's Deadly Nursing Home Policy Likely Cost 10,000 Lives So Far." *PJ Media*, May 27, 2020. https://pjmedia.com/news-and-politics/matt-margolis/2020/05/27/cuomos-deadly-nursing-home-policy-like-cost-10000-lives-so-far-n433483.
12. Matt Margolis. "Cuomo's Deadly Nursing Home Policy Likely Cost 10,000 Lives So Far." *PJ Media*, May 27, 2020. https://pjmedia.com/news-and-politics/matt-margolis/2020/05/27/cuomos-deadly-nursing-home-policy-like-cost-10000-lives-so-far-n433483.
13. Rebecca C. Lewis. "Cuomo Said 'Blame Me,' But He Hasn't Always Taken Responsibility." *City & State New York*, May 26, 2020. https://www.cityandstateny.com/articles/politics/new-york-state/cuomo-said-%E2%80%9Cblame-me%E2%80%9D-he-hasnt-always-taken-responsibility.html.
14. https://coronavirus.health.ny.gov/system/files/documents/2020/03/doh_covid19-_nhadmissionsreadmissions_-032520.pdf.
15. Jill Terreri Ramos. "New York's Nursing Home Policy Was Not Fully in Line with CDC." *Politifact*, June 13, 2020. https://www.politifact.com/factchecks/2020/jun/13/andrew-cuomo/new-yorks-nursing-home-policy-was-not-line-cdc/.

16. Ibid.
17. Bernadette Hogan and Natalie Musumeci. "Gov. Cuomo Blames Sick Nursing Home Staffers for Infecting Residents." *New York Post,* June 23, 2020. https://nypost.com/2020/06/23/gov-cuomo-blames-sick-nursing-home-staffers-for-infecting-residents/.
18. David Sirota. "Cuomo Gave Immunity to Nursing Home Executives After Big Campaign Donations." *The Guardian*, May 26, 2020. https://www.theguardian.com/us-news/2020/may/26/andrew-cuomo-nursing-home-execs-immunity.
19. Mark Weiner. "Digital Views for Cuomo's Daily Coronavirus Briefings Set Records." *Syracuse*, March 31, 2020. https://www.syracuse.com/coronavirus/2020/03/digital-views-for-cuomos-daily-coronavirus-briefings-near-1m-a-day.html.
20. Maurice Carroll. "By M. Cuomo and A.J. Parknson: Aphorisms in Search of an Author." *New York Times*, May 22, 1984. https://www.nytimes.com/1984/05/22/nyregion/by-m-cuomo-and-aj-parkinson-aphorisms-in-search-of-an-author.html.
21. "New York Coronavirus Map and Case Count." *New York Times,* Updated July 22, 2020. https://www.nytimes.com/interactive/2020/us/new-york-coronavirus-cases.html.
22. Kate Sheehy. "'I Hate Bullies': Bicyclist Verbally Attacked by Chris Cuomo Fires Back." *New York Post*, April 14, 2020. https://nypost.com/2020/04/14/long-island-bicyclist-verbally-attacked-by-chris-cuomo-fires-back/.

CHAPTER 9: BOZO DE BLASIO

1. Greg B. Smith. "Mayoral hopeful Bill de Blasio has had three different legal names, court records show," *New York Daily News,* September 22, 2013. https://www.nydailynews.com/news/election/de-blasio-names-de-blasio-article-1.1463591
2. Michael Gartland. "Add morning naps to list of things de Blasio does instead of work," *New York Post,* August 7, 2017. https://nypost.com/2017/08/07/de-blasio-naps-on-his-office-couch-after-workouts-sources/
3. Gino Spocchia. "New York mayor confronted after breaking stay-at-home rules by walking 11 miles from home in overcrowded park," The Independent, April 28. https://www.independent.co.uk/news/world/americas/us-politics/coronavirus-new-york-de-blasio-mayor-prospect-park-brooklyn-wife-snitch-a9487686.html
4. Ronn Blitzer. "De Blasio warning to Jewish community sparks backlash in latest controversy over coronavirus measures," Fox News, April 29. https://www.foxnews.com/politics/de-blasio-warning-to-jewish-community-sparks-backlash-in-latest-controversy-over-coronavirus-measures
5. Ibid.
6. Samuel Smith. "Evangelicals slam NYC's threat to 'permanently' close churches that defy coronavirus order," The Christian Post, April 2, 2020. https://www.christianpost.com/news/evangelicals-slam-nycs-threat-to-permanently-close-churches-that-defy-coronavirus-order.html
7. Mary Kay Linge, Georgett Roberts, and Laura Italiano. "De Blasio urges New Yorkers to snitch on social distance rule breakers," *New York Post*, April 18, 2020. https://nypost.com/2020/04/18/de-blasio-urges-new-yorkers-to-snitch-on-social-distance-rule-breakers/
8. Tina Moore, Gabrielle Fonrogue, and Bruce Golding. "De Blasio's social distancing tip line flooded with penis photos, Hitler memes," *New York Post,* April 21, 2020. https://nypost.com/2020/04/21/de-blasios-social-distancing-tip-line-flooded-with-obscenities/
9. Ibid.
10. Josh Dawsey and Erica Orden. "Cuomo, de Blasio Clash Over Legionnaires' Outbreak," *Wall Street Journal,* August 7, 2015. https://www.wsj.com/articles/cuomo-de-blasio-clash-over-legionnaires-outbreak-1438993349
11. Ibid.
12. Jorge Fitz-Gibbon. "Alleged bank robber freed thanks to bail reform accused of robbing two more banks," *New York Post,* February 12, 2020.
13. Danielle Wallace. "NYC subway thief thanks Democrats after his 139th arrest, release: 'Bail reform, it's lit!'," Fox News, February 16, 2020. https://www.foxnews.com/us/new-york-bail-reform-law-nyc-subway-thief-thanks-democrats-139th-arrest

14. Ibid.
15. Jessica D'Onofrio and Craig Wall. "87 shot, 17 fatally, in Chicago July 4th weekend violence, police say," ABC News, July 6. https://abc7chicago.com/chicago-shooting-shootings-this-weekend-violence-how-many-shot-in/6301523/
16. Ray Sanchez, Brynn Gingras, and Laura Dolan. "Gun violence surges in major American cities in the midst of a pandemic and a policing crisis," CNN, July 1, 2020. https://www.cnn.com/2020/07/01/us/homicides-shootings-spike-us-cities/index.html
17. Ibid
18. Ibid.
19. Jon Levine and Sam Raskin. "AOC: We need to 'slow down' on bail reform fixes," *New York Post,* February 15, 2020. https://nypost.com/2020/02/15/aoc-we-need-to-slow-down-on-bail-reform-fixes/
20. Darcel D. Clark, Eric Gonzales, Melinda Katz, Michael E. McMahon, Anthony A. Scarpino, Jr., Madeline Singas, and Cyrus R. Vance, Jr. "Why We Need to Reform New York's Criminal Justice Reforms," *New York Times,* February 25, 2020. https://www.nytimes.com/2020/02/25/opinion/new-york-bail-reform.html
21. Joe Sexton and Joaquin Sapien. "Two Coasts. One Virus. How New York Suffered Nearly 10 Times the Number of Deaths as California," ProPublica, May 16, 2020.
22. Derrick Bryson Taylor. "George Floyd Protests: A Timeline," *New York Times,* July 10, 2020. https://www.nytimes.com/article/george-floyd-protests-timeline.html
23. Ibid.
24. DISTRICT ATTORNEY OF THE COUNTY OF NEW YORK INTEROFFICE MEMORANDUM, Subject: Police Misconduct and Protest Related Cases, Friday, June 26, 2020

CHAPTER 10: CONGRESS DOESN'T CARE ABOUT YOU

1. Henry Rodgers. "Pelosi Accidentally Calls George Floyd 'George Kirby' During Press Conference." *Daily Caller*, June 26, 2020. https://dailycaller.com/2020/06/26/speaker-nancy-pelosi-george-floyd-kirby-press-conference-legislation-worthy/.
2. Washington Free Beacon Staff. "Pelosi, Schumer Mess Up George Floyd's Name in Same Week." *The Washington Free Beacon*, June 26, 2020. https://freebeacon.com/democrats/pelosi-schumer-both-mess-up-george-floyds-name-in-same-week/.
3. Fred Barbash. "Madison, Hamilton, Dershowitz: One of These Men is Not Like the Others, but for the GOP He's a Better Quote." *Washington Post,* January 29, 2020. https://www.washingtonpost.com/nation/2020/01/29/dershowitz-impeachment-speech/.
4. https://factba.se/topic/calendar.
5. Steve Nelson and Ebony Bowden. "White House Officials Say Trump Works So Hard, He Often Misses Lunch." *New York Post*, April 26, 2020. https://nypost.com/2020/04/26/trump-works-so-hard-he-often-misses-lunch-white-house-officials/.
6. Reuters Fact Check. "False Claim: Nancy Pelosi's Daughter is on the Kennedy Center Board." *Reuters*, April 8, 2020. https://www.reuters.com/article/uk-factcheck-pelosi-daughter-kennedy-cen/false-claim-nancy-pelosis-daughter-is-on-the-kennedy-center-board-idUSKCN21Q2HM.
7. Claudia Grisales. "Stock Trades After Coronavirus Briefing Complicate Loeffler's Reelection Bid." *NPR*, April 13, 2020. https://www.npr.org/2020/04/13/832859747/stock-trades-after-coronavirus-briefing-complicate-loefflers-reelection-bid.
8. Lachlan Markay, William Bredderman, Sam Brodey. "Sen. Kelly Loeffler Dumped Millions in Stock After Coronavirus Briefing." *Daily Beast*, March 20, 2020. https://www.thedailybeast.com/sen-kelly-loeffler-dumped-millions-in-stock-after-coronavirus-briefing.
9. https://efdsearch.senate.gov/search/view/ptr/425096a9-b206-40a7-86b8-67fa4081b252/.

CHAPTER 11: THE OPEN BORDERS LIE

1. Dino Grandoni and Jeff Stein. "Joe Biden Embraces Green New Deal as He Releases Climate Plan." *Washington Post*, June 4, 2019. https://www.washingtonpost.com/climate-environment/2019/06/04/joe-biden-embraces-green-new-deal-he-releases-climate-plan/.

2. Mike Brest. "Biden: 3 Million Deportations Under Obama Were 'A Mistake'." *Washington Examiner*, February 15, 2020. https://www.washingtonexaminer.com/news/biden-3-million-deportations-under-obama-were-a-mistake.
3. Bob Fredericks. "ICE Claims More Illegals Were Deported Under Obama than Trump." *New York Post*, June 21, 2019. https://nypost.com/2019/06/21/ice-claims-more-illegals-were-deported-under-obama-than-trump/.
4. Asma Khalid. "Democrats Used to Talk About 'Criminal Immigrants,' So What Changed the Party?" *NPR*, February 19, 2019. https://www.npr.org/2019/02/19/694804917/democrats-used-to-talk-about-criminal-immigrants-so-what-changed-the-party.
5. Ibid.
6. Peter Beinart. "How the Democrats Lost Their Way on Immigration." *The Atlantic,* July/August 2017 issue. https://www.theatlantic.com/magazine/archive/2017/07/the-democrats-immigration-mistake/528678/.
7. Ibid.
8. Chrissy Clark. "Biden 'Unity Task Force' Features Obama Administration Haters." *The Federalist,* May 15, 2020. https://thefederalist.com/2020/05/15/biden-unity-task-force-features-obama-administration-haters/.
9. Ibid.
10. John Binder. "Joe Biden's Immigration Plan: Amnesty for Illegal Aliens, Free All Border Crosses Into U.S." *Breitbart*, December 11, 2019. https://www.breitbart.com/politics/2019/12/11/joe-bidens-immigration-plan-amnesty-for-illegal-aliens-free-all-border-crossers-into-u-s/.
11. Ibid.
12. Daria Ortiz. "Maria Fuertes' Granddaughter Explains Why She Blames New York's Sanctuary Policies for Her Grandmother's Death." *Fox News*, February 16, 2020. https://video.foxnews.com/v/6132954170001#sp=show-clips
13. https://www.ice.gov/news/releases/ice-lodges-detainer-against-guyanese-national-arrested-murder-92-year-old-new-york
14. Ibid.
15. Annie Correal. "Citing Murder, Top Trump Official Condemns N.Y. Sanctuary Policy." *New York Times*, January 17, 2020. https://www.nytimes.com/2020/01/17/nyregion/reeaz-khan-immigration-maria-fuertes.html.
16. Ibid.
17. Ibid.
18. Ibid.
19. Ibid.
20. President Donald Trump, 2020 State of the Union Address. https://www.whitehouse.gov/briefings-statements/remarks-president-trump-state-union-address-3/
21. Gallup. "Congress and the Public," https://news.gallup.com/poll/1600/congress-public.aspx
22. https://dmv.ny.gov/driver-license/driver-licenses-and-green-light-law
23. Zolan Kanno-Youngs and Jesse McKinley. "Trump Administration Freezes Global Entry Enrollment in New York Over Immigration Law," *New York Times,* February 7, 2020.

CHAPTER 12: COMMANDER IN CHIEF

1. Dexter Filkins. "The Shadow Commander." *The New Yorker*, September 23, 2013. https://www.newyorker.com/magazine/2013/09/30/the-shadow-commander.
2. Mark Bowden. "The Desert One Debacle," *The Atlantic,* May 12, 2006. https://www.theatlantic.com/magazine/archive/2006/05/the-desert-one-debacle/304803/
3. Ibid.
4. Deborah Danan. "Israel to Twitter: Ban Iran's Ayatollah Khamenei Over 'Genocidal' Tweets." *Breitbart*, May 26, 2020. https://www.breitbart.com/middle-east/2020/05/26/israel-calls-for-twitter-to-ban-anti-semitic-genocidal-iranian-leader/.
5. Miriam Berger. "What is Iran's Revolutionary Guard Corps that Soleimani Helped to Lead?" *Washington Post*, January 4, 2020. https://www.washingtonpost.com/

world/2020/01/04/what-is-irans-revolutionary-guard-corps-that-soleimani-helped-lead/.

6. Dexter Filkins. "The Shadow Commander." *The New Yorker*, September 23, 2013. https://www.newyorker.com/magazine/2013/09/30/the-shadow-commander.
7. Ibid.
8. Ibid.
9. A Profile of Combat Injury, *The Journal of Trauma, Injury, Infection, and Critical Care. https://apps.dtic.mil/dtic/tr/fulltext/u2/a480495.pdf*
10. Dexter Filkins. "The Shadow Commander." *The New Yorker*, September 23, 2013. https://www.newyorker.com/magazine/2013/09/30/the-shadow-commander.
11. Ibid.
12. Jay Solomon and Carol E. Lee. "U.S. Transferred $1.3 Billion More in Cash to Iran After Initial Payment." *Wall Street Journal,* September 6, 2016. https://www.wsj.com/articles/u-s-sent-two-more-planeloads-of-cash-to-iran-after-initial-payment-1473208256.
13. Trump gives dramatic account of Soleimani's last minutes before death, *Reuters,* January 18, 2020. https://www.reuters.com/article/us-usa-trump-iran/trump-gives-dramatic-account-of-soleimanis-last-minutes-before-death-cnn-idUSKBN1ZH0G3
14. Ibid.
15. Rosa Brooks. "Obama vs. the Generals." *Politico* Magazine, November 2013. https://www.politico.com/magazine/story/2013/11/obama-vs-the-generals-099379.
16. Ibid.
17. Thom Shanker and Helene Cooper. "Pentagon Plans to Shrink Army to Pre-World War II Level." *New York Times*, February 23, 2014. https://www.nytimes.com/2014/02/24/us/politics/pentagon-plans-to-shrink-army-to-pre-world-war-ii-level.html.
18. Robert H. Scales. "U.S. military planners don't support war with Syria," *Washington Post,* September 5, 2013. https://www.reuters.com/article/us-usa-trump-iran/trump-gives-dramatic-account-of-soleimanis-last-minutes-before-death-cnn-idUSKBN1ZH0G3
19. Ibid.
20. Lindsey Neas. "Undercutting Our Armed Forces." *Washington Post,* April 23, 2015. https://www.washingtonpost.com/opinions/undercutting-our-armed-forces/2015/04/23/dfd2e368-d7d4-11e4-8103-fa84725dbf9d_story.html.
21. Amanda Macias. "Trump signs $738 billion defense bill. Here's what the Pentagon is poised to get," CNBC, December 20, 2019. https://www.cnbc.com/2019/12/21/trump-signs-738-billion-defense-bill.html
22. Bess Levin. "Trump Treatens to Sic Conan the Military Dog on Reporter," *Vanity Fair,* November 25, 2019. https://www.vanityfair.com/news/2019/11/donald-trump-conan-military-dog-reporter
23. Charlie Savage, Eric Schmitt, and Michael Schwirtz. "Russia Secretly Offered Afghan Militants Bounties to Kill U.S. Troops, Intelligence Says," *New York Times,* July 2, 2020. https://www.nytimes.com/2020/06/26/us/politics/russia-afghanistan-bounties.html

CHAPTER 13: CLOSING STATEMENT

1. Joel B. Pollak. "CNN PRAISED MT. RUSHMORE WHEN OBAMA VISITED; ATTACKS WHEN TRUMP VISITS," July 3, 2020. https://www.breitbart.com/the-media/2020/07/03/cnn-praised-mt-rushmore-when-obama-visited-attacks-when-trump-visits/
2. https://twitter.com/nytimes/status/1278387954440904704?ref_src=twsrc%5Etfw%7Ctwcamp%5Etweetembed%7Ctwterm %5E1278387954440904704%7Ctwgr%5E&ref_url=https%3A%2F%2Fwww.foxnews.com%2Fmedia%2Fthe-new-york-times-slammed-as-woke-police-over-mount-rushmore-report
3. Lizzy Acker and Jamie Goldberg. "Protestors pull down Thomas Jefferson statue in front of Portland high school," Oregon Live, June 15, 2020. https://www.oregonlive.com/portland/2020/06/protesters-take-down-thomas-jefferson-statue-in-front-of-portlands-jefferson-high-school.html
4. Ibid.

5. Ron Chernow, "Grant." Penguin Random House, September 2018.
6. Ibid.
7. Amanda Woods. "BET founder Robert Johnson slams protestors for toppling Confederate statues," *New York Post,* June 25, 2020. https://nypost.com/2020/06/25/bet-founder-robert-johnson-slams-protesters-for-toppling-statues/
8. Peter Aitken. "Princeton drops Woodrow Wilson's name from school due to 'racist thinking'," Fox News, June 27, 2020. https://www.foxnews.com/us/princeton-drops-woodrow-wilson-racist-thinking
9. Bradfort Betz. "Shaun King: Statues of Jesus Christ are 'form of white supremacy,' should be torn down," Fox News, June 22, 2020. https://www.foxnews.com/media/shaun-king-jesus-christ-statues-white-supremacy
10. Seth McLaughlin. "Obama praises 'Great Awakening' to challenge social norms during Biden fundraiser," Washington Times, June 23, 2020. https://www.washingtontimes.com/news/2020/jun/23/barack-obama-praises-great-awakening-challenge-soc/
11. Kenneth Garger. "Video shows suspect tossing firework at man sleeping on Harlem sidewalk," *New York Post,* June 22, 2020. https://nypost.com/2020/06/22/video-appears-to-show-man-toss-firework-at-homeless-person-in-harlem/
12. Nicholas Williams, Elizabeth Keogh, and Thomas Tracy. "Man shot dead in Brooklyn while washing car, latest victim in spate of citywide shootings since Friday," New York Daily News, June 20, 2020. https://www.nydailynews.com/new-york/nyc-crime/ny-man-fatally-shot-brooklyn-gun-violence-soars-20200620-pp3uqtsenbf63n4aei3tw265ou-story.html
13. Mike Martindale. "Man charged in Flint Twp. Attack on Macy's employee," Detroit News, June 26, 2020. https://www.detroitnews.com/story/news/local/michigan/2020/06/26/man-charged-flint-twp-attack-macys-employee/3266368001/
14. https://www.whitehouse.gov/briefings-statements/remarks-president-trump-south-dakotas-2020-mount-rushmore-fireworks-celebration-keystone-south-dakota/
15. https://www.justice.gov/opa/speech/attorney-general-william-p-barr-delivers-remarks-china-policy-gerald-r-ford-presidential
16. Yael Halon. "AOC suggests NYC crime surge due to unemployment, residents who need to 'shoplift some bread'," Fox News, July 12, 2020. https://www.foxnews.com/politics/alexandria-ocasio-cortez-nyc-crime-shoplifting
17. Carly Behn and Sam Kelly. "Girl, 10, fatally shot in Logan Square," Chicago Sun Times, June 27, 2020. https://chicago.suntimes.com/2020/6/27/21305839/lena-nunez-logan-square-girl-shot-10-stray-bullet-dickens
18. Joe Biden TRANSCRIPT: 5/14/20, The Last Word w/ Lawrence O'Donnell, May 14, 2020. http://www.msnbc.com/transcripts/the-last-word/2020-05-14
19. Brooke Singman. "Strzok notes show Obama, Biden weighed in on Flynn case even as Comey downplayed it: lawyers," Fox News, June 24, 2020. https://www.foxnews.com/politics/strzok-comey-obama-biden-flynn-case
20. Clare Foran. "What Is the Logan Act and What Does It Have to Do With Flynn?," *The Atlantic,* February 15, 2017. https://www.theatlantic.com/politics/archive/2017/02/logan-act-michael-flynn-trump-russia/516774/
21. Dylan Tokar and Sadie Gurman. "FBI Director Hires New Top Lawyer From Old Law Firm," *Wall Street Journal,* July 17, 2020. https://www.wsj.com/articles/fbi-director-hires-new-top-lawyer-from-old-law-firm-11595011758
22. Ian Schwartz. "Biden: I was "Aware" FBI Had Asked Obama To Investigate Flynn, 'But That's All I Know About It," RealClear Politics, May 12, 2020.
23. http://www.abrahamlincolnonline.org/lincoln/speeches/lyceum.htm